JOHN ADAMS

VOLUME TWO

JOHN ADAMS
VOLUME TWO

JOHN QUINCY ADAMS &

CHARLES FRANCIS ADAMS

COSIMO CLASSICS

NEW YORK

John Adams, Volume Two
© 2005 Cosimo, Inc.

For information, address:

Cosimo, P.O. Box 416
Old Chelsea Station
New York, NY 10113-0416

or visit our website at:
www.cosimobooks.com

John Adams, Volume Two originally published by Lippincott in 1871.

Library of Congress Cataloging-in-Publication Data
A catalog record for this book is available from the Library of Congress

Cover design by www.wiselephant.com

ISBN: 1-59605-102-7

CONTENTS.
VOLUME II

LIFE OF JOHN ADAMS.

CHAPTER VII.

THE NEGOTIATION AND SIGNATURE OF THE TREATY OF PEACE
WITH GREAT BRITAIN.

THE moral trial described in the last chapter, was not yet entirely passed. It had only changed its form. Some time prior to the completion of the labors there narrated, the calls upon Mr. Adams to repair to another great scene of duty, opening at Paris, had become quite urgent. Not much disposed to be subject, without strong necessity, to a renewal of the rude and menacing tone which Count de Vergennes had not forborne again to use on his last visit, Mr. Adams waited to be convinced that the causes were sufficient to require his presence before he went. Nor was the necessity of putting the seal to the treaty, which he had succeeded in negotiating with the States of Holland, without its imperative force in favor of delay. He deemed it wise to make sure of it before he should leave the Hague. But, this great object once gained, he lost not a moment more. The fact had become by this time apparent that Great Britain was making attempts at negotiation. Intimations had also been received of the occurrence of differences of opinion at

Paris, which his intervention would be required to decide. These events contributed to quicken his movements, so that, on the 26th of October, 1782, he was again in the French capital. In order to comprehend the state of things he found there, it will be necessary to go back a little, and explain the several steps which led to the pacification.

Even before the decisive vote given in the House of Commons upon General Conway's motion, which snapped the chain by which Lord North had been so long held to his sovereign, and before that sovereign had been compelled to subject his recalcitrating will to the necessity of receiving the Whigs once more into his counsels, emissaries had been sent to the continent, directed to discover where the Americans were who were understood to have powers to treat, and what was the precise extent of their authority. They succeeded in their object so far, that on the 11th of March, the day after Lord North had given to the king his final decision to resign, but before any successor had been designated, a private individual, by the name of Digges, who had been in more or less communication with the American ministers throughout the war, was dispatched with a message and a letter from David Hartley to Mr. Adams, announcing that a bill was about to be enacted in parliament to enable the crown to conclude a peace *or truce* with America, and desiring to know whether the four commissioners understood to have been appointed by her were empowered to *conclude* as well as to *treat*, and whether jointly or severally. This agent was sent by Lord North, but with the privity of General Conway, Lord Shelburne, and the leaders of the opposition. His real object seems to have been to sound Mr. Adams as to the possibility of a separate negotiation for a truce. The repugnance to admitting, in any way, the intervention of France, was yet all-powerful in the mind of the sovereign, and it existed more or less strongly among all British statesmen, of whatever party. Nor was the hope abandoned that the nation might yet be saved the mortification of a direct acknowledgment of the independence of the United States. Indeed, visions still flitted across the brain of royalty of the possibility, even at this stage, of succeeding in severing the alliance between them and France, and continuing the war with effect upon one or the other division, as the case might be.

There is reason to infer that all these things combined to originate the experiment upon Mr. Adams, whose dissatisfaction with Count de Vergennes, not entirely unknown in Holland, might have reached the ears of the king. Mr. Adams, apparently quite aware of the delicacy of his position, in agreeing to a conference proposed by Mr. Digges, at Amsterdam, on the 20th of March, attached the condition that it should not be conducted without a witness, and that he should be at liberty to communicate all that might pass to Dr. Franklin and the Count de Vergennes; a wise precaution, which proved not without effect in dispelling from the mind of the latter the suspicions of British tendencies which Gérard had first implanted and which subsequent contentions had nourished. The motive assigned by Count de Vergennes for Digges's mission is singular. He called it a hope that " Mr. John Adams's *connection with some independent members* might facilitate an accommodation." At least this was the version of his dispatch furnished verbally to Mr. Livingston by M. de la Luzerne. The effect of the condition was partially to close the mouth of Digges, who was probably charged with communications to Mr. Adams, of the nature of which Mr. Hartley himself had not been made aware, and to deter him altogether from prosecuting the journey to see Dr. Franklin, which Hartley had arranged for him. Instead of this, Digges took Mr. Adams's advice and hastily retraced his steps to London. The fact was, his mission had already failed. Upon his return home he wrote to Mr. Adams, expressing his own doubts of the sincerity of the whole movement, not only on the part of Lord North, but likewise of the incoming ministry. "I could wish," he said, "I had it more in my power than I now have to say I had clearly discovered the intentions of the new set, at least those I have conversed with, to wit, Lord Shelburne, Lord Camden, General Conway, and Lord Keppel, to be that of going to peace with America on the avowed basis of independence. Every voice pronounces it to be their intention, but I like a little more open declaration for so doing. Time will show what is meant, but, I own, appearances do not please me."

Other overtures came through Lord Shelburne to Mr. Adams, but he was yet too incredulous of any good faith to be disposed to put confidence in them. He therefore contented himself with apprising the French court of the facts, through Dr. Franklin, and resumed his labors in Holland, just then culminating to the wished-for point. In truth, the public mind in Eng-

land was teeming with visions of the possibility of yet
succeeding in a disruption of the formidable combinations against her, of drawing off Holland or Spain, of
buying up a reconciliation with America, and even of
a separate pacification with France. An attempt to
effect this last scheme, coeval with the mission of
Digges, was made through an emissary, used more or
less throughout the war, by the name of Forth,* who
visited Count de Vergennes as from Lord North, and
without the privity of the Whigs. The substance of
his conference is given in a dispatch, dated two days
later, from De Vergennes to the French envoy at
Madrid, Count de Montmorin. But in that he, singularly enough, omits to mention one important offer
made to him, the knowledge of which has been gained
from elsewhere. The same omission occurs in the
communication of the overture made by his order to

---

* A history of the various secret agencies, instituted by the
British government on the continent during the struggle, would
make a curious chapter. To them it is doubtless fair to attribute
the efforts made through anonymous letters to tempt the American
ministers, as well as to embroil them with each other. Several
remarkable specimens of this kind remain among Mr. Adams's
papers. Forth had been secretary to Lord Stormont in France
before the war, and had given early warning of the events which
led to it. Dr. Bancroft was kept in pay, doubtless on account of
his intimacy with Dr. Franklin. Paul Wentworth was a good
deal in Holland during the period of Mr. Adams's negotiations
there. The precise date when Silas Deane sold his services, is
not quite made out. The king appears to have hoped much from
his labors at one moment. All these persons, as well as two or
three others, are mentioned as channels of intelligence in the
correspondence with Lord North.

congress. This was the restoration of Canada, as the price of a separate peace. To the Count it raised no temptation, for his line of policy had always been the retention of Canada just where it was as a check on the new American nation. Neither is it at all probable that he regarded it as made in good faith. The mission was symbolical of the distracted councils in which it originated, and of nothing else. For if the nature of these contemporaneous overtures, through Digges and Forth, be analyzed in connection with the fact that during the same time Lord Shelburne alone had been consulted by the king, whilst the Rockingham Whigs were studiously kept out of his confidence, the inference is irresistible that none of them were more than clumsy traps, without a prospect of deluding the object.

Neither does it appear that the uncertainty of purpose, which is visible before the induction of the Whigs into office, entirely ceased even quite down to the moment of pacification. Whatever may be thought of Lord Shelburne's good-will at last to carry through a policy of conciliation with the United States as an independent nation, there is great reason to question it at the outset. In the administration formed under the Marquis of Rockingham, in which the king was finally compelled to acquiesce, the department of foreign affairs had been assigned to Charles Fox, whilst that of the colonies fell to Lord Shelburne. A difficulty immediately occurred, on account of the anomalous condition of America. In the English view, the United States were still dependent and separate colonies, and therefore under the supervision of Shelburne.

In point of fact, their independence and their union as one nation was admitted, and therefore all dealings with them more properly belonged to Fox. This embarrassment was much aggravated by the jealousy already existing from other causes between the two chiefs. Neither was it in any way relieved by the accidental circumstances through which the negotiation took its rise. A private letter, addressed by Dr. Franklin to Lord Shelburne upon the change of administration, expressive of a hope that peace might grow out of it, was made by Shelburne an excuse for sending, without the knowledge of the cabinet, Mr. Richard Oswald, a gentleman described by him as "a pacifical man, conversant in those negotiations which are most interesting to mankind," to Paris, informally to inquire upon what terms a peace with America could be initiated. The notion of a separate peace was yet the predominating one. Neither was it dispelled until Dr. Franklin assured his visitor that a conference with Count de Vergennes was indispensable to any further proceedings. Mr. Oswald accordingly conferred with the French minister, as well as he could without knowing the French language, and offered to become the medium of conveying to his employer propositions for a general negotiation.

It cannot be pretended that this last proceeding was not an encroachment upon the province of Mr. Fox and the action of the cabinet. Mr. Oswald is reported, by Count de Vergennes, to have proposed a scheme of truce, upon the old ground of *uti possidetis*, not unlike that suggested by Spain two years before, at this time when the Rockingham party was notoriously disposed to adopt a more liberal policy of concession.* But Dr. Franklin, wholly unconscious of all these entanglements in the British cabinet, sent Mr. Oswald home with a kind letter to Lord Shelburne, expressive of a hope that he would soon return so amiable a gentleman, armed with powers to treat. The hint, falling in with Shelburne's own desire to control the negotiation, was eagerly taken, and Oswald was sent back with a promise of such powers. Oswald appears to have communicated to Franklin that part of the record of the cabinet council held on the 27th of April, which settled the terms of a general pacification, but, perhaps from a wish not to expose domestic troubles to the eye of so shrewd an observer, he omitted the significant conclusion which Mr. Fox had succeeded in attaching to it.† By that conclusion, Fox had drawn the negotiation with France back into his own hands. Distrustful of Shelburne's agent, he had appointed Mr. Thomas Grenville to confer with Count de Vergennes. This omission, significant of the dissensions at home, was supplied by Oswald's announcement of the fact of that appointment, *verbally, as he was ordered*, towards the

---

* This proposition, intended for the Americans, was made to Count de Vergennes, in order to enlist his authority with them to secure its adoption. No wonder that the Count's fine tact marvelled at the "absurdity" of Shelburne's agent.

Much of the secret history of these events is now furnished to the world from the three sources. The above fact is given in the dispatch of Count de Vergennes to Count de Montmorin, in Spain, April 18, 1782. *Flassan*, tom. vii. p. 331.

† Compare the minutes of council as given by Franklin, from Oswald's reading, with the official copy.—*Sparks's Franklin*, vol. ix. p. 266; *Russell's Memorials of Fox*, vol i. p. 345.

close of the conversation. Thus it appears that, at the very outset of this important proceeding, each of the two rival interests then in the British administration was carrying on a part of the same general duty, without harmony or even a desire to co-operate with the other. The effect of this was not long in making itself felt.

The prudence and statesmanship of Prince Kaunitz had more than once, during this war, proved unavailing to restrain some ejaculations at the diplomacy of his excellent English friends. Frederick the Second, of Prussia, had no opinion of it habitually. But nowhere is the justice of this verdict more palpable than in the opening details of these momentous negotiations. When Mr. Grenville, a person not without abilities, but a novice in such matters, not yet twenty-seven years of age, found his way over to Paris, and opened his business to one of the most expert veterans in Europe, the first inquiry addressed to him was as to the extent of his powers; for France could not treat excepting in conjunction with her allies. But no such question had been provided for or thought of in London. Mr. Grenville's commission empowered him to deal only with France. Yet though the Count at once pronounced this a barrier to his treating, he offered to listen; and the embarrassed Grenville was fain to put up even with this mode of securing an opening for the great offer with which he considered himself charged. In the mind of an Englishman, nothing could be greater than the surrender of the point of American independence; so that, when once uttered, the young man seemed to take it for granted that everything would be settled, and peace ensue as a matter of course. His consternation may be imagined, when the adroit old minister assured him that American independence was but an incidental object of the war, and that many other concessions might be required of Great Britain before peace could be attained. These views the Count repeated the next day upon a renewal of the conference, at which he took the precaution of obtaining the presence of the Spanish minister, Count d'Aranda, in order to confirm and extend the impression he wished to make upon his youthful antagonist.

Greatly discouraged by this imposing exhibition of the temper of France, Grenville wrote home for further instructions and for an extension of his commission, if it was thought best to proceed. From the minutes of the cabinet council held on his application, it seems that a full authority to treat with "all the belligerent powers" was ordered to be sent to Mr. Grenville, though the basis of negotiation was not changed. Yet by some singular inattention on the part of the foreign office, the new commission came, bearing substantially the same restriction as before. Under such circumstances, it can be no cause of surprise that the wary French minister should infer that the whole proceeding lacked good faith. On the other hand, Dr. Franklin had his reasons for a similar conclusion, growing out of a still more extraordinary concurrence of accidents, not easy, from his point of view, to account for in any other way. They were these. At the time of Mr. Oswald's departure from Paris, after his visit of inquiry, Dr. Franklin had seized the opportunity to commit to his care a paper, designed for the eye of Lord Shelburne alone, which contained some reasons why a cession of Canada to the United States should be made an integral part of any basis that might be proposed of reconciliation between the two countries. It is most remarkable that the Doctor, at the same time, imposed upon him a strong injunction of secrecy on this point, particularly as it respected the French ministry, *which did not favor the idea.* The bearing of this material fact will be made visible at a later period of the negotiation. Mr. Oswald, who seems throughout to have displayed the qualities rather of good sense, and a conciliatory temper, than of a trained statesman or advocate, manifested no aversion to the proposal, and cheerfully consented to become the bearer of it to Lord Shelburne. That minister, not over-inclined to favor the idea, yet unwilling to put any unnecessary obstacle in the way of negotiation, preferred to waive the consideration of the subject until things should arrive at a later stage, and he so instructed Mr. Oswald upon his return to Paris. It did so happen, however, that in the course of a conversation with Mr. Grenville, Oswald, forgetting the injunction of secrecy, casually betrayed the fact that such a proposition had been received and considered by his principal. The effect of this disclosure upon Grenville was decisive. Attaching a much worse construction to it than the thing really merited, and yet not an unreasonable one under the peculiar circumstances, this gentleman instantly wrote to Mr. Fox, communicating his discovery, and requesting to be forthwith relieved from the painful position of appearing to conduct a negotiation actually managed by other hands. His desire, he said, was the more positive from the percep-

tion of a marked change in the manner of Dr. Franklin
towards him ever since Mr. Oswald's return. Instead
of opening himself unreservedly, as he had promised,
not a word more could be gained from him on the
topics of the proposed negotiation. This change, however surprising to Grenville, was to be accounted for
naturally enough. Dr. Franklin, looking only from the
outside, saw a duplicate mission, the reasons for which
he could only in part conjecture, but the effect he perceived was to create confusion, and put off action. It
is not, then, to be wondered at, that he should suspect
it was all a contrivance for delay. Count de Vergennes,
as has been already shown, was much in the same state
of mind. It was, therefore, no more than the exercise
of proper caution in Franklin, to decline further confidential conversation until he should be able definitely
to understand what were the true intentions.

The life of Charles James Fox was one long game of
chance, only the scene of which was changed, from
Almack's and Brookes's, with a pack of cards, whenever in opposition; to the cabinet of the sovereign,
with public principles, when put into the administration. It was a game, too, in which the luck was almost
always against him. This time he had only come in to
be tortured with jealousies and suspicions of his colleague, Lord Shelburne, who seemed to have the ear of
the king, which was closed to him. In this state of
mind, the intelligence conveyed by Grenville from
Paris, came to him like confirmation strong of the
duplicity to which he imputed the obvious difference
in the royal favor. One thing was certain, that Oswald had been sent at first without consultation with

the cabinet, to which not a whisper of such a proposal as the cession of Canada had ever been made. To remain a mere pageant, without power in the government, was out of the question. So the Rockingham party, to which Mr. Fox belonged, after consultation, made up their minds to avail themselves of the earliest excuse for retiring. One shade of difference between the factions related to the mode of initiating the negotiations with America. Whilst Fox advocated the more manly way of commencing with a recognition of her independence, Shelburne had wished to make it a condition to chaffer with in the peace negotiation. The question was brought up in the cabinet for a decision. The Rockingham Whigs were outvoted, which Mr. Fox construed as furnishing the desired opportunity; and accordingly their withdrawal was announced.

But before this design could be executed, a new event brought on a crisis of a different kind, which put another face upon affairs. It was the death of the chief of the Whigs, the Marquis of Rockingham, the very day after the cabinet meeting. The question now was, who should succeed him in that position, not less than who should become prime minister. The two situations had been united in Lord Rockingham. But Lord Shelburne, who now advanced very reasonable claims to the lead in the cabinet, claims backed by the preference of the king himself, stood no chance whatever of attaining the other place. The major part of the Whigs, under the influence of Fox, setting aside the pretensions of the Duke of Richmond, determined that, unless the Duke of Portland, whom they had

made their chief, was likewise placed at the head of
the ministry, they would not consent even to form a
part of the same cabinet with Shelburne. The consequence of these selfish and factious counsels was dissension, and an ultimate disruption of the party. The
king, biased, perhaps, by the action at the last cabinet
meeting, selected Shelburne; and the Duke of Richmond, with four other Whigs, decided to retain office,
whilst Fox and the remainder chose to resign. It was
the impulse of wounded pride in the latter, a motive
which will never be found to sustain the action of a
public man, especially at a critical moment in the
affairs of his country. This was a primary cause of
all the later errors of Mr. Fox, errors which must forever forfeit for him a place among Britain's best or
purest statesmen.

The immediate effect of this revolution in the cabinet upon the state of things at Paris was the recall of
Mr. Fox's minister, Grenville, who was only too glad
to get away, but no material change in the double
form of the negotiations. Mr. Oswald obtained his
commission to treat with America, which had up to this
moment been represented solely by Dr. Franklin. But
Mr. Jay, having failed in animating Spain with a single
generous or downright sentiment, now joined him as a
colleague. In the room of Grenville, Thomas Townshend, the new foreign secretary, dispatched Mr. Al-
leyne Fitzherbert as the minister to treat with France.
Besides these avowed agents, another gentleman, Mr.
Benjamin Vaughan, repaired to Paris, with no ostensible
commission, but, in fact, charged by Lord Shelburne
to give him confidential information respecting the

character of the American commissioners, and the easiest terms with which they would be likely to be satisfied.

The position occupied by Mr. Jay in the public affairs of the United States, down to the day of his election to the mission to Spain, has been already explained. It may be recollected that that election was regarded as a triumph by the French minister, bent upon defeating Arthur Lee, and counteracting the influence of the Eastern, or, as he called them, the British party. In the conflict, which raged so long in congress upon the instructions to be given to the negotiator for peace, Mr. Jay had been ranged among those who favored every modification of the *ultimata* that had been pressed by France, and this to such an extent as to bring upon him the most determined resistance on the part of the New England States, as one ready to abandon their darling interest, the fisheries, in case he should be made the pacificator. But, as not infrequently happens in popular governments, the parties, in the vehemence of their struggles for a policy, forgot to measure the character of the man expected to execute it. They are apt to regard him merely as an instrument of the party that supports him. Such indeed, in common times, he too often proves. But these were not common times, and John Jay was no common man. Throughout the contest, his sympathies had never been with New England. The moderation and repose of his character had little in unison with the more stubborn and vehement temper that had carried on the struggle in the East. And so long as he was subjected to the collisions of opinion incident to public assemblies, he had almost instinctively ranged himself on the calmer and more conservative side. But this was very far from making him what the power which had contributed to bring him on the scene in Europe had expected. Jubilant at what he regarded his victory, M. Gérard, about to return to France, and willing perhaps to make an opportunity for intimacy with the new envoy, offered him a passage in the frigate which was to convey himself. The two accordingly embarked together. What happened on the voyage has not been fully explained. Mr. Jay has left enough to justify an inference that something or other then opened a novel train of ideas in his mind. Suspicions of the policy of France took their date from this period with him, which further observation, after he reached his destination, only tended more and more to confirm. Neither was it simply the failure of his wearisome solicitations to Spain for aid, always promised but never given, which weighed so much with him, as the conviction that the co-operation of France was not hearty. The objects of the latter power, at Madrid, were different, and the necessity of humoring her capricious ally, to gain them, overbore all other considerations. They might, in the end, lead even to her acquiescing in a sacrifice of favorite American claims in order to pacify her. Hence, when Mr. Jay found that he made no progress, it was a positive relief to him to receive a letter from Dr. Franklin, saying that the time had come for him to exchange his humiliating position as a rejected mendicant at Madrid, for the more honorable task of negotiating a peace with Great Britain, at Paris.

But if the experience of Mr. Jay, in his first mission, was not altogether agreeable, it was not without its compensations in better fitting him for his share of the task which now devolved upon him. He had at least been warned that Spain, so far from being disposed to yield the free navigation of the Mississippi, was pushing her claims to a boundary on the west of the United States, which would exclude them altogether from that river, and that France had expressed no aversion to the proceeding. With this clue he came to meet Count de Vergennes face to face. The first thing that fixed his attention, was the solicitude of that minister to have him begin with Count d'Aranda, the Spanish minister at Paris, the negotiation which he had in vain tried to conduct at the Spanish court itself. The next was the anxiety manifested by the confidential secretary of the foreign office, de Rayneval, that he should listen to the proposed sacrifice in regard to the boundary, which went to the extent of submitting to his consideration a memoir affirming the reasonableness of the Spanish claim. All this was to be arranged, too, previously to a recognition by Spain of the independence of America. Mr. Jay's cautious nature took the alarm. He began to suspect more than was actually intended. For the motives of France are now tolerably apparent. Foreseeing the greatest obstacles to a pacification from the intractable imbecility of Spain, Count de Vergennes, without wishing to do positive injury to America, was not the less disposed to keep within reach as many means of satisfying it as possible. Among them this cession of boundary was one; but the resolute refusal of Mr. Jay to treat without a prior acknowledgment of his position, put all possibility of resort to it, for the time, out of the question.

In the mean while the British government had gone on very slowly. Misled by the representations of unauthorized persons who had affirmed Dr. Franklin to be disposed to proceed without a recognition of American independence, or cherishing a hope that they might make something out of the concession, as an item in the negotiation, they yet showed a hesitation well calculated to keep alive the distrust of all the parties watching their movements at Paris. So late as the 25th of July, the king's order to the attorney-general, to prepare a commission for Mr. Oswald, specified only an authority to treat with "commissioners of the thirteen *colonies*, or any *person* or *persons* whatsoever," and not with any sovereign state. And this authority was issued under the supervision of the Home, and not the Foreign Department. The phraseology was material, if there was no certainty of good faith behind it ; and neither George the Third nor Shelburne bore an unequivocal reputation in that regard. Under these circumstances a copy of this commission was submitted by Mr. Oswald to Dr. Franklin and Mr. Jay, who, in their turn, laid it before Count de Vergennes, for his advice. That minister, anxious to advance the negotiations, and regarding the precise form of treating as of small consequence, provided Great Britain would consent to treat at all, gave an opinion that it was sufficient, and this opinion Dr. Franklin cautiously seconded. The argument to sustain it was, that it was not to be expected that the effect, independence, should be made to precede its cause, the treaty itself.

But in maintaining this, the existence of the treaty with France, and her own excuse made to Great Britain for negotiating it, which was that the independence of the United States was already established beyond question, were overlooked by Count de Vergennes. Mr. Jay, not convinced by the reasoning, having his experience of the joint Spanish and French representations fresh upon him, and deeply impressed with the responsibility of his position, was unwilling to commit himself to the sanction of a negotiation with so ambiguous a commencement. He declined to proceed.

But in order to acquit himself of his responsibility for this course, he determined on two measures: the one, a strong appeal to Mr. Oswald to exert himself with his government to procure a recognition of the United States; the other, the preparation of an elaborate paper, addressed to Count de Vergennes, giving reasons for thus abruptly closing the way to negotiation. Dr. Franklin, on his side, however, viewed these movements with more or less dissatisfaction, as too distrustful of the French, and too captious with the English. Nobody was left in Europe with the power to settle this difference but Mr. Adams, and he was yet at the Hague, so deeply engaged in his special duties as to be unwilling to leave them for what seemed, at best, a very uncertain overture. Letters had already passed between him and Mr. Jay, in which he had expressed his sentiments decisively. Whilst he had entirely accorded with that gentleman in refusing to accept the language of Oswald's commission, he suggested a modification by which the difficulty might be removed. As it stood, the king assumed that he was to treat only with colonies or individuals. But if, instead of this, the commission should confer authority to treat with the ministers of "the United States of America," that would be acknowledgment enough for him to begin with. The same sentiment had been expressed by him in a letter written to Dr. Franklin on the 2d of May preceding. Mr. Jay ultimately adopted this idea. It was then submitted to Mr. Oswald, who cheerfully welcomed it, and sent it, together with a copy of Mr. Jay's argument, furnished to him for the purpose, by a courier to London, for the decision of his government.

In the mean while, Benjamin Vaughan, Lord Shelburne's secret agent, had been improving his time in sounding the disposition of Franklin and of Jay, and in communicating the result of his observations to his anxious principal. With the former, as an old acquaintance not entirely unapprised of his relations with the minister, he labored assiduously in smoothing down what seemed obstacles in the way of reconciliation, whilst he so far won the confidence of Jay as to obtain from him, to his great joy, a special commission to wait upon Lord Shelburne in person, and urge him to acquiesce in making the concession demanded. This was on the 9th of September. Mr. Jay, however, in soliciting this, does not seem to have known that Shelburne had sent Vaughan to Paris, nor that a letter had already gone from Vaughan by Oswald's courier, earnestly exhorting Shelburne to grant what had been asked.

One reason given for this urgency by Mr. Vaughan is too remarkable to be omitted in this biography. He had found the two commissioners so well disposed, that he considered it safer to hurry the negotiations whilst they were here alone, than to await the arrival of Mr. Adams and Mr. Laurens, from whose ill-will he apprehended much embarrassment. The day before the departure of Mr. Vaughan, a secret and confidential dispatch of Barbé de Marbois, secretary of the French legation, who had been sent out to the United States with the Chevalier de la Luzerne, to Count de Vergennes, which had been intercepted by the British, was put into Mr. Jay's hands. It revealed something of the general course of the French policy, such as it had been ever since M. Gérard had initiated it at Philadelphia, marking out the Eastern States, and Samuel Adams, in particular, as unreasonable in their pretensions for the fisheries, and leaning strongly to the members of the more southern States, as in harmony with France. The object of this disclosure on the part of England was to make Mr. Jay willing to surrender his objection to immediate negotiation on the terms of Oswald's commission. Its effect was directly the reverse of this, for Mr. Jay made it the basis of the strongest representations, communicated through Mr. Vaughan to Lord Shelburne, to secure the modification which was required. It was this last view, reinforced by the written representations made before, and the verbal communication held after Mr. Vaughan's arrival in England, which probably turned the scale in favor of the concession.

Mr. Vaughan left Paris on the 11th of September. By his own account it appears that the cabinet decision was made whilst he was in London. Four days before his departure, another secret agent had been dispatched from the French capital, under an assumed name, on an errand of still greater importance. This was no less a person than Gérard de Rayneval, a *premier commis* in the department of Count de Vergennes, a brother of M. Gérard, who had been in the same department, and had conducted the earlier negotiations with the United States, and, like him, possessed of the principles with a great share of the confidence of his chief. Of this mission, not a hint had been given by the Count either to Dr. Franklin or to Mr. Jay. The latter learned it from other persons the very day before Marbois' intercepted letter came into his hands. The suspicions, that the two events coming so near together generated in his breast, of a design in the Count to defeat his purpose, and to persuade the British to adhere to their first commission, were natural, but they were not well founded. The construction gave much more importance to the objection, in the French view of it, than it really had. But the purpose of De Rayneval's mission was not less important for all that. The whole truth has never yet been disclosed concerning it, nor is it certain that it ever will be. De Rayneval, under his fictitious name, called privately upon Lord Shelburne, who seems, for a time, to have kept the information of the visit secret from all his colleagues. There are reasons to suppose that some irregular interference had occurred with the ministerial policy, which had so far confirmed the French court in its suspicions of duplicity in Lord Shelburne as to justify a demand of a direct explanation.

These suspicions had grown out of the reception, through the hands of the liberated prisoner, Count de Grasse, of a mysterious note, containing certain propositions, purporting to come from Lord Shelburne. The nature of this message, which has never been disclosed, seems to have excited no less surprise than the channel through which it was received. It was the business of De Rayneval to ascertain what it meant, and whether Lord Shelburne had really authorized it. In case of disavowal, his instructions were to return forthwith. But before leaving, he was at liberty to make an opening for such further communications as the minister might be disposed to make, touching his views of the proposed negotiations. Accordingly, after the disavowal, a general examination ensued of the points which should serve as a basis for a treaty, so far as France was concerned. Beyond these, when pressed to answer, he declared himself without authority to speak. For example, when Shelburne expressed a hope that France would not sustain the American claim to the fisheries, Rayneval replied that "he might venture to say, the king would never support unjust demands; that he was not able to judge whether those of the Americans were of that kind or not; and that, besides, he was without authority in this respect." And afterwards, when Shelburne alluded, in the same way, to the American claims of boundaries, Rayneval fell back into the same guarded strain.

The natural inference of an acute statesman from the tone taken by Rayneval could scarcely be other than that perseverance against the American demands would not be objected to by France; an inference, the justice of which receives great confirmation from the fact, now well known, that Rayneval had already officially done what he could to persuade Mr. Jay to give way to Spain on one point, the southern boundary, and that he afterwards equally urged concession to Great Britain in the matter of the fisheries and the northern boundary. These were the two points in the American negotiation, the fisheries and the boundaries, in which France took pains to declare that she had no interest; the very same points, it should be recollected, which M. Gérard had labored so hard to expunge as *ultimata* from the original instructions given to Mr. Adams; and to which M. Marbois, in his intercepted letter, had alluded as unreasonably insisted upon in America. It may fairly be presumed, then, that one of the purposes of De Rayneval's visit was to give the British incidentally to understand how France felt about them, without committing herself by any overt act. But with regard to the question upon which Mr. Jay had fixed his suspicions, it involved an object which had been from the first directly interesting to France. De Rayneval was not tied up so cautiously here, and he therefore urged upon the prime minister a concession in this respect to the demands of the Americans. There is no evidence to show that his action, in this point, had any effect, independent of the representations which were pressing upon Lord Shelburne from Mr. Vaughan, Mr. Oswald, and Mr. Jay. What he gained by his expedition, was the answer he was instructed to obtain, disavowing the message through De Grasse, and a more perfect apprehension of those points which might constitute the serious obstacles to a pacification. Among these, neither the American claim to the fisheries nor to the boundaries was to be ranked, so far, at least, as France had any hand in the negotiation. They were yet held in abeyance, waiting for the period when it might be necessary to deal with Spain as well as with England. In accordance with this understanding, a note was made of the English proposals, which received the sanction of the cabinet, and was then carried, by M. de Rayneval, back to Paris.

From this statement of facts, it appears that although Mr. Jay was in error in suspecting Rayneval to be charged with a commission to thwart him in his demand of the recognition of American independence, a result which had been a principal object of the war on the part of France, and which fell in with her general European policy, he was not so much mistaken in regard to the disposition, rather betrayed than expressed, upon the secondary points in the negotiation. Without uttering a single word that could be used to commit him or his government with America, M. de Rayneval had succeeded in making Lord Shelburne comprehend that France was not inclined to prolong the war by supporting America in *unjust* claims. What sense M. de Rayneval himself attached to the word *unjust,* will appear as the negotiations proceed.

This was the first of three trips made during this period by De Rayneval to England. On the other hand, Mr. Vaughan, who had been the bearer of Mr. Jay's message to Lord Shelburne, was again on his way back to Paris, charged to continue his confidential labors with the American commissioners, and accompanied by the courier bearing Mr. Oswald's amended commission. The obstacles to negotiation being now all removed, the parties, consisting of Dr. Franklin and Mr. Jay on one side, and Mr. Oswald on the other, prepared themselves for the task of constructing the basis of a pacification.

Of all the surprising incidents in this remarkable war, nothing now seems so difficult to account for as the mode in which Great Britain pursued her objects by negotiation. The person first selected to cope with the ablest of French diplomatists was a young man who had never had experience in public life outside of Great Britain. The individual pitched upon to deal with the United States was a respectable and amiable private gentleman, nominated at the suggestion of Dr. Franklin, with whom he was to treat, because the Doctor thought he would get along easily with him, but by no means a match for a combination of three such men as Franklin, Jay, and John Adams. In order to be upon equal terms with them, Great Britain had need of the best capacity and experience within her borders. But it was her fortune, during all this period, and, indeed, almost to the present day, to insist upon underrating the people with whom she had to do, because they had been her dependents; a mistake which has been productive of more unfortunate consequences to herself than an age of repentance can repair.

The first instance of this took place on the preparation of a basis, made out of a project suggested by Dr. Franklin whilst he was alone at Paris, to which Mr. Oswald was persuaded to give his assent so far as to send it home for the consideration of his government. This basis was formed of three propositions. The first acknowledged the independence, and defined the boundaries of the United States. The second provided for the continued use of the fisheries by the people of both countries, in the manner that had been practised before the last war between France and England. The third admitted the free navigation of the Mississippi, and placed trade on the most liberal footing of reciprocity. The United States could, in all reason, ask little more of any nation; and at bottom there was no more than, with a comprehensive view of national policy, Great Britain would have found it for her interest to grant. But neither sovereign, ministers, nor people in that country were at all prepared for what appeared to them such extravagant liberality. To avert the possibility of a similar error, a new person, fresh from the bureau of the foreign office, and experienced in business, Mr. Henry Strachey, was selected and dispatched to assist Mr. Oswald. In other words, the English position was to be fortified by a little more obstinacy. The instructions with which he was charged were to insist upon indemnity for the refugees, to narrow the line of boundaries, and to cut off the reciprocity of the fisheries and of trade.

This arrival gave another turn to the negotiation. And a new element came in to add a shade of gloom. Simultaneously with the mission of Mr. Strachey, designed to give a higher tone to the British demands, Mr. Jay held a conference with M. de Rayneval, in which it soon appeared that so far from retaining the inability to judge of the merits of the American demands, which he had professed in the conference a short month before with Lord Shelburne, he had no scruples in expressing his positive opinion that they were ill founded and should be materially curtailed. If "ill founded," of course they were "unjust." This related to both the questions, that on the fisheries as well as that on the boundaries. And with regard to the latter, his arguments, which had on a former occasion been applied to restrict them on the south and west, were now directed, in the same spirit, towards the north and east. Inasmuch as M. de Rayneval was well understood to be possessed of the entire confidence of Count de Vergennes, extending, as it proved, even to the intrusting him with the successive missions to Great Britain, each of them vitally important to the pacification, it is not to be wondered at, if Mr. Jay drew some inferences of his own as to the probable nature of the advice which the head of the department would give, in the contingency of the Americans being obliged to ask it, for their guidance in the negotiation.

It was precisely at this moment that Mr. Adams, having completed his business in Holland, arrived to take his place in the commission. His advent seems to have been viewed with equal uneasiness by the agents of England and of France. Mr. Vaughan had been imploring his principal to make haste in order "to get out of the reach of interruption from Mr. Adams." For he was not softened, like Franklin, by English connections or conversation, and he was "very warm and ambitious," so that Mr. Vaughan would not answer for the mischief he might do, if there should be a delay. On the other hand, M. de Rayneval, in alluding to the fisheries, had freely expressed to Mr. Jay his fears of "the ambition and restless views of Mr. Adams." The coincidence of this sentiment with that expressed in the letter of Marbois of the temper of Samuel

Adams, must not be overlooked in this connection. The probability is that both the Adamses were classed, in the French mind, under the same head, as their policy had been identical. On the other hand, Mr. Adams felt, on his arrival, the most profound anxiety respecting his own position. He stood between two colleagues in the commission, with neither of whom he had heretofore entirely sympathized. He had concurred as little with the views of domestic policy held in congress by Mr. Jay, as with the foreign system adopted by Dr. Franklin. His most secret feelings are portrayed in his "Diary" for the 27th of October. He already knew that the two were not agreed upon the course proper now to be taken, and that in taking a side one way or the other, he should be assuming the responsibility of the action that would follow; but he had yet no means to ascertain how far the conclusion arrived at might be one to which he should be ready to give a hearty and cordial support.

An occasion for determining this point was at hand. The instructions of congress, given to the American commissioners under the instigation of the French court, were absolute and imperative, "to undertake nothing without the knowledge and concurrence of that court, and ultimately to govern themselves by their advice and opinion." These orders, transmitted at the time of the enlargement of the commission, had just been reinforced by assurances given to quiet the uneasiness created in France by the British overtures through Governor Carleton. Thus far, although the commissioners had felt them to be derogatory to the honor of their country, as well as to their own character as its representatives, there had been no necessity for action either under or against them. But now that matters were coming to the point of a serious negotiation, and the secondary questions of interest to America were to be determined, especially those to which France had shown herself indifferent, not to say adverse, it seemed as if no chance remained of escaping a decision. Mr. Jay, jealous of the mission of De Rayneval, of which not a hint had been dropped by the French court, suspicious of its good faith from the disclosures of the remarkable dispatch of Marbois, and fearful of any advice like that of which he had received a foretaste through M. de Rayneval, at the same time provoked that the confidence expected should be all on one side, the Count communicating nothing of the separate French negotiation, came to the conclusion that the interests of America were safest when retained in American hands. He therefore declared himself in favor of going on to treat with Great Britain, without consulting the French court. Dr. Franklin, on the other hand, expressing his confidence in that court, secured by his sense of the steady reception of benefits by his country, signified his willingness to abide by the instructions he had received. Yet it is a singular fact, but lately disclosed, that, notwithstanding this general feeling, which was doubtless sincerely entertained, Dr. Franklin had been the first person to violate those instructions, at the very inception of the negotiations, by proposing to Lord Shelburne the cession of Canada, and covering his proposal with an earnest injunction to keep it secret from France, because of his belief that she was adverse to the measure.* A similar secret and confidential communication he promised to make to Thomas Grenville, until diverted from his purpose, as Grenville inferred, by the interposition of Oswald in the negotiation. Oswald himself, so early as the 11th of July, had reported to Lord Shelburne Franklin's desire to treat *and end* with Great Britain on a separate footing from the other powers. From all this evidence it may fairly be inferred that, whatever Franklin might have been disposed to believe of the French court, his instincts were too strong to enable him to trust them implicitly with the care of interests purely American.

And, in this, there can be no reasonable cause for doubt that he was right. The more full the disclosures have been of the French policy from their confidential papers, the more do they show Count de Vergennes assailing England in America, with quite as fixed a purpose as ever Chatham had to conquer America in Germany. Mr. Adams had no doubt of it. He had never seen any signs of a disposition to aid the United States from affection or sympathy. On the contrary, he had perceived their cause everywhere made subordinate to the general considerations of continental politics. Perhaps his impressions at some moments

---

* This is stated by Thomas Grenville as disclosed to him by Mr. Oswald. The injunction, probably, was the reason of Lord Shelburne's withholding the knowledge of the proposal from the cabinet, whilst the disclosure of his reception of it, made by Oswald to Grenville, and by the latter in turn, to Mr. Fox, gave rise to the suspicions of Shelburne's good faith, which ultimately dispersed the Rockingham ministry, and led to many important consequences.

carried him even further, and led him to suspect in the
Count a positive desire to check and depress America.
In this he fell into the natural mistake of exaggerating
the importance of his own country. In the great game
of nations which was now playing at Paris under the
practised eye of France's chief (for Count de Maure-
pas was no longer living), the United States probably
held a relative position, in his mind, not higher than
that of a pawn, or possibly a knight, on a chess-table.
Whilst his attention was absorbed in arranging the combinations of several powers, it necessarily followed that
he had not the time to devote that attention to any one,
which its special representative might imagine to be its
due. But even this hypothesis was to Mr. Adams justification quite sufficient for declining to submit the interests of his country implicitly to the Count's control.
If not so material in the Count's eyes, the greater the
necessity of keeping them in his own care. He therefore seized the first opportunity to announce to his colleagues his preference for the views of Mr. Jay. After
some little reflection, Dr. Franklin signified his acquiescence in this decision. His objections to it had
doubtless been increased by the peculiar relations he
had previously sustained to the French court, and by a
very proper desire to be released from the responsibility
of what might from him be regarded as a discourteous
act. No such delicacy was called for on the part of the
other commissioners. Neither does it appear that
Count de Vergennes manifested a sign of discontent
with them at the time. He saw that little confidence
was placed in him, but he does not seem to have made
the slightest effort to change the decision or even to

get an explanation of it. The truth is, that the course thus taken had its conveniences for him, provided only that the good faith of the American negotiators, not to make a separate peace, could be depended upon. Neither did he ever affect to complain of it, excepting at one particular moment when he thought he had cause to fear that the support he relied on might fail.

This important preliminary having been thus settled, nothing remained but to come to an understanding at once with Great Britain upon the points already made. These were simple enough. The boundaries, the fisheries, the recovery of British debts, and some provision for the refugees, made up the whole. Mr. Strachey, who had been sent from England for the purpose of stiffening the easy nature of Mr. Oswald, succeeded only in infusing into the conferences all the asperity which they ever betrayed. It does not fall within the scope of this work to follow up the narrative of the negotiation further than is necessary to elucidate the precise share of it belonging to Mr. Adams. Down to this time his interposition had been effective in two particulars: first, as to the precise shape of Mr. Oswald's commission, upon which the negotiation was opened; secondly, as to the assumption of the responsibility of proceeding without consultation with France. The articles, upon which to treat as a basis, had been agreed upon before his arrival. They were entirely satisfactory to him, so that he entered into the treaty only at that stage in which Mr. Strachey appeared, demanding adverse modifications for the British cabinet. No moment could have been more happily chosen for reinforcing the arguments already presented by Dr.

Franklin and Mr. Jay. Upon the question of the northern and eastern boundary, which the British were attempting to push back to the Penobscot, he came fully prepared with materials especially confided to him by his own State of Massachusetts, intended to establish her rights as far as the St. Croix and the Highlands, the ancient bounds of Nova Scotia. In the matter of the claims of indemnity, he suggested the very proper concession of acknowledging the just debts contracted before the Revolution, and opening the American courts to the full recovery of them, which furnished the British government some grounds at home for concluding the treaty, without which it is doubtful whether they could have ventured on it at all.

The third and the most delicate point was that relating to the fisheries. It was here, and here alone, that there was any appearance of a conflict of interests with France, which was likewise negotiating with Great Britain on that subject ; and it was here that was shown the greatest reluctance to concede any thing to America. On this point the two other commissioners had been tenacious, without making it a vital element of the treaty. Mr. Adams insisted upon an acknowledgment of the right of fishery as indispensable to the durability of any compact that could be made. After a succession of elaborate conferences and mutual propositions, a new set of articles was finally prepared, and sent, by the hands of Mr. Strachey, to England, for the approbation of the cabinet. But so little were they to the taste of that gentleman, that he left behind him a note for the American commissioners, intimating, in a manner not the most courteous, that unless they should immediately reconsider their denial of indemnity to the refugees, and furnish him with the evidence of it before he got to London, little prospect remained of a favorable result from his journey. But neither conciliation nor menaces could avail to shake them from the position which Dr. Franklin had been the most strenuous in assuming. They replied, but not in the way Mr. Strachey desired. The letter and the mode of action both bear the characteristic marks of Dr. Franklin. The real answer, addressed to Mr. Oswald, although firm in its refusal, abounded in terms of kindness and conciliation to him, which were made the more emphatic by contrast with the cold ceremonious note to Mr. Strachey, inclosing the paper for his information.

This was on the 6th of November. It was the 25th before the gentleman returned. In the mean while the indefatigable Vaughan, not content with writing to Lord Shelburne a series of letters, urging, with great good sense and solid statesmanship, the expediency of yielding a little more on the disputed points, acceded to the desires of the Americans, and once more crossed the Channel to reinforce his representations by personal conference. He had seen the unfortunate effect of the interposition of Mr. Strachey at Paris, and dreading the consequences, in widening the breach, of the report that gentleman was likely to make, he left Paris on the 17th, with the hope of counteracting it. Before he reached London, however, the cabinet had decided upon their course, which was to persevere on the main points, but not to break off the negotiation in case the Americans should remain firm. After a confidential interview with Shelburne, in which he was made acquainted with his views, Mr. Vaughan once more followed Strachey back to Paris, arriving there three days after him, and two days before the decisive conference on the 29th of November.

Later disclosures of the secret influences operating upon the prime minister's position, at this time, sufficiently explain the reasons of his course. A peace had become a matter of necessity. No other escape from the difficulties with which he was surrounded, seemed to present itself. On the one side was the condition of Ireland, and the urgency of the Marquis of Buckingham, then the Lord Lieutenant, that something should be done to redeem his engagements to that country;* on the other, the ill-reconciled assemblage within the cabinet, all its members equally feeling that the king himself was scarcely to be depended on from day to day. It may be doubted whether a more distracted state of things ever existed in the councils of that country. And to lead out of the confusion, no clue was so tangible as a peace. It is however doing no more than justice to Lord Shelburne to add that his judgment and his line of policy led him the same way. He felt, and justly felt, that a further perseverance in the war was idle. In com-

---

* The influence of this cause upon the American question has come to light in the confidential letters of W. W. Grenville, afterwards Lord Grenville, addressed to his brother, the Lord Lieutenant. He reports Lord Shelburne as admitting to him that "the situation of Ireland weighed very materially with him in his wishes for peace." The reason why may be fully understood by examining Grenville's letters at large.—*Memoirs of the Court and Cabinets of George the Third*, vol. i. pp. 66–136.

parison with the object of peace, the concession required was insignificant, and no sacrifice was made by it, excepting one of pride. But to the American commissioners, little informed of the true state of things in London, the interval of Mr. Strachey's absence had been one of no little anxiety. No better evidence of this can be supplied than that of Mr. Adams in his "Diary." It must have been then a moment of great interest to them, when they learned that the expected answer had arrived.

The conferences were resumed on the 25th of November, and Mr. Strachey appeared once more. His tone was apparently but little changed. The ministry, he said, continued dissatisfied with the refusal of a provision for the Tories, and they required modifications of the article on the fisheries. On the boundaries alone were they disposed to concede. But discouraging as this announcement seemed, it was actually more than compensated by the introduction of Mr. Fitzherbert, to whom the negotiation with France had already been intrusted, as an assistant to Mr. Oswald. The discussions which ensued for the next four days, were long, animated, often vehement. The great struggle was upon the fisheries. Great Britain was willing to concede the use on the high seas as a privilege, whilst she denied it altogether within its three miles' jurisdiction on the coasts. America, on the other hand, claimed the former as a right, and asked for the privilege of the latter. Here was the place at which Mr. Adams assumed the greatest share of responsibility in the negotiation. He insisted upon placing the two countries exactly on a level in regard to the right to the fishery, a claim, the justice of which few, at this day, would be found to dispute. The energy and effect of his representations, on this point, are so well shown in his "Diary," as to render it unnecessary to dwell further on them here. He further claimed for his countrymen a liberty to cure and dry fish on the unsettled regions of British America, and a privilege of the same kind in the settled parts, with the consent of the proprietors.

These propositions he put in writing in a paper which, on the 29th, he proposed to the conference as an article to be inserted in the treaty. The paper was then subjected to a critical examination, in the course of which many alterations and some limitations were agreed to, but the substance remained unchanged. It was at this stage that the British commissioners made their last demonstration. Mr. Strachey proposed that the word "*right,*" in its connection with the entire fishery, should be changed into "*liberty.*" And Mr. Fitzherbert sustained the movement by remarking that "right" was an obnoxious expression. The suggestion seems to have fired Mr. Adams, and immediately he burst into an earnest and overwhelming defence of the term he had chosen. The British commissioners, not prepared to resist the argument, proposed to sign the preliminaries, leaving this question to be adjusted at the definitive treaty. But neither would Mr. Adams consent to this. He rose, and with the concentrated power which he possessed when excited, declared that when first commissioned as a negotiator with Great Britain, his country had ordered him to make no peace without a clear acknowledgment of the *right* to the fishery, and by that direction he would stand. No preliminaries should have his signature without it. And here he appealed, with some adroitness, to Mr. Laurens, who had just taken his place in the commission, and who happened to have been president of congress at the time when that first commission was given. Mr. Laurens had likewise been in sympathy with the original movement that produced the commission, so that he readily responded to the call, and seconded the position with characteristic warmth. And Mr. Jay, without committing himself to an equal extent, virtually threw his weight into the scale.

This act was the assumption of another prodigious responsibility. For the powers to treat on commerce, in which the instructions referred to were inserted, had in the interval been revoked by congress, and the right to the fisheries, although adhered to in argument, had been abandoned as an ultimatum. But Mr. Adams, knowing that these things had been gained from congress by the importunity of the French ministry, and feeling in the depths of his soul a conviction that his country's interests were safest under his guardianship, ventured to risk a direct appeal to the British commissioners to concede this point rather than put at hazard the reconciliation. The stroke proved decisive. The term of persistence, dictated to the British by their government, had been reached; and after consultation, they announced their readiness to abide by Mr. Adams's article as it stood. Such a victory is not often recorded in the annals of diplomacy.

That the effect thus produced by Mr. Adams was not entirely the result of his action at the last conference, but had been gradually forming in the course of his conversations with the British commissioners, and especially with Mr. Oswald, is proved by the evidence of that gentleman himself in a remarkable paper which he seems to have drawn up for the use of Mr. Strachey in case any justification of the concession should be necessary at home. It is in the form of a postscript to a letter, dated the 8th of January, 1783, explanatory of the mode of conducting the Newfoundland fishery. This paper, as illustrating the conduct of Mr. Adams, on this subject, from a British point of view, is so material as to merit insertion here entire.

"I will next add what was settled as to what passed with the American commissioners, particularly Mr. Adams (the New England member), when we came to treat of this article, and to propose keeping off the Americans to a distance from the shore, in the prosecution of their fishery, as well as drying their fish on the coast of Newfoundland.

" I had sundry conversations with this gentleman on the subject before you came over the last time; when his language was as follows:

"That the fishery was their all, their bread. That other States had staples of production; they had none but what they raised out of the sea; that they had enjoyed a freedom of fishing time out of mind, and their people would never part with it; that in depriving them of the privilege in question, we should strike a deeper stroke into their vitals, than any, perhaps, they had suffered since the war commenced. That our refusal was unfriendly, ungenerous, insidious, since we could not come out in time to overtake them; and when we did come, we could not miss them, there being fish enough for all nations, during the whole time we chose to seek for them. But that we grudged that they should avail themselves of the natural conveniency of their situation, only to prevent our (the British) getting somewhat less for that part which it was convenient for us to undertake. That we made no difficulty in accommodating the French in this matter, which of itself would make their people more sensibly feel the effect of the exclusion. That his constituents were alarmed, and particularly attentive to this question; and sent him instructions that would by no means allow of his signing any treaty in which this privilege should be excepted.* That he would never sign any such treaty; that if he were to do so, he should consider it as signing a declaration of perpetual war between England and America. That if things were to come to the worst, their States would support that war of themselves, without the help of France or any other nation. That if we lost somewhat in the sales of our fish by their interfering with us, it would, in part, be made up in the sale of our (British) manufactures, since the more money they had for their fish, the more they would buy of these manufactures.

"These observations passed (as I have said) at different times in conversation with him (Mr. Adams), some part of which he also mentioned in your hearing.

"And you will remember the other commissioners

---

* This refers to the separate representations of Massachusetts, which were never varied or qualified.

were equally stiff in refusing to proceed in the treaty, while we proposed to deprive their people of the coast or inshore fishery.

"And also that one of these gentlemen said, that if we insisted on keeping their people at a distance of three leagues from our shores, we could not complain if they also forbad our ships from coming within the like distance of the coasts of the thirteen provinces.

"With respect to drying their fish, the same gentleman said he thought, if we would not allow of their landing upon the *unsettled* parts of our shore, at a certain season in the year, they would justly deny us the same privilege in all parts of their country.

"Another of these commissioners (who had all along expressed himself with great resentment at their people being thus unfavorably distinguished from the French) declared that it was a matter of indifference to them as to what prohibitions we should put their people under, since they would easily make reprisals in another way to their advantage, by an act of navigation, that should exclude English ships forever from any participation in the American trade, either inwards or outwards.*

"In answer to all these arguments (some of which, I have said, passed in your hearing), you will remember, we had not much to oppose.   We did not think it proper to insist on the right of the sovereignty of the coast; nor to say any thing as to how such a grant would affect the treaty with France; and, upon the whole, were confined to the single object of preventing quarrels among

---

* Mr. Vaughan, among whose papers this letter is found, attributes these remarks to Mr. Laurens.

the fishermen, as the supposed consequence of allowing the Americans to come within three leagues of the shore of Newfoundland and other places.

"In answer to which Mr. Adams said, that he made little account of squabbles among fishermen, which were soon made up. But that quarrels between States were not easily settled. And which were most likely to happen, since, when we came to send out men-of-war to watch in those seas, so as to keep their ships to the precise distance of three leagues (and which stations they must take in the earliest season in the spring), disputes might arise and men would be killed; and redress could be had only by appeals to government of either side. And, in the end, would be attended with such unpleasant consequences that he should be sorry it should ever happen. And would therefore advise, that we should overlook the loss we apprehended by their interference in the early part of the fishery, and end the matter so as that people should not be put in mind, on all occasions, that they were not Englishmen.

"The above is the substance of what the American commissioners said, at different times, upon the unpleasant subject of this intended exclusion, and as near their words as I can remember. I had put them in writing, from time to time, as they occurred in my conversation with the commissioners; and when you (Mr. Strachey) came over and showed me the altered plan of the treaty, and how the article was guarded in all the instructions and letters, I own I despaired of any settlement with America before the meeting of parliament. But there being, happily, a discretionary power, as well regarding the extent as the manner of dispensing with

this article, in your instructions, I used the freedom of
pointing it out, and insisting on it. And you, very
properly (as well as Mr. Fitzherbert), took the benefit
of it, and gave your consent to my signing the treaty.
To which, if there is still any objection, I must take my
share of the blame, as I took the liberty of mentioning
to the secretary of state, in the letter which I troubled
you with upon your return to London.

"If your wishing for this paper is to answer some
purpose in parliament, in case of challenge on this head,
you can judge what parts will be suitable to be brought
under public review. Perhaps not many. The best
general one is, that, without giving way in this particular, *there would have been no provisional articles.* That
is very certain."

The right to the fisheries, considered as a resource
for the subsistence of the people of New England, has
gradually lost its importance in the progress of time.
But whether it be regarded as an attribute of sovereignty
indispensable to the completeness of the independence
of a nation bordering on the great oceans of the globe,
or as a school of discipline for a maritime people, the
estimate of it remains undiminished down to this day.
The prediction made by Mr. Adams, that so long as
there should remain an opening for a question of the
exercise of this right, just so long would there be danger of a renewal of the conflict with Great Britain, has
been verified by later events. But it has only been
within a very late period that the good sense and practical wisdom of both nations, stimulated by the increasing danger of collisions between them, have so far

overcome the illiberal theories of the last century, as to sweep away all remnants of exclusiveness in the enjoyment of what was evidently designed by Providence as the reward of enterprise alone. Proximity is an advantage of which the subjects of Great Britain enjoy their full share, and on neither side can it be a just cause of complaint. The good use that may be made of it should depend upon the skill and adventure of those who choose to try this field of exertion, and not upon mere claims of exclusive property, resting upon no permanent foundation whatever.

One other obstacle had been in the way, the more difficult to remove, that it rested on a point of honor in the British heart. Those individuals who had taken the side of the mother country in the colonies, and who, for so doing, had been subjected to the mortification, disasters, and personal losses consequent upon a failure to re-establish her authority, naturally looked to her to protect their rights, in any and every attempt that might be made at accommodation. And this was a valid claim on her, in spite of the fact that the difficulties into which the mother country had fallen, were mainly owing to the interested misrepresentations made by leading persons of this class. On this point, the instructions to obtain an acknowledgment of their claims to indemnity, had been most positive. But the American commissioners, on their side, well knowing the impossibility of reconciling their countrymen to the acknowledgment of such odious pretensions, and little disposed themselves to recognize their validity, manifested no inclination to concede any thing beyond what the strict rule of justice would demand. Here

Dr. Franklin took the lead; finding that the British were about to urge their views on this subject and the fisheries together, he prepared an article, making, by way of set-off, a counter-claim of compensation for the severe and not infrequently wanton injuries inflicted upon the patriots by the British troops. Neither did this lose force by its reference to the voluntary acts of those very adherents to the British cause, whose pretensions were set up for consideration. The fact that this contest had, in many of its parts, been marked with the most painful characteristics of civil convulsion, in the course of which the parties had suffered shocking outrages from each other, was too well known to be denied. And the wounds were too fresh to permit the supposition that the victorious side would be prepared at once to replace in their former position those of their brethren, who had not only forfeited their confidence by joining the oppressor, but had been guilty of the greatest barbarities in conducting the struggle. The earnest and strenuous resistance of Dr. Franklin, reinforced by the representations of the other commissioners, at last produced an effect in convincing the British envoys that further urgency in their behalf was useless. To prolong the war a single day only for their sakes, without prospect of a better result, was obviously a waste of means which might be better employed in supplying the very remuneration which was now in agitation. The good sense of Mr. Fitzherbert, confirming that of Mr. Oswald, prevailed, and this troublesome discussion was finally terminated by the preparation of two articles, to which all agreed, providing that further hostility to the Tories should cease, and that congress should earnestly recommend to the States the restitution of their estates to such persons as could be proved to be native British subjects, and such Americans as had not borne arms against the United States.

The difficulties, on both sides, being thus finally removed, the negotiators on the 30th of November, 1782, signed their names to the preliminary articles of a treaty of peace. These were made contingent upon the general pacification, the negotiations for which were now in full activity between the three great powers, but they were signed without the knowledge of the French court. They were, however, communicated to the Count de Vergennes immediately after the signature, who then manifested no dissatisfaction to the commissioners, but, on the contrary, commended their management, and signified his opinion that the greatest difficulty in the way of a general peace, the acknowledgment of American independence, was now removed. Fifteen days elapsed, and his tone had undergone a very great change. He then addressed to Dr. Franklin, who had announced his intention to dispatch immediately to the United States a vessel with the interesting intelligence, and had offered to him the use of the same opportunity, an indignant remonstrance against the proceeding, as a breach of the agreement between the two countries. He particularly complained that the commissioners had been in such haste to send home an account of their own acts, before assuring themselves of the conclusion of the French negotiation.

Two circumstances are particularly deserving of

notice here. One, that so many days had been suffered to elapse before any cause of dissatisfaction was intimated; the other, that a complaint should have been made of the commissioners for not informing themselves of the state of a negotiation, no part of which was voluntarily communicated to them whilst it was going on. Of the details of their own proceedings, Count de Vergennes had been kept informed unofficially even by Mr. Adams himself, to whom he had expressed opinions favorable to the British pretensions on the great points of difficulty, but he seems never to have inclined to reciprocate any part of the confidence. Some explanation is then necessary for the altered language of the note of the 15th of December. It is, perhaps, to be found in a knowledge of the secret influences which had, in the interval, suddenly thrown a cloud over the pacification, and roused, in their full force, all the apprehensions entertained from the outset by the French minister of a reconciliation between Britain and America to be effected at the expense of the isolation of France.

As in the beginning, so throughout, to conciliate the intractable temper of Spain had made a cardinal point of the Count's policy. Her loudest outcry was for Gibraltar, without gratification in which she was very likely to stretch her pretensions over the southern borders of the United States and into the Mediterranean, a proceeding which would tend materially to complicate the chances of a pacification. Nor yet did she abstain from threatening that if France did not gain it for her, she would give her the British for neighbors by ceding the Spanish part of St. Domingo to them as the purchase-money. But Gibraltar, even though Shelburne himself appeared not indisposed to yield it, was so fastened into the prejudices and pride of the British nation, that the good sense of Count de Vergennes early saw the futility of calculating upon its surrender. The only alternative was, to devise some exchange of equivalents between the three powers, with which Spain might be consoled for her disappointment. The mode of doing this had been entrusted to the confidential agency, once more, of the secretary, De Rayneval, who, with the son of De Vergennes and a Spanish secretary, had gone to London for the purpose of more speedily bringing it to a conclusion. It was just in the nick of time, when every thing seemed likely to be arranged, and when, after concessions wrung from all sides, the Count d'Aranda had assumed the responsibility of accepting the Floridas for Spain, that the news came of the signature of the preliminaries by the Americans. For a moment there was chaos in the British cabinet. The remainder of the Rockingham Whigs, headed by the Duke of Richmond, anxious to find an excuse for a breach with Lord Shelburne, which would send them back to their old associates, seized this opportunity to declare their opposition to closing with France; and the idea was started, either by them or, what is more likely, by the king's peculiar friends, of the possibility, in conjunction with the United States, of continuing the war with her.

This it was which roused the suspicions in the minds of the French,* that the American commissioners might

---

* Flassan, t. vii. p. 353. De Sevelinges, Introduction to the French translation of Botta, tom. i. p. lvii. The latter writer

have precipitated a signature of their preliminaries with the view of facilitating such a combination. Hence the sudden change in the language of De Vergennes, perhaps quickened by his sense of the existence of a party in the French cabinet exerting itself to defeat his policy, and thus effect his own fall. There was, however, not a shadow of foundation for any calculations of the kind; a fact which Lord Shelburne and Thomas Townshend, the secretary, knew too certainly to be in the least moved by the flurry among their colleagues. The former had been regularly and industriously supplied by his private agent, Mr. Vaughan, with such minute information respecting the thoughts and feelings of the American commissioners, as to preclude all doubt in his mind of their fixed intention to abide by the alliance with France. His convictions were finally wrung from him in parliament, in his admission that the signature of the preliminaries with America would have been of no effect, unaccompanied by a peace with France. It was impossible to overcome the weight of this evidence; so the cabinet and the nation relapsed into a sullen acquiescence in the march of the general pacification. And with the removal of this obstacle, the alarm of Count de Vergennes became quieted, so that nothing further was heard from him concerning the matter. Not four weeks elapsed from the date of his remonstrance, before he and Mr. Fitzherbert set their

---

affirms that this plan was concerted with some Americans. Whether he found such an intimation in M. Gérard's papers, from which he wrote his account, does not appear. It was natural for the minister to suspect it.

hands and seals to the preliminaries of a treaty, which, in conjunction with a similar agreement with Spain, executed at the same time, gave full force to the American articles, and thus put an end to any further doubt that the time had at last arrived when the United States were, by common consent, to be enrolled in the list of the great principalities of the earth.

Count de Vergennes had taken advantage of Dr. Franklin's civility in offering to transmit his dispatches to America with his own, to send to M. de la Luzerne instructions to express to congress the displeasure of France with the separate action of their commissioners. This once more revived, though in a very qualified form, the party conflicts of the earlier period of the commission. The clause of the instructions, which directed them to be governed by the opinion and advice of the French minister, had not been the offspring of any spontaneous popular sentiment. It sprang from the distrust Count de Vergennes felt of his ability to control Mr. Adams, and the suspicions he entertained of his disposition to treat separately with Britain. This had prompted the instructions to Luzerne, which had extorted from a reluctant majority in congress the revocation of the powers to negotiate a treaty of commerce, the addition of four other persons in the commission for the peace, the retraction of all *ultimata* except independence, and last of all, this substitution of the dubious good-will of a minister of a European power in the place of the discretion, the wisdom, and the integrity of some of the noblest men whom the great struggle had produced. The manner by which this last act was brought about, has been already explained. It had never been heartily concurred in. At two several periods, efforts had been made to rescind it, which were defeated only by the feeblest considerations of sectional jealousy,* and the private remonstrances of the emissaries of France. Hence, when the complaint of the violation of this instruction by the commissioners came at the same time with the news that preliminaries had been actually signed, it met with little real disposition in congress to respond to it. Those who had voted for it well knew that their act itself, if called into question, would have needed more explanation and defence before the people of the States than they were prepared to give, especially in the face of the fact, which the commissioners had to present, that the great objects of the war had all been gained in spite of it. They were, therefore, content to let the matter subside as quietly as a decent regard to the source of the application would permit.

The odious restriction had been received by Mr. Jay and Mr. Adams with the most painful and indignant sensations. The latter, who got the intelligence just on the eve of his entrance into the negotiation, was impelled by it at once to address to Secretary Livingston a letter, resigning all his employments in Europe. A few hours of reflection, however, sufficed to show him the folly of such precipitation. If the issue should prove that there was a disposition on the part of France to surrender any important interests of his

---

* *Madison Papers*, vol. i. p. 241. The strong feeling of Gouverneur Morris is expressed in his letter to Mr. Jay.—*Jay's Life of Jay*, vol. i. p. 130.

country, his resignation would only remove one more
barrier to the execution of the plan. If, on the other
hand, no such disposition should prevail, there was no
occasion for apprehending difficulty from the instructions. Besides, such an act, on his part, at such a critical moment, had too much the appearance of deserting
a post of the highest responsibility, which his experience
in Europe had fitted him to occupy much better than
any new man could. Reasoning thus, he omitted from
the official copy of his dispatch the record of his hasty
determination, and made up his mind to act without
fear of consequences, regulated by this instruction only
so far as it should go hand in hand with his duty to
protect his country. The responsibility was one from
which nothing but a successful issue could redeem his
reputation; but it was one, the assumption of which
was entirely in harmony with the general spirit of his
public life. He had done the same thing in the winter
of 1775, when independence first came in question;
and again in Holland, when he pressed for a categorical
answer to his demand of recognition. He now felt his
stake in the fortunes of his country to be incomparably
greater than that of any representative of France, and
therefore that the care of these should take precedence
of every other consideration.

Entering with such feelings into the negotiation, the
intercepted dispatch of Marbois was put into his hands
at the same time that he heard of De Rayneval's mission to England, secretly undertaken by the French
court for purposes in no way hinted at to the Americans. Surely, these were not indications of a kind
to establish confidence already impaired, or to show

a willingness on the part of France to make common cause of American interests. They were of so decided a kind as to impose great caution in proceeding, as a positive duty. Neither was the tone of her official agents, on either side of the water, upon every question at issue in the negotiation on the part of America, calculated to reassure him. It was decidedly against her on the subject of the cession of Canada, a favorite object with Dr. Franklin and the Northern States. The reason is now disclosed to have been a desire to keep Great Britain as a check upon the United States in that quarter.* It was against her on the navigation of the Mississippi, equally a favorite object of the Southern States. The motive on this side was to keep open a mode of conciliating Spain. It was against her on the fisheries, the objection being there alone a rivalry of interests. And it was against her on the principle of refusing indemnity to the refugees, because that was viewed as a reasonable concession to Great Britain. These constituted the whole of the secondary questions involved in the negotiation. The vital one, of the recognition of independence, was the only thing in which the policy of the two nations exactly coincided. That, under this concurrence of circumstances, the American commissioners were entirely

---

* Given in the memoir of Count de Vergennes read to the king, already quoted, page 439. Opposition to any movement to conquer Canada was likewise made part of the duty of M. Gérard. Yet his successor assured congress that his sovereign *desired* to see Canada and Nova Scotia annexed to the United States.—*Dipl. Corr. of the Revolution*, vol x. p. 366. Is this, too, to be classed among the *mensonges politiques* described by Flassan?

right in maintaining their freedom of action; that, in doing so, they redeemed the dignity of their country in the eyes of all Europe, then inclining to speculate upon its future influence as a make-weight in the scale of France, would seem to be scarcely susceptible of a doubt. Still less can it be questioned that they did wisely in thus acting, if merely considered as a question of policy. For they at once withdrew the interests of their country from the common stock of equivalents, liable to be used like counters to equalize the bargains of the general negotiation. And by saving the pride of the British government, they induced them to offer far easier terms of reconciliation than would have been obtained, had they been passed under the patronage of their most formidable enemy.

The precise character of the policy of the French cabinet in the American Revolution was viewed very differently by different persons at the time, and has of late been once more opened to extended discussion. All the evidence necessary fully to determine it has not yet been submitted to the public eye. But enough has been disclosed to form grounds for a tolerably clear judgment. The memoirs of De Vergennes and Turgot, first sketching out a line of policy for France, and looking at the contest exclusively in the light of its effect upon the power of Great Britain, the confidential dispatches of the former to his envoy in Spain, the policy marked out for M. Gérard, the first minister to the United States, and the way it was executed, as disclosed by the possessor of the papers of that gentleman, and lastly the course of M. Marbois, the real, though not the ostensible, minister to succeed M. Gerard, all, taken together, display a great uniformity from first to last. The intercepted dispatch of Marbois was only an exposition, in terms not guarded against the possibility of exposure, of the same spirit which had animated the policy of M. Gérard. It viewed parties and men in America in exactly the same light in which Gerard had taught his court to see them. It echoed the language of De Rayneval, the brother of M. Gérard, and the man proclaimed by De Vergennes himself* as of all men the most thoroughly possessed of his principles of action, and the most relied on in executing them. It is by no means to be regarded as an accidental and volunteer effusion of an eccentric individual. Such an idea is not to be reconciled either with the earlier or the subsequent career of Marbois. Brought up in the schools of diplomacy, he had served Count de Vergennes with skill and success in various posts at the smaller German courts. From Bavaria, where he had been of great service in a critical moment, he had been transferred to the United States to act an equally responsible part. A man passing through such a training, and acting under a prescribed form of instructions, would scarcely be likely to address to his principal any views based on important principles not in accordance with the general line of policy that had been marked out for him. And if he were, he would not put himself by it in a way to be kept much longer employed. Yet it has been alleged that in this letter

---

* Flassan, t. vii. p. 365. The language is so emphatic that it puts to rest all doubts of De Rayneval's expressing the opinions of the French court.

Marbois had no countenance from the Count de Vergennes, and the language of the latter, excusing it, is quoted in corroboration of this idea. But it is rather a significant proof to the contrary, that the Count not only did not disavow it, but in no way withdrew his favor on account of it. He only said that "the opinion of M. Marbois was not *necessarily* that of the king," a fact which nobody would be wild enough to deny, and further, "that the views indicated in that dispatch had not been followed," a result which might well have been owing to other causes than a disposition to find fault with him for holding them.

Nor yet does the case rest upon the single intercepted dispatch. For Mr. Livingston, whilst foreign secretary, and himself ever disposed to the most favorable construction of the French policy, admits that the views indicated in that dispatch, were in perfect agreement with all of the writer's public language and action whilst he was in Philadelphia. On the other hand, Mr. Adams affirms that they were by no means the views which Marbois, in private conversations during the passage to America, which they took together in the frigate Sensible, had developed to him. To suppose, then, that he would change those views after he got to America, and when placed in a higher post of responsibility, with the knowledge that the change must put him either in opposition to, or at variance with, the opinions prevailing at Versailles, is utterly contrary to all the principles which have ever been understood to regulate the diplomatic movements of modern European courts. That the views indicated were not actually followed, was owing far more to the turn given by the

commissioners of America to the negotiations than to
any other cause.   For there can be no doubt that if the
British had persisted in demanding a greater sacrifice
of American interests, in a negotiation carried on with
the privity of France, and a peace had depended upon
the decision, the advice of Count de Vergennes would
have been on the side of sacrifice.

Yet this minister's policy, though by no means deserving of the praise which some Americans, in the enthusiasm of their gratitude to the people of France, a
very different body from the cabinet, have been disposed
to extend to it; though designed neither to uphold
great general ideas, nor to befriend the struggling
Americans for their sakes alone, may, when tried by the
ordinary standard of European diplomacy, merit to be
considered both liberal and comprehensive.   Liberal,
in its freedom from minor considerations of selfish advantages to be wrung from the necessities of America;
comprehensive, in its aim to restore the power of France,
so seriously impaired by the disasters and calamities of
the preceding war.   The incidental consequences, which
befell that country from this triumph, in the accumulation of a crushing debt, and in the introduction of a
new and potent form of opinion, were not to be foreseen.   Count de Vergennes lived long enough to become profoundly alarmed by the progress that the new
nation, which he had helped into being, was making.*

---

* Marbois, *Histoire de la Louisiane*, p. 163.   Marbois is not
an unfriendly witness.   On the other hand, there is much stronger
testimony to the same effect from the revolutionary party, which,
after an examination of the papers, denounced the policy of De
Vergennes as having been nothing better than "*une vile spécula-
tion.*"

Neither the internal dissensions, nor the external vices, upon the detrimental effects of which he had relied at the outset, proved sufficient to keep down the energies set in motion by the new principle of liberty. The instructions of his successor, Count de Montmorin, to his agents, were to avoid giving more strength to America. On Montmorin he devolved the penalty for his own temporary triumph. He was safe in his grave when the avalanche came down inflicting such a dreadful death upon his disciple. With him departed the brilliant era of Louis the Sixteenth's reign. He is the only minister of that nation, during his time, whose career was untinged with a shade of misfortune. His name will always stand, if not among the list of the great in genius or in learning, at least with those of the most wary and skilful steersmen through the difficult navigation of European diplomacy. Considered in the more restricted attitude of the *French* statesman, he is entitled to peculiar praise. Neither does his American policy deserve to be denominated, as it often is by his countrymen, a great mistake. The severance of Great Britain was indispensable to the maintenance of France as a power of the first class in the present century. He foresaw the danger from an empire which would have controlled all the oceans of the globe, and had the ready energy to seize the happy moment for dividing it forever. And his decision set forward the change which has since been and is yet, slowly but certainly. passing over the face of the world.

But if the statesmanship of De Vergennes merits a share of commendation, it is to be awarded to one trained by a discipline of more than half a century to unweave all the tangled threads of the foreign relations of France, the central nation of Europe. Not so with the American commissioners. To them diplomacy, as a science, was, up to the date when they were called to act as representatives of a new power among the nations, utterly unknown. Yet, although destined to meet many of the ablest men then flourishing in Europe, no one can follow the course of their proceedings without receiving a vivid impression of the great and varied abilities displayed by them in every situation in which they were placed. Notwithstanding the differences of sentiment, having their sources deep down in the peculiarities of their minds and hearts, they appear to have put them all out of sight in every case involving the interests of their common country. Of the purity of their patriotism there cannot be a shadow of a doubt. If each of them found a different field for its exercise, it was only the better to sustain the conclusion to which he arrived with the strength of all. The unity of action thus obtained, did not fail of its effect upon the British agents who were successively sent out to deal with them. Upon every point, on which there was a probability of dispute, they were prepared to reason far more vigorously than those whom they were deputed to meet. And in no case did they manifest more of tact and talent than in that for which they have been sometimes subject to censure. They succeeded in maintaining their own independence without furnishing the least opening for complaint of want of good faith to their ally. Even of Mr. Adams, little as he had cause to be satisfied with the treatment he had previously met with from Count de Vergennes, it was remarked by Mr. Vaughan, in a letter to Lord Shelburne, that nothing could be expected from him, friendly to Great Britain, which was to be obtained at the expense of the alliance with France. As he afterwards significantly remarked, in reply to the rather indiscreet outgiving of George the Third, he had no attachment but to his own country. This was the ruling principle of his foreign policy, not merely during this period, but throughout his life; and it was maintained under still more severe trials, the nature of which will be explained as this narrative proceeds.

When the accounts of the signature of the preliminaries arrived in the United States, they were received both in and out of congress with general joy, not unmingled with apprehensions. The terms obtained by the United States were so satisfactory as to preclude all possibility of complaint on this score. But there were some who disapproved of the violation of the instructions as a breach of good faith towards France, and others who, as yet unapprised of all the circumstances attending the negotiation, were fearful lest their ministers had fallen upon some trap, which might yet be sprung by Great Britain, and destroy at once the alliance with France and the pacification. The greatest embarassment seems to have arisen from the separate and secret article, establishing a boundary on the south, more or less remote, according to the hands into which the ownership of the Floridas might fall. This article was one, in which France could claim no interest excepting as the ally of Spain, and of which she could scarcely make a complaint even in that relation, as no rights of Spain in the tract of land conditionally ceded were to be affected.   From the abstract of the debates, to which this matter gave rise, and in which congress divided much in the usual way, it would appear as if the anxiety to avert possible consequences from what might be stigmatized as rashness in their ministers, was the leading motive in their policy.   Mr. Livingston, with characteristic caution, addressed a letter to the president of congress, dwelling upon the danger of this secret article as an instrument in the hands of Great Britain, and suggesting the adoption of an order instructing him to avert the apprehended evils, by communicating the article at once to the French minister, by directing the ministers to agree to the least favorable line of boundary, without any contingency as to the ownership of the adjacent territory, and by disclaiming any validity of the preliminaries unless in conjunction with a treaty between Great Britain and France.   The timidity of this proceeding, in surrendering a considerable tract to Spain without any consideration whatever, as well as in volunteering a disavowal of a construction to which the negotiators themselves had never dreamed of giving countenance, is its most striking feature.   Mr. Madison, among others, showed clearly enough, in the debate, that the alarm at the secret article, as a violation even of the well-known restrictions on the American commissioners, was without just foundation.   As Mr. Livingston's proposal did not meet with much favor in congress, three others were successively offered by different members, Mr. Williamson, Mr. Peters, and Mr. Alexander Hamilton, neither of which seemed exactly to meet the views of a majority.   On the other hand, Mr.

John Rutledge, of South Carolina, declared himself with so much warmth and earnestness against any action of the kind at all, and the New England members manifested so general a determination to sustain him, that the subject was not then further pressed. The arrival of later intelligence dispelled uneasiness as to possible consequences, so that the question lost its interest, and was forgotten in the general congratulations upon the glorious issue of the contest.

Mr. Livingston, however, anxious not to be wanting in courtesy to France by utterly neglecting the remonstrances which had at last arrived from that country, and sincere in his own belief of their soundness, seized the opportunity of the first dispatch to the commissioners to give his sentiments at large, and to express his dissent from the reasoning upon which they rested their separate action. This paper was received by a majority of them with not a little indignation. The task of framing a reply was devolved upon Mr. Jay, who accordingly prepared a draft, the substance of which was finally adopted and signed by them all. But a portion of the commencement, objected to by Dr. Franklin as unnecessary in the existing state of things, was stricken out. Mr. Jay, unwilling to lose it altogether, embodied it as an expression of his own sentiments in a private letter to Mr. Livingston, which has been since given to the world in the biography written by his son. Another form, proposed by Mr. Laurens as a substitute for that of Mr. Jay, met with no better success, and was also laid aside. But as these suppressed passages were deemed of sufficient consequence to be recorded in the book kept by the secretary of the commission, together with the reason given for not adopting them, it may subserve the purpose of completing the evidence of all the movements in this most important negotiation, to give them to the world.*

The general pacification was effected by the signature of the preliminaries between the three great powers on the 21st of January, 1783. But Great Britain, which had demanded at the hands of Lord Shelburne some sort of a peace, was by no means disposed to receive any sort with favor, much less to approve that which he was compelled to present. Of the factions into which parliament was then divided, not one but acknowledged the necessity under which he had acted, yet not one was averse to making it a cause of reproach to him that he had done so. History does not furnish an instance of a more gross perversion of public professions to private ends than this. The remnant of the Rockingham Whigs, which had continued in the cabinet at the time of Mr. Fox's resignation, now deserted Shelburne, so that, when the time came to meet parliament, he was left almost without support. It is difficult to find in the public policy of that minister any justification for the course adopted towards him by all sides. The only objection of a serious nature urged against him was a personal one, of duplicity in his relations with his colleagues. But although his isolated habits gave some color to the accusation, the instance most relied on by Mr. Fox to establish it, is now clearly proved to have been greatly misconceived. He certainly was not to

---

* See Appendix to the first volume of the collected works of J. Adams.

blame, in saying nothing of the proposal made to him to cede Canada by Dr. Franklin ; a proposal which he never manifested any inclination seriously to entertain. Yet the experiment served to show the impossibility of keeping a cabinet together upon his plan of imperfect confidence in its head on the part of its members. Lord Shelburne was quite as jealous of the influence of Fox, as Fox was suspicious of him. Yet he brought himself at last to offer to Fox, through the agency of the younger Pitt, a free opening to power. · The refusal to accept this proposal on any terms short of the removal of the chief, was the selfish act which determined the character of the rest of Fox's political life. Fearful of a union, in which there would have been a general harmony of principles, as likely to shut them out for a long time from place, the faction of Lord North, on their side, made overtures to their bitterest opponents, the Rockingham Whigs, which they, forgetful of their own self-respect, and listening only to the promptings of their favorite leader, were tempted, in an evil hour, to accept. Thus originated the ill-starred coalition, in which Fox began by condemning a treaty, the legitimate consequence of his own policy whilst a member of the ministry, the mere hesitation to accept which in its fullest extent by Shelburne had been his pretext for deserting it ; and in which he ended by approving, when he got to be a minister, the very same articles, in the shape of a definitive treaty, against which he made his victorious assault when offered in the form of preliminaries by Shelburne. The extent to which a contemporary age can be biased in its judgments by the authority of a man of leading character in the political

arena, it is almost impossible to measure by any standard
of abstract morality. There is no more striking instance
of it in English history, than that of Mr. Fox. But
posterity cannot be so far blinded by such influences as
to leave uncondemned those great delinquencies of his
life, both public and private, which forfeit for him the
honor of being set down as a benefactor of his own
generation, or an example for imitation by those that
are to come.

CHAPTER VIII.

IMMEDIATELY after the signature of the preliminary
articles, in the manner already mentioned, Mr. Adams,
in a dispatch to Mr. Livingston, transmitting them,
announced his desire to resign all his employments.
The principal objects for which he had consented to
come to Europe at all, having been accomplished, and
the definitive treaty being likely to be completed before
a reply could return, he felt warranted in asking to be
released from further service.   Congress, however, was
in no humor to comply with the request.   Satisfied with
the action of the commissioners in procuring the peace,
they were now desirous to enlist them in the work of
superadding a treaty of commerce with Great Britain.
This idea had taken its rise in a suggestion made by
Mr. Adams himself in a later dispatch, which lamented
the revocation of the commission formerly given to him,
and urged a re-establishment of it at this auspicious moment, in the hands of one or more of the official representatives of the country, who might be left in Europe.
Congress adopted it by giving the necessary powers to
Messrs. Adams, Franklin, and Jay.   And the receipt of
this intelligence determined Mr. Adams to remain,
after the signature of the definitive treaty.

But the labors, anxieties, and excitement of the trials through which he had passed, had acted strongly upon his physical frame, already weakened by one violent fever taken during his residence in Holland, two years before. Scarcely were the necessary dispatches, transmitting the history of the treaty of peace, fairly in the hands of Mr. Thaxter, his secretary, who was about to return home, when he was brought down again, in Paris, with a severe illness. Inasmuch as he has himself given a familiar, careless narrative of his adventures during the few months that ensued, which makes the last of the reminiscences supplied by him for the columns of the Boston "Patriot," and in which one or two curious anecdotes are related, it may afford a refreshing transition to insert whatever portions of it may appear to be of interest.

"Whether the violence of exercise in riding more than a hundred miles a day, for so many days together, on my journey to Holland, in a sultry season, or whether the deleterious steams of marshes and canals in that country, so pestilential to foreigners, had filled me with the seeds of disease, I found myself, on my return to Paris, very unwell, and continued in a feeble, drooping condition till Mr. Thaxter's departure. My disorder was, in part, occasioned, perhaps, or at least aggravated, by the sedentary and inactive life to which I was obliged to submit after my return from Holland. Travellers ought never to forget that, after a course of long journeys and uncommon exercise, their transition to a sedentary life and total inactivity ought not to be sudden. My duty demanded it of me, as I thought; for every moment of time that could be spared from meals and sleep was required of me and two clerks, Mr. Thaxter and Mr. Charles Storer, to copy my own papers, and those of Mr. Jay, who had no clerk or secretary.

" Mr. Thaxter was gone, and I soon fell down in a fever, not much less violent than that I had suffered two years before at Amsterdam. Sir James Jay, who had been some time in Paris, and had often visited at my house, became my physician, and I desired no better. The grand *Hôtel du Roi, Place du Carrousel,* where I had apartments, was situated at the confluence of so many streets, that it was a kind of thoroughfare. A constant stream of carriages was rolling by it over the pavements for one-and-twenty hours out of the twenty-four. From two o'clock to five in the morning there was something like stillness and silence, but all the other one-and-twenty hours was a constant roar, like incessant rolls of thunder. When I was in my best health, I sometimes thought it would kill me ; but now, reduced to extreme weakness, and burning with a violent fever, sleep was impossible. In this forlorn condition, Mr. Thaxter, who had been to me a nurse, a physician, and a comforter at Amsterdam, was separated from me forever. My American servant, Joseph Stevens, who had been useful to me in Amsterdam, had fallen in love with a pretty English girl (how she came there, I know not), and married her. Consequently he left my service, and soon after embarked for America, and perished at sea ; at least he has never been heard of since. With none but French servants about me, of whom, however, I cannot complain, for their kindness, attention, and tenderness surprised me, I was in a deplorable condition, hopeless of life in that situation. In this critical and desperate moment, my friends all despairing of my recovery in that thoroughfare, Mr. Barclay offered me apartments in his *hôtel* at Auteuil, and Sir James Jay thought I might be removed, and advised it. With much difficulty it was accomplished. On the 22d of September I was removed, and the silence of Auteuil, exchanged for the roar of the *Carrousel*, the pure air of a country garden, in place of the tainted atmosphere of Paris, procured me some sleep, and, with the skill of my physician, gradually dissipated the fever, though it left me extremely emaciated and weak.

"As I have never found, in the whole course of my life, any effectual resource for the preservation of health when enjoyed, or the recovery of it when lost, but exercise and simplicity of diet, as soon as I had strength, by the assistance of two servants to get into my carriage, I rode twice a day in the *Bois de Boulogne*. When my strength was sufficiently increased, I borrowed Mr. Jay's horse, *i.e.* my colleague's horse, and generally rode twice a day until I had made myself master of that curious forest. . . . . .

"Lost health is not easily recovered. Neither medicine, nor diet, nor any thing would ever succeed with me, without exercise in open air. And although riding in a carriage has been found of some use, and on horseback still more, yet none of these have been found effectual with me in the last resort, but walking ; walking four or five miles a day, sometimes for years together, with a patience, resolution, and perseverance, at the price of which many persons would think, and I have been sometimes inclined to think, life itself was scarcely worth purchasing. Not all the skill and kind assiduity of my physician, nor all the scrupulous care of my regimen, nor all my exercise in carriage and on the saddle, was found effectual for the restoration of my health. Still remaining feeble, emaciated, and languid to a great degree, my physician and all my friends advised me to go to England, and to Bath, to drink the waters and to bathe in them. The English gentlemen politely invited me, with apparent kindness, to undertake the journey.

"But before I set out, I ought not to forget my physician. Gratitude demands that I should remember his benevolence. His attendance had been voluntarily assiduous, punctual, and uniformly kind and obliging; and his success had been equal to his skill in breaking the force of the distemper, and giving me a chance of a complete recovery in time. I endeavored to put twenty guineas into his hand, but he positively refused to accept them. He said the pleasure of assisting a friend and countrymen in distress, in a foreign country, was reward enough for him, and he would have no other. I employed all the arguments and persuasions with him in my power, at least to receive the purchase of his medicines. He said he had used no medicines but such as he had found in my house among my little stores, and peremptorily and finally refused to receive a farthing for any thing.

"As my health, though still very feeble, was now thought sufficient to bear the journey, on Monday, the 20th of October, 1783, I set out, with my son and one servant, on a journey to London. . . . . .

"The post-boy (who, upon asking where I would be

carried, was answered 'to the best inn in London, for all are alike unknown to me') carried us to the Adelphi buildings in the Strand. Whether it was the boy's cunning, or whether it was mere chance, I know not, but I found myself in a street which was marked John's Street. The postilion turned a corner, and I was in Adam's Street. He turned another corner, and I was in John Adam's Street! I thought, surely we are arrived in Fairy-land. How can all this be?

"Arrived at Osborne's Adelphi Hotel, and having engaged convenient apartments, which was all I desired, and as much as my revenues could command, I inquired of Mr. Osborne, our landlord, about the oddity of meeting my own name in all the streets about his house. I was informed that the Adelphi Hotel and all the streets and buildings about it had been planned and executed by two architects by the name of Adams, two brothers from Scotland, the name of the oldest of whom was John, both under the protection and probably the support of the great Earl of Mansfield; that the hotel and many other of the buildings were elevated to a height in the air, so that the rooms for stables, stores and cellars, apparently under ground, were more spacious and capacious than all the buildings above ground; and that the elder brother, John Adams, had been permitted by Lord Mansfield to give his own name to all the streets he had erected, and the name of the Adelphi, the brothers, to the hotel.*

"I was not long at the Adelphi, but soon removed

---

* There were four brothers instead of two; a street was named for each of them. The surname was Adam.

to private lodgings, which, by the way, were ten times more public, and took apartments at Mr. Stockdale's, in Piccadilly, where Mr. Laurens had lately lodged before me. Here I had a great opportunity of learning (for Dr. Brett was at the next door) the state of the current literature of London. I will not enlarge upon this subject at present, if ever. I found it exactly similar to what I had seen in Paris. The newspapers, the magazines, the reviews, the daily pamphlets were all in the hands of hirelings, men of no character. I will sum up all upon this subject in the words of one of the most active and extensive among the printers and booksellers to me. 'Sir,' said he, 'the men of learning are all stark mad. There are in this city at least one hundred men of the best education, the best classical students, the most accomplished writers, any one of whom I can hire for one guinea a day to go into my closet and write for me whatever I please, for or against any man or any cause. It is indifferent to them whether they write *pro* or *con*.' These were the men, both in Paris and London, who preached about the progress of reason, the improvements of society, the liberty, equality, fraternity, and the rights of man. They made their experiment in France, and came very near it in England, Holland, Germany, Switzerland, Geneva, and, indeed, in all the rest of Europe. It is no wonder that so many of them concurred with Tacitus and Quintilian, in avowing their doubts whether the world was governed by blind chance or eternal fate. If they had not discarded a much better and more divine philosophy, they would never have reduced the world to this anarchy and chaos.

"Curiosity prompted me to trot about London as fast as good horses, in a decent carriage, could carry me. I was introduced, by Mr. Hartley, on a merely ceremonious visit, to the Duke of Portland, Mr. Burke, and Mr. Fox; but finding nothing but ceremony there, I did not ask favors or receive any thing but cold formalities from ministers of state or ambassadors. I found that our American painters had more influence at court to procure all the favors I wanted, than all of them. Mr. West asked of their Majesties permission to show me and Mr. Jay the originals of the great productions of his pencil, such as Wolf, Bayard, Epaminondas, Regulus, etc., which were all displayed in the queen's palace, called Buckingham House. The gracious answer of the king and queen was, that he might show us 'the whole house.' Accordingly, in the absence of the royal family at Windsor, we had an opportunity, at leisure, to see all the apartments, even to the queen's bedchamber, with all its furniture, to her Majesty's German Bible, which attracted my attention as much as any thing else. The king's library struck me with admiration. I wished for a week's time, but had but a few hours. The books were in perfect order, elegant in their editions, paper, binding, etc., but gaudy and extravagant in nothing. They were chosen with perfect taste and judgment; every book that a king ought to have always at hand, and so far as I could examine and could be supposed capable of judging, none other. Maps, charts, etc., of all his dominions in the four quarters of the world, and models of every fortress in his empire.

"In every apartment of the whole house, the same

simplicity, without the smallest affectation, ostentation, profusion, or meanness. I could not but compare it, in my own mind, with Versailles, and not at all to the advantage of the latter. I could not help comparing it with many of the gentlemen's seats which I had seen in France, England, and even Holland. The interior of this palace was perfect. The exterior, both in extent, cost, and appearance, was far inferior not only to Versailles and the seats of the princes in France, but to the country houses of many of the nobility and gentry of Great Britain. The truth is, a minister can at any time obtain from parliament a hundred millions to support any war, just or unjust, in which he chooses to involve the nation, much more easily than he can procure one million for the decent accommodation of the court. We gazed at the great original paintings of our immortal countryman, West, with more delight than on the very celebrated pieces of Vandyke and Rubens, and with admiration not less than that inspired by the cartoons of Raphael.

"Mr. Copley, another of my countrymen, with whom I had been much longer acquainted, and who had obtained, without so much royal protection, a reputation not less glorious, and that by studies and labors not less masterly in his art, procured me, and that from the great Lord Mansfield, a place in the House of Lords, to hear the king's speech at the opening of parliament, and to witness the introduction of the Prince of Wales, then arrived at the age of twenty-one. One circumstance, a striking example of the vicissitudes of life and the whimsical antitheses of politics, is too precious for taste, the same judgment, the same elegance, the same its moral to be forgotten. Standing in the lobby of the House of Lords, surrounded by a hundred of the first people of the kingdom, Sir Francis Molineux, the gentleman usher of the black rod, appeared suddenly in the room with his long staff, and roared out, with a very loud voice: 'Where is Mr. Adams, Lord Mansfield's friend?' I frankly avowed myself Lord Mansfield's friend, and was politely conducted, by Sir Francis, to my place. A gentleman said to me the next day: 'How short a time has passed since I heard that same Lord Mansfield say, in that same House of Lords, My Lords, if you do not kill him, he will kill you.'* Mr. West said to me that this was one of the finest finishings in the picture of American Independence.

"Pope had given me, when a boy, an affection for Murray. When in the study and practice of the law, my admiration of the learning, talents, and eloquence of Mansfield had been constantly increasing, though some of his opinions I could not approve. His politics in American affairs I had always detested. But now I found more politeness and good-humor in him than in Richmond, Camden, Burke, or Fox.

"If my business had been travels, I might write a book. But I must be as brief as possible.

"I visited Sir Ashton Lever's museum, where was a wonderful collection of natural and artificial curiosities from all parts and quarters of the globe. Here I saw

---

* This remark, applied to the Americans generally, was made at the beginning of the struggle, 20 December, 1775.

again that collection of American birds, insects, and other rarities, which I had so often seen before at Norwalk, in Connecticut, collected and preserved by Mr. Arnold, and sold by him to Governor Tryon for Sir Ashton. Here, also, I saw Sir Ashton and some other knights, his friends, practising the ancient, but, as I thought, long-forgotten art of archery. In his garden, with their bows and arrows, they hit as small a mark and at as great a distance as any of our sharp-shooters could have done with their rifles.

"I visited, also, Mr. Wedgwood's manufactory, and was not less delighted with the elegance of his substitute for porcelain, than with his rich collection of utensils and furniture from the ruins of Herculaneum, bearing incontestable evidence, in their forms and figures, of the taste of the Greeks; a nation that seems to have existed for the purpose of teaching the arts, and furnishing models to all mankind of grace and beauty in the mechanic arts, no less than in statuary, architecture, history, oratory, and poetry.

"The manufactory of cut glass, to which some gentlemen introduced me, did as much honor to the English as the mirrors, the Sèvres china, or the Gobelin tapestry of France. It seemed to be the art of transmuting glass into diamonds.

"Westminster Abbey, St. Paul's, the Exchange, and other public buildings did not escape my attention. I made an excursion to Richmond Hill to visit Governor Pownall and Mr. Penn, but had not time to visit Twickenham. The grotto and the quincunx, the rendezvous of Swift, Bolingbroke, Arbuthnot, Gay, Prior, and even the surly Johnson and the haughty Warburton, will never be seen by me, though I ardently desired it.

"I went to Windsor, and saw the castle and its apartments, and enjoyed its vast prospect. I was anxiously shown the boasted chambers where Count Tallard, the captive of the Duke of Marlborough, had been confined. I visited the terrace and the environs; and, what is of more importance, I visited the Eton school. And if I had been prudent enough to negotiate with my friend West, I doubt not I might have obtained permission to see the queen's lodge. But as the solicitation of these little favors requires a great deal of delicacy and many prudent precautions, I did not think it proper to ask the favor of anybody. I must confess that all the pomps and pride of Windsor did not occupy my thoughts so much as the forest, and comparing it with what I remembered of Pope's Windsor Forest.

"My health was very little improved by the exercise I had taken in and about London; nor did the entertainments and delights assist me much more. The change of air and of diet, from which I had entertained some hopes, had produced little effect. I continued feeble, low, and drooping. The waters of Bath were still represented to me as an almost certain resource. I shall take no notice of men or things on the road. I had not been twenty minutes at the hotel in Bath before my ancient friend and relation, Mr. John Boylston, called upon me, and dined with me. After dinner he was polite enough to walk with me about the town, showed me the Crescent, the public buildings, the card-rooms, the assembly-rooms, the dancing-rooms, etc., objects about which I had little more curiosity than about the bricks and pavements. The baths, and the accommodations for using the waters, were reserved for another day. But before that day arrived, I received dispatches from America, from London, and from Amsterdam, informing me that the drafts of congress, by Mr. Morris, for money to be transmitted in silver through the house of Le Couteulx, at Paris, and through the Havana, to Philadelphia, together with the bills drawn in favor of individuals in France, England, and Holland, had exhausted all my loan of the last summer, which had cost me so much fatigue and ill health; that an immense flock of new bills had arrived, drawn in favor of Sir George Baring, or Sir Francis Baring, I forget which, of London, and many other persons; that these bills had been already presented, and protested for non-acceptance; and that they must be protested, in their time, for non-payment, unless I returned immediately to Amsterdam, and could be fortunate enough to obtain a new loan, of which my bankers gave me very faint hopes.

"It was winter. My health was very delicate. A journey and voyage to Holland at that season would very probably put an end to my labors. I scarcely saw a possibility of surviving it. Nevertheless, no man knows what he can bear till he tries. A few moments' reflection determined me; for although I had little hope of getting the money, having experienced so many difficulties before, yet making the attempt and doing all in my power would discharge my own conscience, and ought to satisfy my responsibility to the public. I returned to London, and from thence repaired to Harwich. Here we found the packet detained by contrary winds and a violent storm. Detained in a very uncomfortable inn, ill accommodated and worse provided, I and mv son, without society and without books, wore away three days of *ennui*, not a little chagrined with the unexpected interruption of our visit to England, and the disappointment of our journey to Bath ; and not less anxious on account of our gloomy prospects for the future.

" On the fourth day, the wind having veered a little, we were summoned on board the packet. With great difficulty she turned the point and gained the open sea. In this channel, on both sides the island of Great Britain, there is, in bad weather, a tremulous, undulating, turbulent kind of irregular tumbling sea that disposes men more to the *mal de mer* than even the surges of the Gulf Stream, which are more majestic. The passengers were all at extremities for almost the whole of the three days that we were struggling with stormy weather and beating against contrary winds. The captain and his men, worn out with fatigue and want of sleep, despaired of reaching Helvoet Sluys, and determined to land us in the island of Goree. We found ourselves, upon landing, on a desolate shore, we knew not where. A fisherman's hut was all the building we could see. There we were told it was five or six miles from the town of Goree. The man was not certain of the distance, but it was not less than four miles, nor more than six. No kind of conveyance could be had. In my weak state of health, rendered more impotent by bad nourishment, want of sleep, and wasting sickness on board the packet, I thought it almost impossible that in that severe weather I could walk through ice and snow four miles before I could find rest. As has been said before, human nature never knows what it can endure before it tries the experiment. My young companion was in fine spirits; his gayety, activity, and attention to me increased as difficulties multiplied, and I was determined not to despair. I walked on with caution and moderation, and survived much better than could have been expected, till we reached the town of Goree. When we had rested and refreshed ourselves at the inn, we made inquiries concerning our future route. It was pointed out to us, and we found we must cross over the whole island of Goree, then cross the arm of the sea to the island of Over Flackee, and run the whole length of that island to the point from whence the boats pass a very wide arm of the sea, to the continent, five or six miles from Helvoet Sluys.

But we were told that the rivers and arms of the sea were all frozen over, so that we could not pass them but upon the ice, or in ice-boats. Inquiring for a carriage of some kind or other, we were told that the place afforded none better, and, indeed, none other than boor's wagons. That this word *boor* may not give offence to any one, it is necessary to say that it signifies no more in Dutch than peasant in France, or countryman, husbandman, or farmer in America. Finding no easier vehicle, we ordered a wagon, horses, and driver to be engaged for us, and departed on our journey. Our carriage had no springs to support, nor cushions to soften, the seats. On hard benches, in a wagon fixed to the axletree, we were trotted and jolted over the roughest road you can well imagine. The soil upon these islands is a stiff clay, and in rainy weather becomes as soft and miry as mortar. In this state they had been trodden by horses, and cut into deep ruts by wagon wheels, when a sudden change of the weather had frozen them as hard as rocks. Over this bowling green we rolled, or rather hopped and skipped, twelve miles in the island of Goree, and I know not how many more in Over Flackee, till we arrived at the inn at the ferry, where we again put up. Here we were obliged to wait several days, because the boats were all on the other side. The pains of waiting for a passage were much alleviated here by the inexpressible delight of rest, after such violent agitations by sea and land, by good fires, warm rooms, comfortable beds, and wholesome Dutch cheer. And all these were made more agreeable by the society of a young English gentleman, not more than twenty, who, happening to come to the inn, and finding we had the best room and the best fire, came in, and very modestly and respectfully requested to sit with us. We readily consented, and soon found ourselves very happy in his company. He was cheerful, gay, witty, perfectly well bred, and the best acquainted with English literature of any youth of his age I ever knew. The English classics, English history, and all the English poets were familiar to him. He breakfasted, dined, supped, and, in short, lived with us, and we could not be dull, and never wanted conversation while we stayed. As I never asked his name or his history, I cannot mention either.

"We were obliged to bid high for a passage, and promise them whatever they demanded. Signals were made, and at last an ice-boat appeared. An ice-boat is a large ferry-boat, placed and fastened on runners. We embarked early in the morning. The passage is very wide over this arm of the sea. We were rowed in the water till we came to the ice, when the skipper and his men, to the number of eight or ten, perhaps, leaped out upon the ice, and hauled the boat up after them, when the passengers were required to get out and walk upon the ice, while the boatmen dragged the boat upon her runners. Presently, they would come to a spot where the ice was thin and brittle, when all would give way, and down went the boat into the water. The men were so habituated to this service that they very dexterously laid hold of the sides, and leaped into the boat; then they broke away the thin ice till the boat came to a part thick enough for the passengers to leap in, when the men broke away the thin ice forward, and rowed the boat in the water till she came to a place again strong enough to bear, when all must disembark again, and march men and boat upon the ice. How many times we were obliged to embark and disembark, in the course of the voyage, I know not, but we were all day and till quite night in making the passage. The weather was cold; we were all frequently wet; I was chilled to the heart, and looked, I suppose, as I felt, like a withered old worn-out carcass. Our polite skipper frequently eyed me, and said he pitied the old man. When we got ashore, he said he must come and take the old man by the hand and wish him a safe journey to the Hague. He was sorry to see that I was in such bad health, and suffered so much as he had observed upon the passage. He had done every thing in his power, and so had his men, to make it easy and expeditious; but they could do no better. This I knew to be true. We parted very good friends, well satisfied with each other. I had given them what they very well loved, and they had done their best for me.

"I am weary of my journey, and shall hasten to its close. No carriage was to be had, and no person was to be seen. But, by accident, a boor came along with an empty wagon. We offered him any thing he would ask to take us to the Briel. Arrived there, we obtained a more convenient carriage, but the weather was so severe and the roads so rough that we had a very uncomfortable journey to the Hague. Here I was at home in the *Hôtel des États Unis*, but could not indulge myself. My duty lay at Amsterdam, among undertakers and brokers, with very faint hopes of success. I was, however, successful beyond my most sanguine expectations, and obtained a loan of millions enough to prevent all the bills of congress from being protested for non-payment, and to preserve our credit in Europe for two or three years longer, after which another desperate draft of bills from congress obliged me once more to go over from England to Holland to borrow money. I succeeded also in that; which preserved our credit till my return to America, in 1788, and till the new government came into operation and found itself rich enough.

"Here ends the very rough and uncouth detail of my voyages, journeys, labors, perils, and sufferings under my commissions for making peace with Great Britain.

"I had ridden on horseback often to congress, over

roads and across ferries, of which the present generation have no idea; and once, in 1777, in the dead of winter, from Braintree to Baltimore, five hundred miles, upon a trotting horse, as Dean Swift boasted that he had done, or could do. I had been three days in the Gulf Stream, in 1778, in a furious hurricane and a storm of thunder and lightning, which struck down our men upon deck, and cracked our mainmast; when the oldest officers and stoutest seamen stood aghast, at their last prayers, dreading every moment that a butt would start, and all perish. I had crossed the Atlantic, in 1779, in a leaky ship, with perhaps four hundred men on board, who were scarcely able, with two large pumps going all the twenty-four hours, to keep water from filling the hold, in hourly danger, for twenty days together, of foundering at sea. I had passed the mountains in Spain, in the winter, among ice and snow, partly on mule-back and partly on foot; yet I never suffered so much in any of these situations as in that jaunt from Bath to Amsterdam, in January, 1784. Nor did any of those adventures ever do such lasting injuries to my health. I never got over it till my return home in 1788."

Among the singular coincidences which occurred in the life of Mr. Adams, down to its very close, that which is alluded to in the preceding reminiscence is deserving to be dwelt upon for a moment. He came to England, for the first time, in no official capacity, but merely as a visitor, for the sake of his health. Here he saw the Duke of Portland, Mr. Fox, and Mr. Burke, in the short-lived enjoyment of office through the coalition, whom he found shy of acknowledging much acquaintance with the triumphant rebels; whilst, on the other hand he, one of the most distinguished of them, was indebted to the interference of a refugee for the privilege of being admitted by the Tory, Lord Mansfield, to witness the confession made to his parliament and people by George the Third himself, that he had made a treaty of peace with the colonies no longer, but now the independent States of North America. How different must have been the feelings of the two persons most deeply interested in the scene; the sovereign, who felt that he had lost the brightest jewel of his crown, and whose instinctive pride, rather than his forecast, taught him that he was marking the epoch of culmination in the fortunes of Britain; and the subject, at first reluctantly drawn in to resistance, but impelled by his sense of injustice, at every personal sacrifice, to undertake a part of the gigantic task of calling a new empire into being, and, once undertaken, to follow it up, in the face of every discouragement, with a soul undaunted by the comminations lanced against him as a traitor, who could securely occupy a place in the heart of Britain's proudest assembly, in the very presence of the monarch, to hear him confess to the world that he had thrown away an empire. And instead of dishonoring the humble name of his American auditor, that name was henceforth to go out indelibly graven by his act upon the list of those who, by upholding fundamental principles at critical moments, originate the beneficial movements of the world!

The reckless and hap-hazard manner in which the financial officers of congress continued to overdraw the accounts of their bankers in Europe, had once more placed the credit of the United States at Amsterdam in the utmost jeopardy. It was the announcement of this fact, made to Mr. Adams by Messrs. Willink and others, the undertakers of the former loan, which had called him from London, to undertake, in the dead of winter, the journey to Amsterdam described in the preceding extract. On his first arrival he seems to have entertained no hope of being able to raise further means in season to meet the approaching liabilities. The United States had shown few signs of restoration from the exhaustion consequent upon the war, or of energy in reorganizing their finances. Neither did their practice, of drawing at random, recommend itself to the shrewd and careful habits of the Dutch. It is not too much to say that, had the operation been then to begin, scarcely any house would have been found daring enough to undertake it. But in the lucky moment of confidence inspired by the successful issue of the struggle, one loan had been taken up. This created in the creditors a new and strong class of motives to maintain, if possible, the solvency of the debtor State, and in the undertakers to exert themselves to persuade them to come to their aid. As a consequence, propositions for a new loan were started, varying from the old one only in the less advantageous terms obtained by the United States. Under the circumstances, nothing could be expected for a country which had placed itself so rashly at the mercy of its creditors, to save it from mercantile dishonor, better than that it should be made to pay a price for its improvidence. Mr. Adams, finding himself reduced to the painful dilemma of suffering the bills to be protested or of accepting the terms offered, very wisely decided for the latter. For this and all his services of the same kind in Holland, as well before as afterwards, by means of which the United States were carried through the period of social disorganization that intervened between the peace and the establishment of the federal constitution, Mr. Adams received the repeated thanks of Mr. Morris and his successors in the direction of the finances.

Whilst thus engaged in Holland, Frederick the Second, of Prussia, who had not been an inattentive observer of the course of events, directed his minister at the Hague to make overtures to Mr. Adams for the negotiation of a treaty of commerce. This proposal, so complimentary in its nature, was cordially received by him, though he had no powers to treat. With this understanding, and the assent of his colleagues in Europe, the form of the treaty just entered into with Sweden, by the agency of Dr. Franklin, was transmitted for the consideration of the king as a suitable basis of negotiation. The monarch soon returned it with but one or two material changes, drawn up by his own hand. After passing forward and backward once or twice, the plan was finally agreed upon and transmitted to congress for their approval. That body, however, had already established a new commission, by virtue of which Mr. Adams, Dr. Franklin, and Mr. Jefferson, who was sent out to take the place of Mr. Jay, were empowered to negotiate treaties of commerce with any and all foreign powers who should be disposed to enter into them. And on them the duty was devolved of continuing the Prussian negotiation upon a basis somewhat altered from that agreed upon in Europe.

Thus it was that Mr. Adams found himself engaged in new labors, that might extend his residence abroad for an indefinite time. How he might have welcomed this under other circumstances, is uncertain. Happily he had written out to America directions to Mrs. Adams, in case of any such event, to come out, with his only daughter, and join him, which she accordingly did during the summer of 1784. Her arrival completely altered the face of his affairs. He forgot the ten years of almost constant separation which had taken place, and became reconciled at once to a longer stay abroad. No man depended more than he upon the tranquil enjoyments of home for his happiness. He took the house at Auteuil, to which he had been removed in the preceding year for recovery from his illness, and returned to a state of life placid and serene. The anxieties and responsibilities, which had so long and so severely pressed upon him in his public life, were all removed. His country was free, and his mind was not so absorbed in what remained of his public avocations as to be closed against the impressions to be received from the neighborhood of the most refined, brilliant, and intellectual community in the world. Paris was just then in that stage of transition from the old to the new, which is apt to quicken whatever there may be of sprightly in society, without having yet materially impaired its stability. Literature and philosophy had become the rage even in fashionable circles. And the flippant ridicule of all things, sacred and profane, of which Voltaire had set a fascinating example, had supplied in zest what was subtracted from the dignified proprieties of ancient France. Mr. Adams saw something of the literary men of the day, of Marmontel, and Raynal, and De Mably, and he became quite intimate with the Abbes Chalut and Arnoux, and Count Sarsfield, men who lived for society, and who were fully able to open to him a view of its springs, ordinarily little obvious to foreigners. Deriving great enjoyment as he unquestionably did from these opportunities, his quick sagacity was not however less active in determining for himself the question, how far the nation he saw before him would be fitted for any other form of government than the one they had. From the opinion then formed he never changed through all the later vicissitudes which made the maintenance of it sometimes of serious import to himself. The lapse of three-quarters of a century, during which almost every variety of experiment has been tried without success, has thus far only proved the correctness of his judgment.

The commissioners assembled, for the first time, for the transaction of business, at Paris, on the 30th of August, 1784, and they immediately adopted the requisite measures to apprise the representatives of the different maritime nations residing in Paris, of the nature and extent of their powers. Favorable answers were received from several governments; but Frederick the Second seems to have been the only sovereign who prosecuted the object with earnestness. Besides the continual exchange of official dispatches, touching the details of the proposed treaty, Baron de Thulemeier maintained his friendly private communications with Mr. Adams as the individual through whom the overture had first been made, and through whom he could best obtain the modifications his sovereign had at heart. Much time elapsed before all the trifling points of difference were adjusted, and in the interval Mr. Adams had been transferred to another scene, so that he was unable to meet the wishes of the worthy baron, to have the last act, the signature of the papers, executed on the same spot and by the same persons under whose auspices the first had been commenced. This treaty is sufficiently remarkable to merit to be distinguished from every other yet made. Free trade, freedom of neutrals, respect for private property of enemies at sea, the abolition of privateering, and the limitation over the power to confiscate contraband of war, were new and bold steps in the progress of international civilization. Much of the honor of the suggestions designed to soften the ferocity of warfare is due to the original mind of Dr. Franklin. But, as Mr. Adams justly remarks, the lesson which they furnish to mankind will derive its greatest force from the fact that they were adopted by the hero of the seven years' war.

It must be conceded that as yet the principles laid down have met with little response from the philanthropic ardor of the world. But in the progress of mankind the vicissitudes of nations play an important part. And Great Britain, which for a time formed the great obstacle to the improvement of the maritime law, has latterly shown a spirit auguring better things. The signature of the treaty was followed by a period, in which, instead of softening the harshness of the ancient rules, it seemed as if all restraints upon the passions of men had lost their force. Slowly does the statesman of any age resist the tendency of his position to fix skepticism in the possibility of any good. The hard realities of mortal conflict repel the gentle monitions of charity and brotherly love, as wild dreams of the enthusiast. And, what is worse, the hand which has grown to wield a giant's strength, directs its power in a very different spirit from that which guided it in the weakness of infancy. Unfortunately the United States, at the time when they executed this treaty, were in a situation in which its provisions, if generally adopted, would have effectually protected their interests from the haughty domination of the sea, assumed by their ancient mistress. Hence their philanthropy was not wholly free from suspicion of incidental benefit to ensue to themselves. Time has altered this. The nation has now attained a great stature. It yet remains to be seen whether, in its mature vigor, it will adhere to a policy which shall protect the weak against it, as it sought to be protected against the strong, and, by voluntarily setting bounds to its ability to do mischief, furnish a real example of disinterestedness and magnanimity, for the benefit of all futurity.

It has been remarked that this time was to Mr. Adams one of the periods of his life of the most unmixed enjoyment. With his wife, his eldest son, John Quincy, then just rising into a youth of the greatest promise, and a daughter in whom anybody would have felt a pride, about him, near the society of a cultivated metropolis, into which his official position gave him free admission, he had little to do but to enjoy the day as it passed, heedless of the morrow. Some little notion of his way of life may be gathered from the fresh and sprightly letters of Mrs. Adams, addressed, during this time, to her friends and relatives at home, which have been already given to the world. He was not, however, reserved for satiety in this enjoyment. On the 24th of February, 1785, congress, not insensible of the injury committed by the revocation of his former commission, elected him to the post of Envoy to the court of St. James's. The position was interesting and important. Count de Vergennes observed to him, that it was a marking event, to be the first representative of his country to that which had been its sovereign. The Duke of Dorset, then the British ambassador at Paris, remarked to him, that "he would be stared at a great deal." Trifles indicate character. Without going the length of De Retz, in his judgment pronounced upon Cardinal Chigi, it will not be unsafe in this instance to measure the relative stature of those two men by this single specimen. Mr. Adams, on the other hand, saw in the result not simply a post of honor, but likewise a position of heavy responsibility.

In May of this year (1785) he transferred himself and his family to the other side of the Channel, prepared to undertake the new duties to which he had been appointed. The first thing to be done was to go through the ceremony of presentation to the sovereign; to stand face to face with the man, whom he had for the first forty years of his life habitually regarded as his master, and who never ceased to regard him, and the rest of his countrymen, as no better than successful rebels against his legitimate authority. In his dispatch to Mr. Jay, then secretary of foreign affairs, Mr.

Adams has left a very interesting account of this meeting. That paper is so easily accessible in the collected edition of his writings that its repetition here is needless. It is not difficult to conceive the varying and opposite emotions by which the parties must have been agitated. On the one side was the king, whose life was one resolute effort to maintain his will above all opposition, until his nervous structure sunk under the struggle. Never reconciled to failure, never yielding cheerfully to defeat, never abandoning a conviction, he was now condemned to the bitter mortification of recognizing an insurgent, whom he thought a traitor, as the representative of a country, the defection of which was, in his eyes, the great calamity of his reign. On the other side was a man with a will quite as stern, with opinions quite as deeply rooted, and a capacity incomparably more profound, all, however, subordinated, at the moment, to a sense of the necessity of uniting suitable deference to the monarch with the dignity becoming the representative of an equal power, so far as neither to offend Great Britain nor to degrade the United States. This delicate task was to be executed, too, in the home of George the Third, where every one around was a courtier sympathizing with his master's mortification, and curious rather than concerned as to the mode in which the rebel might acquit himself. The Duke of Dorset knew his countrymen well when he predicted their stare, but there is discrimination even in that practice, which at all courts is apt to depend upon the presumed temper of the ruler.

All this, however, was outside of the conference, no witness to which was admitted, excepting Lord Carmarthen, the official secretary of foreign affairs. The addresses are reported only by Mr. Adams. That made by himself, as he admits, with visible agitation, though concise, appears extremely appropriate. It is conciliatory in spirit, without betraying any sense of inferiority; holding out a hand as to a distinguished friend, but not to a patron. George the Third was not quite so successful. He betrayed that he had learned something of Mr. Adams's lack of good-will to the French court; and this impression, confirmed by the words of civility to himself as well as the allusion to ancient ties, appears to have raised in his mind an implication which the terms of the address itself did not justify. The difficulty was increased by the few sentences afterwards spoken to Mr. Adams. They made his position very delicate. It was of the utmost consequence to escape the imputation even of acquiescing in any idea derogatory to the impartial attitude of his countrymen as well as to his own, whilst it was equally important to avoid appearing to slight a civility. Mr. Adams extricated himself with great presence of mind. Apparently falling in with the sense of the king's language, he nevertheless added the significant words: "I must avow to your Majesty, I have no attachment but to my own country." They naturally harmonized with the rectitude of George's character as a British statesman, and therefore brought from his heart the immediate reply: "An honest man will never have any other." In this sense two more accordant minds were not to be found in the broad surface of both hemispheres. The meeting fitly terminated here. Seldom has it happened, with the empty ceremonials of court presentation, that

the individualities of the respective actors have signified
so much.

But although George the Third had submitted with
dignity to the painful necessity of this conference, it
was a sacrifice attended with no permanently favorable
result either to America or to Mr. Adams. The Revolution and all connected with it was an unpleasant topic
to which he never voluntarily turned his attention.
The band of king's friends, for which his reign is memorable in the British constitutional history, was sure to
reflect the color of his opinions so long as he held the
reins. Hence the obvious wisdom of conciliating the
young and rising nation on the other side of the Atlantic was forgotten, and the error of supercilious neglect
was preferred. Throughout the whole political history
of Great Britain this marked fault may be traced in its
relations with foreign nations, but it never showed itself
in more striking colors than during the first half century after the independence of the United States. The
effects of the mistake then committed have been perceptible ever since. Mr. Jefferson, who soon joined
Mr. Adams in London, for the purpose of carrying out,
in the case of the British government, the powers vested
in the commission to negotiate commercial treaties, has
left his testimony of the treatment he met with at court.
The king turned his back upon the American commissioners, a hint which, of course, was not lost upon the
circle of his subjects in attendance. Who can measure
the extent of the influence which even so trifling an insult at this moment may have had in modifying the later
opinions of the two men who were subjected to it?
And in view of their subsequent career in the United

States, who can fail to see how much those opinions have done to give to America the impressions respecting Great Britain that have prevailed down to this day? Often has it happened that the caprices of men in the highest stations have produced more serious effects upon the welfare of millions than the most elaborate policy of the wisest statesmen.

In truth, the leading minds in the government of Britain had been much occupied in deciding upon the course proper to adopt towards the new American nation, and on this subject a wide difference appeared among them. It was a critical moment. There was a choice to be made between opposite ideas: one, leading to hearty conciliation and the establishment of relations of true reciprocity; the other, removing further and further the distance between the kindred peoples, and confirming the alienation which warfare had begun. The majority decided; and they preferred the latter. A generous hand extended to the struggling young country, a liberal construction of treaty stipulations, and a frank concession of commercial privileges, might have won back the confidence of America, and have become the means of imposing upon her chains quite as durable, though by no means so galling, as any which Great Britain could ever have desired her to wear. Instead of this, she relapsed into a cold, distrustful, passive state, offering nothing, requiring every thing, waiting for events in order to see how much could be made out of the distresses of America, and indulging a hope that the prize might yet, by some accident or other, be thrown back into her hands. The policy which the three American negotiators of the

treaty of peace marked out to Mr. Oswald, had it been
followed out, would have kept the United States tribu-
taries to the mother country for a century.   That
which was adopted by British ministers, under the instigation of discontented refugees who ever proved
their most fatal counsellors, nursed the feelings of enmity already engendered, in such a manner as to break
out a quarter of a century later into another conflict of
arms, and as even now, after forty years of profound
peace and much more conciliatory treatment, not to be
altogether at rest.*

It is no more than common justice, however, to one
eminent statesman of that day, to add that this unfortunate decision was made in opposition to his better
judgment.   William Pitt, whilst acting as the youthful
chancellor of the exchequer to Lord Shelburne, and
not yet overwhelmed by the embarrassments that
crushed him in after-life, had shown an inclination to
follow alike the impulses of his heart and the dictates
of his education.   His system, as first declared, was
highly liberal, and, could he then have carried it into
full execution, would have placed his name on a level
quite as high as his father's ever deserved to stand.
Among its marked features, was the introduction of a
bill into parliament, which, though it placed the ships
of the United States on the footing of all other independent nations, at the same time laid no higher duties
upon their products than those levied upon the British

---

* Since these words were written, another marked illustration
of their truth has occurred, the evil consequences of which it
remains for circumstances only to develop.

themselves. And with yet greater liberality, it threw open to them the commerce with the British colonies in America, thus removing at once a source of irritation which from the failure of this measure remained in activity for half a century. Regarded as a mere question of self-interest, this bill would have been of great advantage to Great Britain, independently of its effect in conciliating the temper of America. Perseverance in the policy it indicated would have anticipated the events of the last ten years, and averted the conflicts, and the waste of blood and treasure on both sides, which have occurred in the interval.

But the liberal ministry of Lord Shelburne survived the proposition scarcely a month; and its coalition successors listened to very different counsels. Lord Sheffield gave expression to the remonstrance of the navigating interest, which predicted its own downfall in the colonial trade as a consequence of such a policy. He borrowed the language of Deane, Galloway, and Oliver, when he painted in vivid colors, not quite harmonizing with the other picture, the ruin and confusion in which the colonists were involved by the state of anarchy consequent upon their independence. And then he ventured to whisper the prediction that, out of this chaos, New England, at least, would, in the end, solicit to come back as a repentant child to the maternal embrace. These arguments finally carried the day. In July of the year 1783, the exclusive system was decreed, first by orders in council, then by temporary acts of parliament. The United States were treated as utter strangers, and carefully shut out from trade with the colonies. Restriction and commercial jealousy were the order of the day. The demonstrations were viewed by all Americans as hostile in spirit, and therefore to be met in the same manner. The failure of all efforts to establish an effective counter-system of restriction went a great way to rouse them to a sense of the necessity of a better form of government. Pride came in aid of principle, stimulating the sluggish and quickening the timid, until the cry for a new confederation became general. The pamphlet of Lord Sheffield had its effect upon the formation and adoption of the federal constitution in 1788. Thus it often happens with nations that think to make a gain out of the embarrassments and miseries of their neighbors. Indignation at once supplies the vigor to apply a remedy, which, had the matter been left to reason alone, might have been put off a great while or never been resorted to at all. Lord Sheffield's interference must be classed among the secondary misfortunes which befell Great Britain in the disastrous record of the American war; whilst, among the people of America, it deserves to be remembered with satisfaction as a conversion of what was intended to be a poison into a restoring medicine.

The restrictive policy having been thus determined upon before Mr. Adams's arrival, little prospect was left to him of effecting any beneficial change. His labors during his stay in Great Britain were therefore confined to fruitless solicitations for the execution of several articles of the treaty of peace. The posts which were to be surrendered had been retained, and no provision had been made to compensate for the slaves and property carried away by the military commanders, contrary to agreement. These complaints were certainly founded in justice; but, on the other hand, the British government were not without reasonable grounds of complaint for similar short-comings permitted by the Americans. So far from facilitating the recovery of British debts, several States had interposed further obstacles by legislation. The exhaustion of the people was great, and their feelings were still bitter. Poverty united with passion to keep up the hatred of refugees and Tories. The claims advanced by English creditors for interest during the whole period of the war, against merchants whose property had been sacrificed in the struggle, were regarded as little better than the demand of Shylock for the whole pound of flesh nearest the heart. Superadded to all this was the effect of the utter relaxation of the bonds of government, rendering a remedy for any existing evil difficult of attainment. No State was responsible for the acts of its neighbor, and each had within its power the means of rendering null the best-intended legislation of the rest. The confederation, hooped together by the bands of a common war, was falling to ruins in peace. In real truth, America could not, and Great Britain would not, because America did not, execute the treaty. Under such circumstances, effective negotiation was out of the question. Mr. Adams confined himself to the painful duty of remonstrating almost equally with both governments. His correspondence was of more service at home than abroad, for the letters, communicated from time to time by congress to the separate States, for the purpose of stimulating them to perform their duties, served to accelerate the state of public opinion which, in good time, brought effectual relief.

The situation of an envoy from one nation to another is likely to be made imposing as well as agreeable in direct proportion to the impression that prevails in the world of the power and the energy of the government by which he is sent. For a short time after the close of the struggle, the different sovereigns of Europe awaited with curiosity the results that were to follow the successful establishment of American independence. But as the accounts came, symptomatic of nothing but anarchy and confusion, the inference grew general that the experiment of self-government had failed, and that the new nation would prove of little account in the affairs of the globe. To an indifferent observer looking from the English point of view, Mr. Adams soon ceased to appear as representing any thing but disorder. His people, impoverished by a nine years' struggle for a fancied good, seemed plunged into an abyss of irremediable evil. The causes for this state of things were too far off to be analyzed. It was enough that the attempt to re-establish the ordinary course of justice had been met with resistance, to convince a European that an aversion to paying debts honestly contracted had much more to do with American notions of liberty than principle. Hence he held up his hands in amazement at the profligacy of a community which refused to execute its recognized contracts, and determined to waste no more sympathy upon a people thus proving itself beneath his contempt. In Great Britain, especially, this spectacle was witnessed with a mixed feeling of disgust and exultation. No disposition existed to palliate faults or to overlook errors. The observation of them served rather as a relief to wounded pride. It was just what might have been expected. The contemptible rebels were served right. They were paying the penalty of their sedition and treason. Here was the natural end of all the fine professions about the love of liberty. The liberty wanted was of that kind which means license, which abhors the restraints of well-ordered society, which revels in impunity for crime. To communities thus showing their incompetency to take care of themselves, what was the need of paying the smallest regard? And of him who came to London to represent them, what could be the importance? It might not be a great while before they would all be seen on their knees, supplicating to be taken back on any terms, repenting of their past sins, and promising that they would never commit the like again. Then would be the hour of just retribution. And the ways of Great Britain would go forth justified over the earth.

Such being the state of opinion, the situation of Mr. Adams may be easily imagined; a situation which, instead of growing better, became more hopeless of good in every hour of his stay. The monarch, never well reconciled to the triumph of his subjects, became less and less disposed to put restraint on his feelings. He was cold. Of course, his family were cold. Of course, the courtiers were freezing. What is not in vogue with the quality in England, is sure to be slighted by the commons. There was no cordiality anywhere excepting among the dissenters and the very few who leaned to republican doctrines: no better association than this to prove how unfashionable was every thing American. Of civility, rigidly formal, such as only the

English know how in perfection to make offensive, there was enough.   No marked insult; nothing but supercilious indifference.   Official representations lay long unheeded.   The courtesy of sending out a minister to America was left unregarded.   Last of all, the commercial policy, which had been thus far kept in operation by temporary acts, was made permanent by parliament. This was in 1788, a few months after Mr. Adams had solicited permission to return home.   His mission had only served to convince him that nothing was to be looked for in Great Britain but ill-will.   Neither could he indulge even in the luxury of complaint, for he had it not to say that America had placed herself in a position void of offence.

Yet, apart from the embarrassments occasioned by the mortifying condition of his own country, the period passed by Mr. Adams in England was not without its agreeable compensations.   The presence of his wife and daughter, and the marriage contracted by the latter with Colonel William Stephens Smith, whom, after many years of honorable service in the army, congress had sent out as secretary to the legation in London, afforded him the domestic society without which he never could be happy; and the leisure he enjoyed from pressing public business yielded an opportunity to turn his mind to other useful objects.   Nothing affected him more than the accounts of the condition of the States, threatening, as they seemed to do, the failure of all the bright hopes he had cherished of their career as a united and independent nation.   The difficulties in their way were clearly enough to be traced to one source, the want of energetic government.   It seemed therefore of importance that the true principles, at the foundation of a well-ordered system, should be fully explained. In the formation of the draft of a constitution for Massachusetts, in 1779, Mr. Adams had first labored to embody favorite ideas, which his later opportunities to view the practical operation of the British government had only tended more fully to confirm. He now directed his attention to the analysis of the theory upon which it rested, and to the possibility of stripping it of those appendages which foster a great inequality of social condition, so as to adapt it to purely republican habits. The experiment promised to be of use in confirming the popular mind in the United States, now showing tendencies to wild and dangerous errors, and he determined to make it. Inasmuch as later events tended greatly to distort a proper conception of his views, traces of which are thickly scattered in the writings left by some of his contemporaries, it will not be out of place here to give a brief and impartial summary of the principles that appear to constitute his system.

Unlike most speculators on the theory of government, Mr. Adams begins by assuming the imperfection of man's nature, and introducing it at once as an element with which to compose his edifice. He finds the human race impelled by their passions as often as guided by their reason, sometimes led to good actions by scarcely corresponding motives, and sometimes to bad ones rather from inability to resist temptation than from natural propensity to evil. This is the cornerstone of his system. And any substitute for it which involves a different idea, such, for example, as that men will certainly do right from their love of it, or that

they can only be deterred from evil by the fear of punishment; any substitute that omits to provide in as
many ways as possible for the tremendous working of
the passions which attends all contests for the possession
of power, must, according to him, end in failure. The
problem to be solved is, to what extent these adverse influences, not less than the virtues of all the citizens, can
be made to subserve the purpose of supporting government instead of shaking it. This cannot be expected
to be done by concentrating power in one place, to
be acquired by efforts all exerted in one direction; for
such a plan would expose the whole edifice to be sub-
merged by every successive wave of opinion. Neither
can it be hoped from the setting in opposition of forces
nearly equal; for the conflicts that might result would
inevitably be so violent as to threaten total ruin. The
true end is, to find the means so to decentralize power,
so to distribute it in a multiplicity of parts, as to give
no undue preponderance in any single one, and yet to
maintain the healthy co-operation of all.

To arrive at practical results, it is necessary, then, to
classify powers. The *interests* of men in society lie at
the foundation of the attachment to property, through
the unequal operation of which arises the distinction
between the rich and poor. Their *passions* make themselves felt in the ambition of place as well as in the desire for fame. Out of these causes issue three concentrated forms of social energy: the multitude, who must
ever represent poverty and numbers; the rich, who
represent education and property; and the chief, who
symbolizes the aspirations of the whole. A wise forecast would then provide free play for the legitimate ex-

ercise of these several forces, in some shape or other; thus making each subservient to the common support, and yet placing careful limitations and restrictions around them all. Mr. Adams thought this admirably arranged in the constitution of Great Britain, and therefore worthy of imitation. The distribution of power in the three parts, executive, legislative, and judicial, with the introduction into the second of two opposing elements likely to reduce its otherwise dangerous preponderance over the others, seemed to promise security without the risk of feebleness. All this appeared quite as easy of execution under a system deriving its origin from the people, as under one born of feudal tenures. The required changes would only limit the extent of the powers conferred, and multiply the neutralizing forces. The subdivision as well as the balancing of opposite interests to effect the great purpose of preventing a concentration of too much power at any one point, might be carried as far as could be, consistently with the general good. Yet the rule was not to be applied in all cases equally. The executive, for example, was not to be subdivided in such a manner as to injure its energy, nor weakened so far as to impair its capacity of self-protection; whilst into the legislative was to be introduced a recognition of the interests of property so far as it might tend to keep in check the dangerous tendency to appeal exclusively to numerical force.

Such is, in brief, the theory of Mr. Adams, as drawn from a review of his writings on the subject throughout his life, and illustrated as well by the early sketch which he drew for the use of the Southern States as by the more mature model which he presented for the consideration of the Convention of Massachusetts. It fell in with the habits and prepossessions of his countrymen so far as to be made the foundation of most of the constitutions adopted in the several States. But there were great differences between them in the degree of attention paid to the organic principle, and two or three departed from it altogether. Not a few persons were disposed to regard the complicated machinery which it called into action as cumbrous, and its operations as unnecessarily expensive. The simplicity of an absolute monarchy or of a pure democracy will always have its charm with minds not kept awake to its susceptibility of abuse. As between these extremes, the Americans tended much the most towards democracy. One representative body, vested with powers barely sufficient to supply the need of government in every department, became not an uncommon demand. And it had been latterly growing into popular favor from the dissatisfaction prevailing with all existing institutions, upon which the responsibility for every grievance of the body politic was cast, without the smallest regard to the causes that might have really produced them.

But in addition to the various springs of discontent, which were combining to shake the doctrines of Mr. Adams in America, the state of affairs in Europe, and especially in France, was superinducing a novel disturbing force of extraordinary strength. Staggering under the combined weight of the moral corruptions and the financial complexities of the preceding reign, with religious institutions sapped by the indefatigable assiduity of the most brilliant minds of the kingdom, moved by the popular sympathies with the victory of liberty effeçted by French aid in America, that great edifice of European society, which it had taken ten centuries to consolidate, was toppling to its fall. This terrific event was, as usual in such cases, giving out its heralding signs. Prominent among them were the discussions touching the origin of government, in which the natural dryness of the topic was relieved to the general sense by fascinating charms of style and seductive pictures for the imagination. The dreamy enthusiasm of Rousseau combined with the epigrammatic wit of Voltaire to prepare a favorable reception for the more stately speculations of Turgot, De Mably, Mirabeau, and Condorcet. Differing in almost every other particular, there was one point in which these writers were found to agree. The iron hands and hearts of Louis the Eleventh and Henry the Fourth, Richelieu, and Mazarin, by rigidly adhering to one policy for two centuries, had succeeded in eradicating almost every germ of provincial or departmental independence out of France, and in sowing in its place a fixed attachment to centralization.

As a consequence, little favor has since been extended to any theory based upon a complex subdivision of powers, and still less to any form of federation whatever. The fancy displayed by Montesquieu for the English system, though caught up by a limited number of disciples, has at no time taken root in the popular mind of France. Turgot, one of the clearest thinkers of his nation, seeing no possible benefit in it, took advantage of the publication by Dr. Price of his pamphlet upon the American governments, to address to him a

letter, commenting with regret upon what he called the
servility of the States in following the precedent set by
the mother country. He was not disposed to admit
merit in any system that departed from the utmost simplicity. Neither could he recognize a safer guide than
that obtained by concentrating all power in one body
directly representing the nation. The specious doctrine
thus put forth was taken up and immediately repeated
in the eloquent declamations of Mirabeau and the more
logical reasoning of Condorcet, as it has of late been
reproduced in the poetic prose of Lamartine; all equally
symbolic of the ruling idea of France, but all, so far
from proving its soundness, that it has condemned their
country twice within a century to pay a fearful price for
the lesson that the simplicity aimed at can only come,
in its perfect form, in the person of an absolute king.

Alarmed, by the indications of opinion in various
countries of Europe and in America, for the consequences that might ensue to his native State, then showing the most unequivocal tendencies to disorganization,
Mr. Adams thought he might do service if, from his
point of view, he should attempt to lay before the
world something in the nature of a general defence of
the theory so extensively assailed. He fixed upon the
passage of Turgot's letter which referred to the American States, as the text upon which to frame his observations. But not content with fortifying the reasons
upon which their system rested, it occurred to him that
a secondary class of arguments could be obtained from
a wide examination and historical review of the operation of all known forms of government, ancient as well
as modern. If, in the process, the truth could be made

to appear, that many of them had owed their misfortunes and final ruin to the improper distribution of power, it might be of use as a warning against the repetition of similar experiments. The results of his labor were embraced in a work, entitled *A Defence of the Constitutions of the United States of America against the attack of M. Turgot.* It comprehended an analysis of the various free governments of ancient and modern times, with occasional summaries of their history, to illustrate the nature of the evils under which they had suffered and ultimately perished. It was comprised in three volumes, composed, printed, and published during the author's residence in England. The first volume, which was issued before the others, came to the United States just as the convention to frame a federal constitution was on the point of commencing its labors at Philadelphia. It was at once put to press in the principal towns, and, owing to the excitement immediately occasioned by the anxiety for the success of that assembly, it was read by a number of persons far greater than is in ordinary times attracted to such discussions. Happening to fall in with the popular current just then setting with force against the disorders and commotions that had broken into open violence in some of the States and threatened them all, it did much to confirm many minds in the course of thought which ensured the acceptance of the constitution. This was particularly the case in Massachusetts, where the sentiments of the people were by no means settled. There was a wide diversity of opinion among them, one side, frightened by the prospect of anarchy, leaning to the conviction of a necessity of strong government almost

like monarchy, whilst the other, relaxed by the license
of the period, regarding with aversion any tendency to
more positive restraints.   The form of constitution
agreed upon at Philadelphia, whilst it was hailed with
delight by the commercial interests of the seaboard,
was by no means equally relished in the agricultural
regions, or by those who had been the most active in
the early struggles of the Revolution.   The consequence
was, that the convention summoned to decide upon its
merits on the part of Massachusetts, contained many
hesitating members.   Much depended upon the course
taken by John Hancock and Samuel Adams, neither of
them prepossessed in its favor.   At this crisis, the voice
of John Adams, warning them of the risk attending ill-
balanced and feeble governments, came in happily
from the other side of the water, to reinforce the argument for adopting something, and to dispel scruples of
opponents, at least so far as to induce acquiescence in
an experiment.   It was only thus that the federal constitution escaped the jaws of death at its beginning; for
there can be little doubt that, in the wavering state of
opinion, the example of a positive rejection by Massachusetts would have been fatal to all prospect of its
ratification by the requisite number of States.

If the eye of the critic be turned to the composition
of this work, it must be conceded that it will be found
defective in many particulars.   No one was more conscious of this than the author.   His own ideas of it
are so characteristically expressed in a letter written at
the time to his brother-in-law, Richard Cranch, himself a member of the Massachusetts convention the
next year, as to deserve insertion at this place.

"GROSVENOR SQUARE, 15 January, 1787.

"MY DEAR BROTHER,—Dr. Tufts will give you a strange book. I know not whether the sentiments of it will be approved by the men of sense and letters in America. If they are, they will make themselves popular in time. If they are not, our countrymen have many miseries to go through. If the system attempted to be defended in these letters is not the system of the wisest men among us, I shall tremble for the consequences, and wish myself in any obscure hole in the world. I am myself as clearly satisfied of the infallible truth of the doctrines there contained as I am of any demonstration in Euclid; and if our countrymen are bent upon any wild schemes inconsistent with the substance of it, the sooner they remove me out of their sight the better; for I can be of no service to them in promoting their views. I shall be anxious to know how it is received, and shall be obliged to you to inform me.

"I lament that it is so hasty a production. It is only since my return from Holland, in September, that I began to collect the materials. But the disturbances in New England made it necessary to publish immediately, in order to do any good. My friends in Holland were much employed in revolutions. In several conversations there, I had occasion to mention some things respecting governments which some of those gentlemen wished to see on paper. Their desire, falling in with the seditious meetings in the Massachusetts, determined me to write. The field is vast enough, the materials are splendid enough, and the subject is of weight enough, to employ the greatest scholar of the age for seven years. I am no great scholar, and have had but a few months' time; but I hope the men of genius and science in America will pursue the subject to more advantage. By the hurry and precipitation with which this work was undertaken, conducted and completed, I have been obliged to be too inattentive both to method and the ornaments of style for the present taste of our countrymen; for I perceive that taste and elegance are the cry. This appears to me like establishing manufactures of lace, fringe, and embroidery in a country, before there are any of silk, velvet, or cloth. Our countrymen are by no means advanced enough in solid science and learning, in mathematics and philosophy, in Greek and Latin, to devote so much of their time to rhetoric. The ignorance of old Mummius, who threatened a master of a ship to compel him to replace the paintings of Apelles, if he lost them, would become us much better. I am no enemy to elegance, but I say no man has a right to think of elegance till he has secured substance; nor then, to seek more of it than he can afford. That taste which, for its gratification, will commit knavery and run in debt beyond the ability to pay, merits execration. That elegance which devours honor, truth, and independency, which scorns reputations and can reconcile itself to ignominy, public or private, is a monster that Hercules ought to destroy. If the courts of justice must be stopped at the point of the bayonet, if the laws must be trampled under foot to satisfy elegance, it is a demon that ought to be sent back to hell.

"'*Libertatem, amicitiam, fidem, præcipua humani animi bona*'—these are essential to human happiness.

Finery of every kind may be dispensed with, until it can be reconciled to the other.''

It may be observed, in passing from this letter, that the passage from Tacitus, quoted at the close, became such a favorite with Mr. Adams that he selected the first three words and the governing verb *retinebis*, as a motto for himself, which he caused to be engraved in various forms for his private use. They are taken from the address put into the mouth of the Emperor Galba by the historian, upon the adoption of Piso, as his heir, according to the forms of the Roman law ; a fatal gift, as it proved, but conveyed in an address breathing so much of the early spirit of the republic as to elevate the speaker far above those either before or after him on the imperial throne.

A few words more will close all that it is deemed necessary to say of the ''Defence of the American Constitutions.'' The transient interest in its pages, awakened by a sense of the necessities of government at the time, passed away with the adoption of the federal constitution. Another motive for perusing them succeeded, in the desire of political antagonists to find materials for impairing the influence of the author. To this end, not only the general tendency of the work was denounced as monarchical, but every passage in it was sedulously hunted up, which could be made to bear an invidious meaning. The obvious approbation of the distribution of powers in the British constitution was used to justify an accusation, at one moment of a desire to introduce absolutism, at another, of favoring an aristocracy. These representations were attended with a considerable share of success for the time. But a calmer examination of the whole work will serve to show that there is no just ground for them. The object of it is to show the great danger of power concentrated in any one quarter, whether it be in the hands of a single chief, or in a select number, or in the multitude, as well as to recommend precautions against it by subdividing and thus neutralizing as much of the excess as possible. Hence the book, if studied for that object, would be found to yield quite as many texts against absolutism or aristocracy as against democracy. Such a result must inevitably flow from any discussion of the rights of men carried on with regard only to general principles, and independent of all local or temporary considerations. In this, as in other instances in his life, Mr. Adams followed his own convictions, without seeking to accommodate them to prevailing ideas of any kind. His speculations have now gone into the immense reservoir of human thought accumulated by ages, there to take the chance of confirmation or otherwise, as the cumulative experience and the passionless judgment of later generations shall see fit to determine. No interest remains to pervert them. Whether pronounced right or wrong, the verdict can only affect the correctness of his doctrines. It can make no difference with the estimate of his motives or of his character.

Passing from the view of the substance to the form, it must be admitted, that as a specimen of style, it has few attractions for the general reader, being in this respect inferior to most of the author's productions. It is defective in the arrangement, and in exposition of the arguments to establish the general conclusion. Much too great space is given to the minor details of the history of the small Italian republics of the Middle Ages, which were not necessary to prove what is made clear enough without them. For these reasons, it is not likely that it will attract to its pages many readers out of the limits of the very small class who study the science of government on a comprehensive scale. To these, this book will still recommend itself as a profound examination of the principles upon which mixed forms, like those of Great Britain and America, are established, and as a treasury of just reflections and striking illustrations, appropriate to the general subject. Nobody has done so much to prove the fatal effect of vesting power in great proportions in any single agency. No one has shown so clearly the necessity of enlisting the aid of the various classes of society in the support of a common cause, by giving to each a legitimate field of exertion; and no one has more impressively warned posterity of the consequences of permitting the growth of distinctions, thus setting the rich and the poor, the educated and the ignorant, the gifted and the dull into opposition, without preserving ready means of neutralizing the excesses of each. Over and above these recommendations, there are scattered here and there maxims of policy, and observations upon events and characters in history, both ancient and modern, well worthy to be stored in the mind of every man called to the duties of a statesman. Strange as it may seem, this work supplied, in part, what was then a vacuum in literature, and what is not yet entirely filled. The later labors of Brougham, and Guizot, and De Tocqueville have added much to the stock of useful materials; but a philosophical and comprehensive treatment of all practicable forms of government, the joint offspring of learning and experience, remains to task the powers of some future genius, who, with the analytic power and the sententious wisdom of Montesquieu, will have a care to avoid his errors of precipitate generalization.

Whilst the leisure of Mr. Adams was thus absorbed in this interesting pursuit at home, it is not to be inferred that he did not derive much enjoyment from many of the events which were taking place in the world around him. The indifference of the court and ministers could not prevent him from enjoying the opportunities presented of witnessing the contests of eloquence almost daily occurring in the two houses of parliament. Mr. Adams heard Burke, and Pitt, and Fox, and Sheridan, and Camden, and was present at the opening of the solemn proceedings against Warren Hastings. It was the age of strong intellect in England. Nothing like it had occurred since the reign of Queen Anne, and nothing like it has been seen since. For the mind of the human race seems to be, in this respect, like the surface of the earth it inhabits, which must lie fallow at intervals between periods of excessive productiveness, in order to recruit from its exhaustion. In addition to all these occupations and diversions, Mr. Adams was engaged, in conjunction with Mr. Jefferson, then minister to France, with whom he had established agreeable social relations, in the duty of negotiating treaties with the Barbary powers and procuring the liberation of many unfortunate prisoners taken by them. This relation gave rise to an interesting correspondence between the two gentlemen, a large portion of which has been already laid before the world.

But much as Mr. Adams might enjoy these superior opportunities for study and recreation in Great Britain, there was a single drop of bitterness apart from every thing in Europe, which came in to spoil his pleasure. For the love or hate, the kindness or neglect of the English he cared little, so long as he could feel that the country which he represented, and for whose cause he had staked so much, was doing her duty in the new position assumed by her before the nations. It was during his residence here that he was compelled daily to receive new proofs of her reluctance to fulfil her solemn engagements, and of her neglect to sustain her honor as he would have wished her to do. In his situation, all the arguments in extenuation of her deficiencies, her poverty, her exhaustion, her inability to unite the several States in one policy, would have been of no avail, had he condescended to use them; but he never did. He would have been proud to defend her to the last drop of his blood against every unjust charge, but he would not stoop to palliate or equivocate about her short-comings, when they were undeniable. His feelings upon this subject he did not seek to conceal from his friends at home. In a letter, addressed to Dr. Tufts, an uncle of Mrs. Adams, at the time a member of the senate of Massachusetts, he thus expressed himself on this topic:

"As to politics, all that can be said is summarily comprehended in a few words. Our country is grown, or at least has been dishonest. She has broke her faith with nations, and with her own citizens; and parties are all about for continuing this dishonorable course. She must become strictly honest and punctual to all the world before she can recover the confidence of anybody at home or abroad. The duty of all good men is to join in making this doctrine popular, and in discountenancing every attempt against it. This censure is too harsh, I suppose, for common ears, but the essence of these sentiments must be adopted throughout America before we can prosper. Have our people forgotten every principle of public and private credit? Do we trust a man in private life who is not punctual to his word? Who easily makes promises and is negligent to perform them? Especially if he makes promises knowing that he cannot perform them, or deliberately designing not to perform them?"

This was severe language towards his countrymen, but not unwarranted by much of the doctrine prevalent among the people of America at this period. A large number growing daily more restless under the curb of the law, were encouraging each other to the last step of throwing it off, whilst others were resorting to more indirect but not less decisive means of annulling their obligations altogether. It was this relaxation of morals which gave Mr. Adams his moments of deep mortification as minister of the United States in London. Through life, his code as a public man was, on this subject, perfectly uniform. He never favored that species of logic, not infrequent among political leaders of all nations, whereby a different standard of right can be assumed at home from that which is proclaimed abroad, another rule acted upon individually from that which is prescribed in official station. He wished his country to be all that his dreams had pictured when advocating her independence; and finding that, as time went on, the prospect of his usefulness in his station became less and less, he determined, in 1787, to ask leave of congress to resign his trusts and to return home to private life. Letters of recall were accordingly sent out by congress in February, 1788. Not one of the important objects he had sought to gain in England had been effected. Supercilious indifference prevailed in the British councils. Alienation and not conciliation was the order of the day. The only compensation for a disappointment, which events rendered it utterly out of his power to prevent, was found in the receipt of a copy of a resolution adopted by congress, expressive of the sense entertained by that body of the value of his services during the ten years of his residence abroad. It was in these words:

"Resolved, that congress entertain a high sense of the services which Mr. Adams has rendered to the United States, in the various important trusts which they have from time to time committed to him; and that the thanks of congress be presented to him for the patriotism, perseverance, integrity, and diligence, with which he hath ably and faithfully served his country."

CHAPTER IX.

ON the 20th of April, 1788, Mr. Adams bade fare-
well to the shores of the ancient world. He returned
to his native land to find it permanently freed from all
dangers, excepting those which had their origin from
within. He had quitted it the first time at the very
crisis of the war. He came back to see it in the most
critical moment of the peace. The political world had
undergone, in the interval, a great revolution. Those
questions which had agitated the people, so long as
independence was in doubt, had all passed away, and
many of the men who appeared to lead at the beginning had vanished from the scene. But four of the
members of congress who had signed their names to
the Declaration in 1776 were members of the same
body when the treaty of peace was submitted for ratification in 1783. It may fairly be doubted whether, in
any modern government having a semblance of free
institutions, the state of public feeling or the motives
and principles that affect action ever continue for three
years together the same. The passions of men cannot
long endure a high degree of tension, and the decline
of an excitement is invariably followed by indifference
to a revival of the same emotion, as well as indisposi-

tion immediately to enter upon any new one. The peace had been received with joy, because it was regarded as a final object. Nothing further was needed to make America happy and prosperous. Hence there was little disposition to exertion. It was expected that the country would go on of itself. Great was then the disappointment to discover, at the end of four or five years, that independence had not done all that was hoped of it, that the people were not prosperous, that law and order were not so well established as they had been in the colonial days, that instead of improving with time, things were visibly growing worse; and, lastly, that something was left to be done, or else the cherished independence was likely to turn out like the service of a wooden idol, an idle waste of labor and of emotions.

Neither was it difficult to understand what was the sort of action called for. The want was plain. There was no common principle harmonizing the action of the different States. The attempt to incorporate one in the old form of confederation had utterly failed. More vigorous restraint upon liberty was seen to be necessary by some, however reluctantly the idea might be welcomed by the great body of their disappointed countrymen. Forthwith a field of action opened itself, very different from the old one in 1774, and new persons came forward as leaders of opinion on one side and on the other. The first occasion upon which this change became outwardly visible, was upon the assembling of the convention to form a federal constitution. Here Mr. Madison and Mr. Hamilton attained the prominence which produced such important effects in

the course of later events.   Here is found the nucleus
of the sentiments which led to subsequent party divisions.   Mr. Adams arrived at home only in time to
witness the popular ratification of the instrument which
emanated from these consultations.   To him most of
the actors who combined to frame it were almost, if
not quite, strangers.   But inasmuch as they had a powerful influence upon the remaining portion of his public
life, it seems necessary to go into some explanation of
the causes that operated to bring them into the places
which they were called to fill.

The revolution of 1776, as has been mentioned heretofore, was effected through a union of colonies and
individuals marching by no means with an equal pace
to a common point, the rupture with Great Britain.
The advance had been taken by Massachusetts, which
led New England, and by a section of the planters of
Virginia, headed by the Lees, Patrick Henry, Wythe,
George Mason, and Jefferson, under whom rallied all
the citizens of other colonies south of Maryland who
sympathized with them.   In the three southernmost
States of New England only, was the whole community so inoculated with republican principles as to
make the transition from the colonial to an independent state simple and easy.   The emigration of the
few who had formed connections with government or
with commercial interests at home, was not felt excepting as it removed the last restraint upon opinions
always substantially democratic.   The political power
had ever been in the hands of the people.   Such had
not been the case elsewhere.   The institutions of New
York, Pennsylvania, and Virginia, had cherished a

privileged class, which formed an obstacle to the reception of the new ideas, not to be removed without a serious rent in the social system, at least in the first-named States. That removal, gradually effected by the disappearance of numbers of the wealthy and more intelligent, left a deficiency which was scarcely made good by the elevation to influence of persons of less education and experience. The transition to democracy, being sudden, was attended with a good deal of social disorder, rendering itself most visible in the violent contentions in Pennsylvania about the crude constitution, and the oaths against alteration, which had been so thoughtlessly adopted. Yet, before the peace, the new ideas had become well established, and the people, under their influence, had grown to be not less impatient of every restraint of individual action than jealous of the arrogation of any, even the most necessary power. They had therefore arrived at about the same anarchical condition, into which the Eastern people, for a different reason, soon after fell. Exhausted by the war and the derangement of all useful industry, the forms which enforced justice soon became equally hateful with those which had labored to impose a tyranny. It was the upheaving of the poorest classes to throw off the relation of debtor and creditor, which brought about the successful effort to organize the federal government anew, as a bridle upon their license. They never favored it beforehand, nor cordially approved it afterwards, during their day and generation. The federal convention was the work of the commercial people in the seaport towns, of the planters of the slaveholding States, of the officers of the revolutionary army, and the property holders everywhere. And these parties could never have been strong enough of themselves to procure the general adoption of the instrument which they matured, had it not been that the open insurrection in Massachusetts, and the assemblages threatening to shut up the courts of justice in other States, had thrown the intermediate body of quiet citizens of every shade of opinion, in panic, all on their side. It was under the effect of this panic, that the delegates had been elected, and that they acted. The vibration of the pendulum may be most distinctly measured by the language of such men as James Madison and Elbridge Gerry, at all other periods of their lives the exponents of popular opinions. And taking these as the type of the most moderate party, the extent to which the ideas must have reached among the habitual advocates of a strong government, may readily be conceived. The federal constitution was the offspring of compromises made under these circumstances. Although reduced in tone far below the level of opinion of one class, there can be no doubt that it was still considerably above that which prevailed in the country at large. And it may very fairly be questioned, whether any period has occurred before or since, with perhaps one brief exception of extraordinary unanimity, when it could have succeeded, even as it did then, in fighting its way through the ordeal of the ratifying conventions.

From this moment is then to be dated a new epoch in the history of the United States. And in the friends of the new constitution, denominated *federalists*, as well as in its opponents, called *anti-federalists*, are to be seen the germs of the great political division of the country, which now sprang up and continued to prevail during the existence of at least one generation of men.

In the distribution of individuals upon one side or the other of this line, it is not to be supposed that many anomalies did not occur. That among the opponents of the constitution are to be ranked a great majority of those who had most strenuously fought the battle of independence of Great Britain, is certain. The sentiment that animated them having its nourishment in a single root, the jealousy of power, imparted a homogeneous character to their movements, which the opposite side never could possess. Among the federalists, it is true, were to be found a large body of the patriots of the Revolution, almost all the general officers who survived the war, and a great number of the substantial citizens along the line of the seaboard towns and populous regions, all of whom had heartily sympathized in the policy of resistance. But these could never have succeeded in effecting the establishment of the constitution, had they not received the active and steady co-operation of all that was left in America of attachment to the mother country, as well as of the moneyed interest, which ever points to strong government as surely as the needle to the pole. As a consequence, there was from the beginning a line of division within the ranks of the government party, which did not fail to make itself more and more visible with the progress of time. The course of John Adams, like that of Jefferson and Samuel Adams, previous to 1783, had been much the most closely allied with that of the enemies of the constitution, of whom Patrick Henry, and the Lees, and Gerry, and George Clinton were the most prominent representatives; but his bitter experience of the want of a government to sustain the national honor in Europe, and his lifelong attachment to the tripartite or English theory, combined, on his return, to place him warmly on the side of its friends. He, too, had felt the reaction, which had carried even Jefferson, and Madison, and Gerry into the approbation of sentiments rather out of line with the rest of their public life. And embracing the cause with his customary ardor, he was naturally brought into greater prominence as a supporter of the new system in Massachusetts, from the fact that there it had met with much difficulty to make its way. Almost on the instant of his return, he had been elected to a place in the old congress. But that body had fallen into the last stages of dissolution, with its sessions continued only for form's sake, so that he never took his seat. In the mean while, the necessary elections were in progress to set agoing the new organization, and the time approached to determine the important question, who should be the two men selected by the general voice to fill the most prominent posts established by the plan.

The constitution, in its original form, required that the votes of the Electoral Colleges should point out these two persons, without assigning their relative places. That question was left to be determined by the greater or less number of suffrages which they might respectively obtain. The obvious motive for this arrangement was, to secure a second person in the far inferior place, who might be depended upon, in case of necessity, suitably to fill the first. And in this it was certainly more successful than the provision since substituted has proved. Here, however, its beneficial nature ended, for in every other respect it became the fertile mother of abuses, some of which were not slow to show themselves even on the very first opportunity. With respect to the nomination of one of the two individuals, and him whom it was the desire alike of the electors and the people at large to see placed at the head of the government, there was no shadow of doubt in any mind. George Washington was the man, and there could be no other. No similar unanimity was to be expected in the selection of any second person; hence there could be no ambiguity about his destination. The question then fell down to the comparatively small matter, who should be the Vice-President. Geographical considerations prompted the selection in a quarter opposite to that which was to give the President, and the prominence of Massachusetts in the revolutionary struggle pointed out that State as the one from which it might properly be made. Among the distinguished statesmen within her limits, three stood forth broadly in the public eye. These were Hancock, and Samuel and John Adams. But neither Hancock nor Samuel Adams had manifested a very hearty good-will to the new constitution, or had done much more than to acquiesce in supporting it as a dubious experiment. Nor yet had they the advantage of the long and brilliant course of foreign service rendered before the eyes of the whole country, which recommended the third individual. As a consequence, John Adams united a far greater number of votes than either, or than any other man. But he did not obtain a majority. Only thirty-four out of sixty-nine electors named him. The other thirty-five votes were scattered at random among ten individuals, no one of whom obtained more than nine. But by the terms of the constitution, even this was decisive; so that Mr. Adams became the first Vice-President of the United States.

This narration is of great importance to the right conception of the later history, because in it is to be found the first trace of the opposition of sentiment which ultimately destroyed the federal party. Had the choice been left entirely to the predilections of the electors, without an effort to direct it, or to regulate the mode in which it was to be made, there can be no doubt that, whatever the issue might have been, everybody would have cheerfully acquiesced in it. In New England, and throughout the Union, the great body of those friends of the constitution who had been in the habit of reposing confidence in Mr. Adams as a leader in the Revolution, would probably have found a voice in the Electoral Colleges, which might or might not have decided the choice in his favor. At any rate, they would have proved hearty in supporting him. The case was widely different with another class, who had not harmonized with him during the struggle, and who now regulated their course upon very different considerations from those of personal preference. Of this class, Alexander Hamilton was rapidly becoming the representative and the spokesman. Active and energetic in promoting the adoption of the constitution itself, in the success of which, as an experiment, he entertained but a feeble confidence, his natural ardor impelled him to the exercise of what influence he could command in the further and more delicate task of shaping the manner in which, and designating the men through whom, it should first be carried into operation. Coinciding with the rest of the world in the nomination of Washington for the chief position, his activity seems to have been exerted mainly to the point of determining the relation the second officer was to bear to the first. Towards the prominent men of Massachusetts, between whom his sagacity perceived the choice to lie, he was, at best, indifferent. But he had not lost the old impressions obtained in the army, first against New England generally, and next against the Lees and the Adamses as caballing against Washington in the Revolution, and therefore looked with great distrust upon the prospect of placing one of the latter in a situation of power to embarrass the new government. Reassured on this point by his friend Sedgwick, of Massachusetts, as well as by his own belief, that "to a sound understanding Mr. Adams joined an ardent love for the public good," he determined upon giving him the preference. But he did it, subject to a refinement in policy, by which Mr. Adams was to be brought into place with as little of the appearance of equality with the President in the popular esteem as possible. The idea of any equalization of electoral votes, from which a possible danger to Washington's election could be apprehended, was preposterous. It is plain that he never entertained it. His exertions, to subtract votes from the number which would otherwise have been given to Mr. Adams, must then be traced to some other motive; and there is none, on the whole, so probable as the desire to keep a check over the political influence of the second officer in the new government, should he prove to incline at last to embarrass the chief by his opposition.   They were effective in New Jersey and Connecticut, not to say elsewhere, and to the extent of giving to Mr. Adams the appearance of being chosen by less than a majority of the electors.

In the remarkable correspondence on this subject between Mr. Hamilton and his friends, a portion of which has been lately disclosed, it is a singular coincidence that Mr. Adams should have been recommended by Mr. Sedgwick, though not among his partisans, on the ground that he was "a man of unconquerable intrepidity and of incorruptible integrity," and that the same gentleman should, twelve years later, have been one of the leading actors in, as well as the most discontented with the issue of the greatest trial to which that intrepidity was ever subjected.   He little foresaw, that in urging Mr. Hamilton to prefer Mr. Adams for these qualities, he was opposing to that gentleman's natural aspirations for command the only effectual barrier remaining within the reach of the federalists, and sowing the seeds of a division which was to end in the complete overthrow of the power of them all.   The peculiar mode in which Mr. Hamilton thought it proper to concede that preference was the first great political error which he committed.   Mr. Adams very naturally felt that the process of deducting, in a clandestine manner, from the votes which but for that would have been given to him, was ominous of imperfect faith ; and he complained that he had been exposed to the world as the choice of a minority of the electors, when, except for positive interference, he would have received at least forty-one, and probably more, of the sixty-nine. This complaint, scarcely unreasonable in itself, it would have been more prudent in a public man not to express even in the privacy of the domestic circle; but Mr. Adams, never a calculating politician, was not in the habit, excepting in the most critical cases, of suppressing his feelings. The consequence was, that his unguarded language was tortured to justify the inference that he was dissatisfied at not having been permitted the chance to receive as many votes as General Washington. This again came back to his knowledge, and another element of mutual distrust entered into the counsels of those who were destined to act together.

Yet these causes, though beginning to operate at this time, produced no perceptible effects until long afterwards. Neither is it just to suppose that Mr. Adams attached much importance to them at first. He was satisfied with the honors conferred upon him, little as the labors of the post were adequate to a man of his abundant energies. No high situation in the government of the United States could now be so easily lopped off without missing it, as that of the Vice-President. Its only consequence depends upon the contingency of a succession to the chief office. It was not by any means so insignificant, however, when Mr. Adams was first chosen, as it has been in later times. Mr. Hamilton had not overrated the importance of filling it with a steady friend. At that moment, the machine of government was to be set in motion, and it was material that all the principal parts should be put in a condition to work kindly together. The grand fact, of a serious division of public opinion upon its merits, and of the existence of a large body of the people ready from the outset to condemn it, was universally understood. It made itself painfully visible in the return of the individuals selected to serve in both branches of the legislature. Although the lines were not then so sharply defined as afterwards, and in spite of the overruling influence of the name of Washington, there was reason to apprehend that the men who feared the constitution, would be nearly if not quite as numerous in congress as those who trusted it. This was particularly the case in the senate, over which body the Vice-President was required to act as the presiding officer. The assembly consisted, at the outset, only of twenty-two, out of whom the number of those who had favored the policy of enlarging the powers of government scarcely exceeded that of those who maintained the propriety of restricting them. This difference, from which the constitution had narrowly escaped shipwreck at the start, made itself felt in every part of the organizing process that formed the main business of the first congress. The creation of the various subordinate branches of the executive department, especially that of the treasury, the establishment of order in the finances, where nothing of the kind could be made to prevail under the old system, the construction of a plan for raising a revenue, the consolidation of all outstanding obligations that had been incurred during the struggle, and the marking out of the complicated channels for the administration of justice in the federal courts, all devolved upon it. The first instance in which opposition developed itself by close divisions in both Houses, occurred in the case of the law proposed to organize the Department of Foreign Affairs. The question most earnestly disputed turned upon the power vested by the constitution in the President to remove the person at the head of that bureau, at his pleasure. One party maintained it was an absolute right. The other insisted that it was subject to the same restriction of a ratification by the senate which is required when the officer is appointed. After a long contest in the house of representatives, terminating in favor of the unrestricted construction, the bill came up to the senate for its approbation.

This case was peculiar and highly important. By an anomaly in the constitution, which, upon any recognized theory, it is difficult to defend, the senate, which, in the last resort, is made the judicial tribunal to try the President for malversation in office, is likewise clothed with a power of denying him the agents in whom he may choose most to confide for the faithful execution of the duties of his station, and forcing him to select such as they may prefer. If, in addition to this, the power of displacing such as he found unworthy of trust had been subjected to the same control, it cannot admit of a doubt that the government must, in course of time, have become an oligarchy, in which the President would sink into a mere instrument of any faction that might happen to be in the ascendant in the senate. This, too, at the same time that he would be subject to be tried by them for offences in his department, over which he could exercise no effective restraint whatever. In such case, the alternative is inevitable, either that he would have become a confederate with that faction, and therefore utterly beyond the reach of punishment

by impeachment at their hands, for offences committed
with their privity, if not at their dictation, or else, in
case of his refusal, that he would have been powerless to
defend himself against the paralyzing operation of their
ill-will.   Such a state of subjection in the executive
head to the legislature is subversive of all ideas of a
balance of powers drawn from the theory of the British
constitution, and renders probable at any moment a
collision, in which one side or the other, and it is most
likely to be the legislature, must be ultimately annihilated.

Yet, however true these views may be in the abstract,
it would scarcely have caused surprise if their soundness
had not been appreciated in the senate.   The temptation to magnify their authority is commonly all-powerful with public bodies of every kind.   In any other stage
of the present government than the first, it would have
proved quite irresistible.   But throughout the administration of General Washington, there is visible among
public men a degree of indifference to power and place,
which forms one of the most marked features of that
time.   More than once the highest cabinet and foreign
appointments went begging to suitable candidates, and
begged in vain.   To this fact it is owing, that public
questions of such moment were then discussed with as
much of personal disinterestedness as can probably ever
be expected to enter into them anywhere.   Yet even
with all these favoring circumstances it soon became
clear that the republican jealousy of a centralization of
power in the President would combine with the *esprit
de corps* to rally at least half the senate in favor of subjecting removals to their control.   In such a case, the re-

sponsibility of deciding the point devolved, by the terms of the constitution, upon Mr. Adams, as Vice-President. The debate was continued from the 15th to the 18th of July, a very long time for that day in an assembly comprising only twenty-two members when full, but seldom more than twenty in attendance. A very brief abstract, the only one that has yet seen the light, is furnished in the third volume of Mr. Adams's collected works. He appears to have made it for the purpose of framing his own judgment in the contingency which he must have foreseen as likely to occur. The final vote was taken on the 18th. Nine senators voted to subject the President's power of removal to the will of the senate: Messrs. Few, Grayson, Gunn, Johnson, Izard, Langdon, Lee, Maclay, and Wingate. On the other hand, nine senators voted against claiming the restriction: Messrs. Bassett, Carroll, Dalton, Elmer, Henry, Morris, Paterson, Read, and Strong. The result depended upon the voice of the Vice-President. It was the first time he had been summoned to such a duty. It was the only time, during his eight years of service in that place, that he felt the case to be of such importance as to justify his assigning reasons for his vote. These reasons were not committed to paper, however, and can therefore never be known. But in their soundness it is certain that he never had the shadow of a doubt. His decision settled the question of constitutional power in favor of the President, and consequently established the practice under the government, which has continued down to this day. Although there have been occasional exceptions taken to it in argument, especially at moments when the executive power, wielded by a strong hand,

seemed to encroach upon the limits of the co-ordinate
departments, its substantial correctness has been, on the
whole, quite generally acquiesced in.   And all have
agreed, that no single act of the first congress has been
attended with more important effects upon the working
of every part of the government.

But though this was the first and the most important
case in which the casting vote of the Vice-President was
invoked to settle the details of organization, it was by
no means the only one during the time Mr. Adams pre-
sided over the senate.   Very seldom was the majority
on disputed points more than two; and four times,
during this session, the numbers stood nine against
nine.   At the second session his casting vote was called
for, twelve, at the third, four times, making twenty
times during the first congress, and always upon points
of importance in the organic laws.   The services thus
rendered make little figure on the records; but the
effect of them, in smoothing away, at a critical moment,
many of the obstacles to the establishment of the government, will continue to be felt so long as the form
itself shall endure.

President Washington, anxious to unite the feelings
of the people, began his administration by calling into
his cabinet the leading exponents of opposite opinions.
In this way, Thomas Jefferson was placed at the head
of the foreign office, and Alexander Hamilton took the
direction of the finances.   The harmony hoped for did
not follow.   No possible circumstances, short of a renewal of the struggle for independence, could have
availed to produce it.   Both the persons named were
men of the first class of minds, but they had little else

in common. Neither could bear the ascendency of the other, or submit to be overruled without resentment. The consequence was, in the secret councils of the first administration, a perpetual conflict of opinions, which the imposing presence of the chief could barely prevent from breaking over every limit. Neither could this state of feeling continue in the cabinet without soon extending itself into the ranks of those who sympathized with the respective combatants, and spreading from them among the people at large. For they were both representatives of ideas, and not merely of persons. The forms which this antagonism took, naturally followed the two lines of action in which the abilities of the combatants had been called into exercise; but unforeseen and extrinsic circumstances contributed greatly to increase its intensity. To Mr. Hamilton the difficult task had been assigned of drawing order out of the chaos of the finances. He did so by proposing plans for funding the public debt, for the assumption of the State debts, for a national bank, a system of revenue from taxation internal and external, and a sinking fund. These plans all equally bristled with points of irritation to a large class of men, of whom Mr. Jefferson was soon regarded by the public as the natural head. They were opposed in both houses of congress with such pertinacity as barely to escape defeat.

Here again the influence of Mr. Adams became important. There can be no doubt that it would have turned the scale, had it been exerted in opposition. But though not in all cases entirely agreeing in sentiment with Mr. Hamilton on these subjects, and in some particulars holding very strong opposing opinions, he felt the necessity, to the very salvation of the machine of government, of sustaining some general system at once, and therefore gave a cordial and hearty support to this as the most practicable plan. The steady and uniform manner in which he rendered it, always valuable to a public man when seeking the attainment of important results against active resistance, seems to have worked so far on the feelings of Mr. Hamilton as for the moment to dispel the distrust he had entertained of him at the outset of the government. When the time approached at which it became necessary to point out candidates for re-election to the chief offices, he not only desisted from any further attempt to subtract from the number of electoral votes Mr. Adams might be likely to obtain, but he even solicited for him a general support, as "a firm, honest, and independent politician." This tribute it is important to bear in mind in a later stage of the narrative, when Mr. Hamilton found occasion for dissatisfaction with the exercise, in his own case, of those very qualities which he now commended.

But whatever may have been the state of the public mind caused by the financial questions which were determined in the course of the first administration of General Washington, it did not, nor, with the exception, perhaps, of direct taxation, can such matters in themselves ever, excite a very deep agitation of the popular passions. Neither is it possible to expect much duration of discontent after the measures in dispute begin sensibly to connect themselves with the national prosperity. It could not be denied that the revival of confidence consequent upon them acted like magic upon industry, and began that great development of material wealth which has gone on with almost unbroken continuance to this day. Whether Mr. Hamilton's plans caused this change, or whether, if they did, they were the best that could have been devised, became speculations only for the curious. At all events, they were followed by the desired effect. The commercial and moneyed interests, which were the first to feel it, at once rallied around Mr. Hamilton as their benefactor, and they never deserted him afterwards. A new power arose, that of the fundholders, the rapid increase of which inspired Mr. Jefferson with alarm and a determination to resist it. But all his opposition would have availed little, had it not been for a new and extraordinary disturbing force, which came in to aid him by giving another course to the public feeling. This was the French revolution.

This moral earthquake was, at the outset, hailed by the people of America, with Washington at their head, as the harbinger of a new era of republican liberty. Their sympathies, quickened by the remembrance of the aid received in the days of their own tribulation, and warmed by visions of a brilliant futurity, not only prompted earnest prayers for the success of the French republicans, but dictated assistance, in case of emergency growing out of the pressure of the monarchical combinations against them. On the other hand, the supercilious and neglectful conduct of Great Britain towards them since the peace, had only contributed to confirm their sentiments of alienation and dislike in that quarter. Of this attraction towards the one nation and repulsion from the other, Thomas Jefferson was the natural exponent in America; whilst his official position made him necessarily prominent as a guide and adviser in framing the incipient relations of the country with both. A brilliant rather than a just thinker, the necessary consequence of a mind more comprehensive than true, the sanguine visions of a glorious issue from the French revolution were slow with him in vanishing. Neither did they disappear at last without leaving an impression upon his mind, and upon that of the large class in America who followed him, that his calculations had been well founded, and that the disastrous failure, which so grievously disappointed him, was chargeable to accident rather than any intrinsic cause.

Here is the great point of divergence in the action of Mr. Adams, which most strongly illustrates the difference of character between him and Mr. Jefferson. Not called, in his official position, to take any part in directing the opinions of others, he could not forbear to express his own. The phenomena in France had never, from the outset, roused his enthusiasm, for he had early detected the element of destructiveness which they contained. Before Burke had ever ventured to interpose, with his giant's strength, to stay the torrent of passion then threatening to submerge all Europe, he had predicted that the experiment of self-government, upon which the French had entered, would fail. In a letter to Dr. Price, acknowledging the reception of a copy of the discourse, which first drove Burke into this field of controversy, he used these memorable words:

"I know that encyclopedists and economists, Diderot and D'Alembert, Voltaire and Rousseau, have contributed to this great event more than Sidney, Locke, or Hoadly, perhaps more than the American Revolution; and I own to you, I know not what to make of a republic of thirty million atheists." . . . . . "Too many Frenchmen, after the example of too many Americans, pant for equality of persons and property. The impracticability of this, God Almighty has decreed, and the advocates for liberty who attempt it will surely suffer for it."

It would be difficult, in smaller compass, to point out the sources of the calamities that followed. The writer had never sympathized with the speculations of the class of French writers to which he refers. Mr. Jefferson, on the contrary, naturally coincided with their views. Their want of a warm and yet restraining religious faith raised no ripple of distrust, for no image of the sort ever came reflected from his own mind; whilst Mr. Adams's strong convictions of the impossibility of maintaining an equality of condition in any civilized society, savored to him of a backsliding into absolutism, which he ever afterwards laid to his charge. But this suspicion of Mr. Jefferson was really founded in a misconception of Mr. Adams's whole cast of mind, which had been formed in the mould of the English writers, some of whom he names in his letter to Dr. Price, and which never relished the vague and fanciful speculations of the French school.

There was, in this particular, a clear opposition in the systems of the two men; the only one, it should be remarked, that was really developed in the course of their singularly blended career. So long as the causes

of this division continued to operate, the separation
between them grew wider and wider.   Mr. Adams took
up his pen, and furnished to the columns of a newspaper in Philadelphia a series of papers containing an
analysis of Davila's History of the civil convulsions of
France in the sixteenth century, which he wrote to illustrate more fully the dangers from powerful factions
in ill-balanced forms of government.   In this doctrine,
Mr. Jefferson saw visions of an impending monarchy,
which he sought to dissipate, not directly, but by
secretly instigating the adoption, as an antidote, of
Thomas Paine's " Rights of Man," just then published
in Great Britain.   The accidental exposure of this
interference, on the first page of that pamphlet, as
reprinted in Philadelphia, brought another champion
into the field to complicate the action.   The papers
of Publicola, written by John Quincy Adams, then a
young lawyer in Boston, without any communication
with his father, and first printed in a newspaper of that
town, attracted great attention everywhere.   They were
reprinted in New York and Philadelphia, afterwards
collected and editions issued in London, in Edinburgh,
and in Dublin, as the work of John Adams.   They
were not his, however, excepting so far as the son
might have imbibed with his growth the principles
which animated the father through life.   Those principles were widely remote from the doctrines of Paine.
They seemed to Mr. Jefferson like adding fuel to the
funeral pile of liberty; and the whole force of his
friends was soon concentrated to resist their progress.
The Adamses, on the other hand, denying the justice
of this imputation, regarded Mr. Jefferson's support of

Paine as bordering too closely upon social disintegration, and favoring a mere popular tyranny. Thus came about the joining of that issue upon fundamental principles in America, which must ever take place under all forms of free government, so long as human society shall remain what it is. The conservative and the democratic republic may be considered as the general types which have from that day to this marshalled the respective divisions of the people of the United States in opposition to each other, when not affected by disturbing influences from without.

The habits of Washington, his military life and his social relations, naturally placed him in the conservative class; and as the wild disorders of the revolution more and more developed themselves in France, as well as through the troublesome intrigues of M. Genest nearer home, he became more and more alienated from the views which Mr. Jefferson was known to favor. That gentleman had, as Secretary of State, nevertheless persevered in executing the policy laid down for the administration during its first term of office, and had very faithfully maintained the reputation of the country, equally well against the impertinent aggressiveness of M. Genest, the envoy of democratic France, and the supercilious arrogance of Mr. Hammond, the representative of British aristocracy. This had not been done, however, without the occurrence of dissensions within the cabinet, and a sense of the growing preponderance of opinions opposite to his, that threatened daily to fix him more firmly the champion of a policy with which he had no sympathy, and the promotion of which was felt by his friends as

well as himself to be fatal to the maintenance of
his own.

The second election of President and Vice-President
passed away; and Mr. Adams, against whom the only
demonstration of opposition was made, came in over
George Clinton, set up as his competitor, by a decided
preponderance in the Electoral Colleges. For Mr.
Jefferson to continue longer in the cabinet in which his
influence was sinking, was not only distasteful to himself, but was putting a restraint on the ardor of opposition, and impairing the energies of his friends, without any compensating prospect of good. He determined
to withdraw; and his act became the signal for the
consolidation of the party, which looked to him as its
chief. Broad and general ground was now taken
against the whole policy of the administration, and the
arrows, shut up within the quiver so long as he remained liable to be hit, were now drawn forth and
sharpened for use even against Washington himself.

Neither was Jefferson wanting, in this crisis, to his
duty of a commander in the war. As he stepped from
the threshold of office, he gave the requisite plan of the
campaign. It was contained in his celebrated report
upon the commercial relations of the country with
foreign nations, the drift of which was favorable to
France and adverse to Great Britain. The able reasoning which it contained, received new force from the
hostility manifested by the latter country to American
commerce. No sooner was war declared by her with
France, than she began to play the tyrant over weaker
nations on the ocean, by Orders in Council designed
to harass the trade of neutrals with her enemy. Of

course, the sympathy with France and the disgust with England proportionally increased in America, and naturally struck into the channel formed for them by Mr. Jefferson. Fortunately for him, he had an auxiliary then in the house of representatives, possessed of singular judgment and skill, upon whom the lead of the opposition devolved, and to whose dexterity and calmness, as a legislator, in tempering in action his own tendencies to extravagance in theory, much of his success must be ascribed. With far less of original genius, Mr. Madison was a more cautious counsellor and a more prudent administrator. The house of representatives assembled in 1794, in a temper to adopt any measures against Great Britain, however hostile. It was soon evident that some discriminating act to favor the commerce with France at her expense, a natural consequence of the reasoning of Mr. Jefferson's report, would meet the approbation of a majority. The only question was upon the extent to which it should be carried. Considering the violence of the various propositions brought to light, General Washington felt at once the embarrassments into which they might plunge him. He had already defined for the country a policy of absolute neutrality. But here was, on the other hand, what threatened to entail upon it an indefinite entanglement in war. Some immediate action was necessary in order to avert the danger. He determined upon resorting to an extraordinary measure.

This measure was the nomination of the chief justice of the supreme court of the United States, John Jay, as a special ambassador to the court of Great Britain, for the purpose of attempting some settlement of the

questions in dispute by a treaty. It checked, without
extinguishing the ardor of the majority, who went on,
nevertheless, to adopt a bill prohibiting the admission
of all the commodities of Great Britain, until the
grievances complained of should be entirely redressed
by her. Had this measure been carried through both
branches of the legislature, there can be little doubt
that it would have rendered the mission of Mr. Jay
wholly abortive. The effect must have been to involve
the United States, as a party, in the terrific contest
then just beginning between the great powers of
Europe. Peace depended upon the action of the
senate, and the senate was almost equally divided.
When the question came up for decision, on the
28th of April, upon two or three preliminary divisions, the opposition did not appear to rally; but,
on the passage of the bill to a third reading, the
vote stood thirteen to thirteen. The Vice-President
then exercised his privilege of a casting vote, and the
measure was defeated. Only second in importance
to this was his action, a month or more before that
time, upon a bill from the Lower House, designed
to put a stop to daring violations of neutrality, like
those which M. Genest, relying upon the popular con-
nivance, had already perpetrated with impunity. Such
a measure was demanded by government, as a proof of
its good faith, in issuing the proclamation which it had
done, declaring its policy to be rigid neutrality. But
it met with a stiff resistance in the senate, and three
times the casting vote of the Vice-President was required and given to secure its safety.

This great power lodged with the Vice-President

has never been brought into exercise by any subsequent
occupant of the presiding chair of the senate to the
same extent that it was whilst Mr. Adams filled the
office. An examination of the journals shows that this
took place almost entirely during his first term of office.
It happened to him, however, to be called upon six
times during the session now in question, after which
the federalists gained enough upon their opponents to
prevent its use so often. But three cases occur in the
remaining three years.

Though in some respects irksome, the duties of the
second office in the United States are not laborious.
They give no scope to the peculiar talents in debate
which had distinguished Mr. Adams in the early congress, and they impose silence, calmness, and impartiality, virtues, the practice of which was by no means
in unison with his natural disposition strongly to take
a side, and ardently to advocate it. Yet, difficult and
delicate as was his situation between parties so equally
balanced, he seems to have succeeded in performing
his task to the acceptance of all. And although complaining from time to time of the meagre compensation
allowed him upon which to maintain his family, as well
as himself, on the scale which had been established at
the outset of the new government, he seems never at
any period of his life to have been more happy and
light-hearted. The best idea of it may be obtained
by extracts taken from his private correspondence with
Mrs. Adams at such times as she was not with him at
Philadelphia. They abound in quiet strokes of humor
and keen observation, which do not appear in his other
writings, interspersed with the same characteristic truth

and nobleness of feeling which are found elsewhere. They come in particularly well at this time, to break the monotony of the narrative, whilst they help to illustrate the history of the events that were taking place. They date from the commencement of the congressional session of 1793–94, some acts of which have been already noticed.

> "PHILADELPHIA, 5 December, 1793.

"The President's speech will show you an abundance of serious business which we have before us. Mr. Jefferson called on me last night, and informed me that to-day we should have the whole budget of foreign affairs, British as well as French. He seems as little satisfied with the conduct of the French minister as any one.

"The Viscount Noailles called on me, and I inquired after all his connections, in a family which I knew to be once in great power, wealth, and splendor. He seems to despair of liberty in France, and has lost, apparently, all hopes of ever living in France. He was very critical in his inquiries concerning the letters which were printed as mine in England. I told him candidly that I did not write them, and as frankly, in confidence, who did.* He says they made a great impression upon the people of England; that he heard Mr. Windham and Mr. Fox speak of them as the best thing that had been written, and as one of the best pieces of reasoning and style they had ever read. The Marquis (de Lafay-

---

* The papers signed Publicola, heretofore mentioned as written by John Quincy Adams.

ette), he says, is living, but injured in his health. Your old friend, the Marchioness, still lives in France in obscurity in the country. He thinks that a constitution, like that of England, would not last three days in France, and that monarchy will not be restored in a dozen years, if ever. The partitioning and arbitrary spirit of the combined powers will contribute more than any thing towards uniting the French under their old government. Frenchmen cannot bear the partition of their country; and rather than see it divided among their neighbors, they will unite in something or other.

"It will require all the address, all the temper, and all the firmness of congress and the States, to keep this people out of the war; or, rather, to avoid a declaration of war against us, from some mischievous power or other. It is but little that I can do, either by the functions which the constitution has intrusted to me, or by my personal influence; but that little shall be industriously employed, until it is put beyond a doubt that it will be fruitless; and then I shall be as ready to meet unavoidable calamities as any other citizen."

"19 December, 1793.

"Citizen Genest made me a visit yesterday while I was in senate, and left his card. I shall leave mine at his hotel to-morrow, as several of the senators have already hastened to return their visits. But we shall be in an awkward situation with this minister. I write you little concerning public affairs, because you will have every thing in print. How a government can go on, publishing all their negotiations with foreign nations, I know not. To me it appears as dangerous and pernicious as it is novel; but upon this occasion it could not, perhaps, have been avoided. You know where I think was the error in the first concoction. But such errors are unavoidable where the people, in crowds out of doors, undertake to receive ambassadors, and to dictate to their supreme executive.

" I know not how it is, but in proportion as dangers threaten the public, I grow calm. I am very apprehensive that a desperate anti-federal party will provoke all Europe by their insolence. But my country has in its wisdom contrived for me the most insignificant office that ever the invention of man contrived or his imagination conceived. And as I can do neither good nor evil, I must be borne away by others, and meet the common fate.

" The President has considered the conduct of Genest very nearly in the same light with Columbus,* and has given him a bolt of thunder. We shall see how this is supported by the two Houses. There are, who gnash their teeth with rage which they dare not own as yet. We shall soon see whether we have any government or not in this country. If the President has made any mistake at all, it is by too much partiality for the French republicans, and in not preserving a neutrality between the parties in France, as well as among the belligerent powers. But although he stands at present as high in the admiration and confidence of the people as ever he did, I expect he will find many bitter and desperate enemies arise in consequence of his just judgment

---

* Other papers written by J. Q. Adams, at this time, in the *Boston Centinel.*

against Genest. Besides that a party spirit will convert white into black, and right into wrong, we have, I fear, very corrupt individuals in this country, independent of the common spirit of party. The common movements of ambition every day disclose to me views and hopes and designs that are very diverting; but these I will not commit to paper. They make sometimes a very pretty farce, for amusement after the great tragedy or comedy is over.

"What I write to you, must be in sacred confidence and strict discretion."

"2 January, 1794.

"Our anti-federal scribblers are so fond of rotation, that they seem disposed to remove their abuse from me to the President. Bache's paper, which is nearly as bad as Freneau's, begins to join in concert with it to maul the President for his drawing-rooms, levees, declining to accept of invitations to dinners and tea-parties, his birthday odes, visits, compliments, etc. I may be expected to be an advocate for a rotation of objects of abuse, and for equality in this particular. I have held the office of libellee-general long enough. The burden of it ought to be participated and equalized, according to modern republican principles.

"The news from France, so glorious for the French army, is celebrated in loud peals of festivity, and elevates the spirits of the enemies of government among us more than it ought; for it will not answer their ends. We shall now see the form of the French republic. Their conventions will have many trials to make before they will come at any thing permanent. The calamities of France are not over. I shall claim the merit of some little accuracy of foresight when I see General Lincoln, who, you remember, was inclined to think the Duke of Brunswick's march to Paris certain; while I was apprehensive that the numerous fortified towns in his way would waste his army and consume the campaign.

"We shall soon see the operation in France of elections to first magistracies. My attention is fixed to this object. I have no doubt of its effects; but it is a curious question, how long they can last. We have lately seen how they have succeeded in New York, and what effect that election has had upon the votes for President. Cabal, intrigue, manœuvre, as bad as any species of corruption, we have already seen in our elections; and when and where will they stop?"

"9 January, 1794.

"The news of this evening is, that the Queen of France is no more. When will savages be satiated with blood? No prospect of peace in Europe, and therefore none of internal harmony in America. We cannot well be in a more disagreeable situation than we are with all Europe, with all Indians, and with all Barbary rovers. Nearly one half the continent is in constant opposition to the other, and the President's situation, which is highly responsible, is very distressing. He made me a very friendly visit yesterday, which I returned to-day, and had two hours' conversation with him alone in his cabinet. The conversation, which was extremely interesting, and equally affectionate, I cannot explain even by a hint. But his earnest desire to do right, and his close application to discover it, his deliberate and comprehensive view of our affairs with all the world, appeared in a very amiable and respectable light.

The anti-federalists and the frenchified zealots have nothing now to do, that I can conceive of, but to ruin his character, destroy his peace, and injure his health. He supports all their attacks with great firmness, and his health appears to be very good. The Jacobins would make a sortie upon him in all the force they could muster, if they dared.''

The allusions in the next extract are to Samuel Adams, at this time lieutenant-governor of Massachusetts, but whom the recent death of the governor, Hancock, had placed in the executive chair for the remainder of the political year. At the opening of the winter session of the legislature he had made a speech, the greater part of which was taken up with comments on the proposition that "all men are created equal." The "other preacher of *égalité*," the Duke of Orleans, had lately perished under the guillotine.

"4 February, 1794.

"I hope my old friend will never .meet the fate of another preacher of *égalité*, who was, I fear, almost as sincere as himself. By the law of nature, all men are men, and not angels—men, and not lions—men, and not whales—men, and not eagles—that is, they are all of the same species; and this is the most that the equality of nature amounts to. But man differs by nature from man, almost as much as man from beast. The equality of nature is moral and political only, and means that all men are independent. But a physical inequality, an intellectual inequality, of the most serious kind, is established unchangeably by the Author of nature; and society has a right to establish any other inequalities it may judge necessary for its good.   The precept, however, *do as you would be done by*, implies an equality which is the real equality of nature and Christianity, and has been known and understood in all ages, before the Lieutenant-Governor of Massachusetts made the discovery in January, 1794.

"I am pleased to hear that the court appointed again their late State attorney.   Mr. Dalton called on me, a few weeks ago, to communicate to me a great secret. The President had the evening before taken him aside, and inquired of him very particularly concerning the Vice-President's son at Boston, his age, his practice, his character, etc., etc., at the same time making great inquiries concerning Mr. Parsons, of Newburyport. From. all which Mr. D. conjectured that Mr. Gore was to be appointed attorney-general of the United States, and J. Q. Adams, attorney for the district.   I was somewhat alarmed, and was determined to advise my son to refuse it, if it should be so, though I did not believe it.   I would not advise Mr. J. Q. A. to play at small games in the executive of the United States.   I had much rather he should be State attorney for Suffolk.   Let him read Cicero and Demosthenes—much more eloquent than Madison and Smith.

"The rascally lie about the Duke of York in a cage at Paris, and Toulon and all the English fleet in the hands of the republic, was fabricated on purpose to gull the gudgeons; and it completely succeeded, to my infinite mortification.   An attempt was made to get me to read the red-hot lie in senate, in order to throw them into as foolish confusion as that below them;* but I was too old to be taken in, at least by so gross an artifice, the falsehood of which was to me palpable.

"You apologize for the length of your letters, and I ought to excuse the shortness and emptiness of mine. Yours give me more entertainment than all the speeches I hear. There are more good thoughts, fine strokes, and mother-wit in them than I hear in the whole week. An ounce of mother-wit is worth a pound of clergy; and I rejoice that one of my children, at least, has an abundance of not only mother-wit, but his mother's wit. It is one of the most amiable and striking traits in his composition. It appeared in all its glory and severity in 'Barneveldt.'†

"If the rogue has any family pride, it is all derived from the same source. His Pa renounces and abjures every trace of it. He has curiosity to know his descent, and comfort in the knowledge that his ancestors, on both sides, for several generations, have been innocent. But no pride in this. Pomp, splendor, office, title, power, riches, are the sources of pride, but even these are not excuse for pride. The virtues and talents of ancestors should be considered as examples and solemn trusts, and produce meekness, modesty, and humility, lest they should not be imitated and equalled. Mortification and humiliation can be the only legitimate

---

* All the bells of Philadelphia, on the occasion of this false report, are said, in the newspaper language of the day, to have "re-echoed the glorious sound of *downfall of tyrants—the rights of man forever.*"

† A signature attached to some articles printed in a Boston newspaper.

feelings of a mind conscious that it falls short of its ancestors in merit.   I must stop."

It may be interesting to some to know how this intelligence was received by the person to whom it was addressed.   Her letter, in reply, will show.   She proved to be right in her conjecture.   The prince alluded to was the person afterwards Duke of Kent, and the father of the present Queen of England.

Quincy, February, 1794.

"You say so many handsome things to me, respecting my letters, that you ought to fear making me vain; since, however we may appreciate the encomiums of the world, the praises of those whom we may love and esteem are more dangerous, because we are led to believe them the most sincere.

"When I read in your letter the communication made you by Mr. Dalton, I drew a very different conclusion from it from what he did.   I believe the President had some hint of the writer of certain pieces, and was led to make those inquiries respecting the master and the pupil, that he might the better judge whether the pupil alone was capable of writing them.   I am much better pleased that this should have been his object, than that the appointment Mr. D. suggested should have taken place.   If I have pride and ambition, it would not have been gratified by that; for instead of benefiting or advancing our son, it would have created envy, and injured him in his present prospect of increasing business.   It would have been a feather whose point would have proved a sting.   He has acquired to himself by his writings, his abilities, and his general character for information, a reputation which his enemies fear, and which cannot be combated by any imputation upon his life and manners.

.   .   .   .

"Prince Edward sailed last Sunday. He sent his aids to visit the Lieutenant-Governor, but would not go himself. He dined with Mrs. Hancock, and was visited by many gentlemen in town. He went to the assembly with Mr. Russell, and danced with Mrs. Russell. He went to visit the college, but I did not hear that he had any curiosity to see Bunker Hill. He related an anecdote at the table of the English consul. As he was coming from Quebec, he stopped at an inn, where an elderly countryman desired to see him. After some bowing, etc., the countryman said: 'I hear you are King George's son.' 'They tell me so,' said the prince. 'And, pray, how do you like this country?' 'Why, very well,' replied his highness. 'And how do you think your father liked to lose it?' 'Why, not half so well as I should like to live in it,' replied the prince, which answer pleased the countryman. I hear he took notice of all the French refugees, and offered any of them a passage with him to the West Indies. His stay here was very short; and it was best it should be so."

In the following extracts, Mr. Adams gives some idea of the movements of the time:

"8 February, 1794.

"Congress have been together more than two months, and have done nothing; and will continue sitting two months longer, and do little. I, for my part, am wearied to death with *ennui.* Obliged to be punctual by my habits, confined to my seat, as in a prison, to see nothing done, hear nothing said, and to say and do nothing. O, that my rocks were here within a mile or two, and my little habitation, and pretty little wife above all! Ah, I fear that some fault unknown has brought upon me such punishments, to be separated both when we were too young and when we are too old.

"I don't believe we shall adopt Mr. Madison's motions,* or build a navy. But if we do not purchase a peace with the Algerines, we shall all deserve to become their captives.

"The Genetians had a frolic on the 6th, in commemoration of the treaty,† and drank toasts enough to get merry. So cordial, so loving, so fraternal, so neat and elegant, so sweet and pretty! Have you read them? Franklin, Bryan, Reed, Hutchinson, and Sergeant, the heroes. Fit company for Dallas, Mifflin, and Genest! No harm done, however, that I hear of. A sharp shot or two at the President.

"The havoc made in our trade, I fear, will distress us. I suspect that immense sums borrowed of banks have fallen a sacrifice in France, as well as on the seas; and when the day of payment comes, more credits must be given, or bankruptcies ensue. Borrowing of banks for a trading capital is very unmercantile. How-

---

* They had been postponed, on the 5th, by a vote of 51 to 47, regarded as a test of the sense of the House.

† The alliance with France, 6 February, 1778.

ever, we shall not go to war, and nothing is to be dreaded so much as that.

"I fear the English will have all the West Indies, leaving a little to Spain. This I don't like at all. We shall see what another campaign will do in Europe. If the English assist La Vendée, which, if they had been cunning or wise, they would have done last year, it is thought that Brittany, Normandy, and Picardy will declare for a king. But of this there can be no certainty."

"9 February.

"So the tables are turned on the French faction; and the English faction will exult, in their turn, in the prospect of the West India Islands a conquest to England, the French navy wholly ruined, and insurrection spreading from province to province. Alas! I see no cause of joy in all these exultations on either side. I am compelled to console myself as well as I can.

> "'Durum! sed levius fit patientiâ
> Quicquid corrigere est nefas.'

"'Est aliquis et dolendi decor. Hic sapienti servandus est. Et quemadmodum in ceteris rebus, ita et in lacrimis aliquid sat est. Imprudentium ut gaudia, sic dolores exundavere. Æquo animo excipe necessaria.'

"Don't be impatient for the meaning of these mysteries. Wait till John comes up to translate them.

"Indeed, and in truth, I see no consolation upon these occasions but in stoicism or Christianity. I am no more delighted with the idea of the West Indies in the hands of the English, than I was with Brabant and Flanders in the power of Dumouriez."

"23 February.

"The birthday was celebrated yesterday with as much joy, affection, and festivity as ever; and, as it happened, the new French minister was then presented. Poor Genest, I fear, is undone. Bad as his conduct has been, I cannot but pity him. What will become of him, I know not. The name of his successor is Fauchet. Gloomy as I was, in expectation daily of afflicting news from home, I contented myself with paying my respects to the President, with the senate; but I thought it would not become me to be present at the ball, of a Saturday night, especially at a time when I could not get it out of my thoughts that my venerable parent* might be closing her eyes forever.

"The senate has been several days trying a contested election of Mr. Gallatin, with their doors open. It is, at length, determined that a gallery is to be built, and our debates public at the next session of congress. What the effect of this measure, which was at last carried by a great majority, will be, I know not; but it cannot produce greater evils than the contest about it, which was made an engine to render unpopular some of the ablest and most independent members. Some of the younger members may descend from their dignity so far, perhaps, as to court popularity at the expense of justice, truth, and wisdom, by flattering the prejudices of the audience, but I think they will lose more esteem than they will acquire by such means."

---

* Mr. Adams's mother was still living at a very advanced age.

The question which the writer decided, as mentioned in the next extract, is the one heretofore alluded to, upon the bill to prevent violations of neutrality.

"12 March.

"I have all along flattered myself with hopes that I might with propriety have taken leave of the senate, and returned home as soon as the roads might be settled; but such is the critical state of our public affairs, and I daily hear such doctrines advanced and supported by almost and sometimes quite one half of the senate, that I shall not prevail on myself to abandon my post. This day, the senators were equally divided upon a question which seemed to me to involve nothing less than peace and war; and I was obliged to decide it, to the no small chagrin of a number. If this country is involved in war, it shall not be my fault. But if it comes either from the malice of our enemies or the imprudence of our own people, it may perhaps be found that I shall not shrink from its difficulties sooner than some who now seek it in disguise. Business is now carried on with rapidity in both Houses, and I shall have a month of severe duty. I have not been absent a day. It is, to be sure, a punishment to hear other men talk five hours every day, and not be at liberty to talk at all myself, especially as more than half I hear appears to me very young, inconsiderate, and inexperienced."

The President *pro tempore*, spoken of in the next letter, was John Langdon, of New Hampshire, who soon after this time went into open opposition.

" 15 March.

"I know not how to throw off the lassitude that hangs upon me. Weary of a daily round, which to me is more confined and more insipid than to any other, I would gladly go home; but at a time so critical as this, it would not be justifiable to quit my post, if there were no particular reasons against it. But as the senate is nearly divided in all great questions, and the President *pro tem.* has lately taken it in his head to shift his box, my retirement would give an entire new complexion to the government. This circumstance, however, must not be repeated from me; but it is true.

"Great pains have been, and still are, taken to inflame the populace of Philadelphia and New York; and they have no method to correct this but by a town meeting, and by the temperate reasonings of the soundest part of the community, as they have at Boston; the consequence of which is that club meets to counteract club, merchants to undo what merchants have done, and the public opinion is a chaos, a Proteus—any thing, every thing, and nothing. Yet all sides trumpet and dogmatize about the public opinion.

"If the New England people suffer themselves to be artfully drawn into a war, they will be dupes indeed; for all the men and most of the money must be forced from them; and while others will throw off the burden of British debts, and obtain all the advantages of fur and peltry trades, and western lands, we have not the smallest thing to hope, unless it be by privateering; and such is now the tremendous naval superiority against us that we shall lose more than we gain by that.

. . . .

"Raynal prayed that, rather than men should always be knaves and fools, the species might be annihilated. At present, it seems in a fair way to be so. I love them too well, with all their faults, to be glad to see their present rapid progress towards destruction. All that I have and all that I am would I cheerfully give to prevent it. But I see no means. Havoc must have its perfect work, and then eyes will begin to open."

"SENATE CHAMBER, 27 March.

"Yesterday an embargo passed both Houses, for thirty days. I am afraid congress will sit late in May. I cannot think of leaving it in so critical a moment.

"I have one comfort: that in thought, word, or deed I have never encouraged a war. I will persevere in doing all in my power to prevent it. If it is forced on us by England, or even if it is brought on us by our own imprudence, I must stand or fall with my country.

"If the French had a better government and better morals, I should feel easier."

The violent measure spoken of in the next extract was the motion of Mr. Dayton, as found in the journal of the House for that day:

"1 April.

"The people here are much cooler than they were last week. The embargo begins to be felt by many who have been the most noisy and turbulent. Speculation mingles itself in every political operation, and many merchants have already made a noble *spec.* of the embargo by raising their prices. But the foolish trades-

men and laborers, who were so ready to follow the heels
of their scheming leaders, are now out of employment,
and will lose thirty dollars a head by this embargo. If
they had been taxed half the sum to the most necessary
and important measure, they would have bitterly complained. I can see little benefit in the embargo, except
that it may cool down the courage of such kind of people.
It may be expected that we shall soon have a clamor
against the renewal of it, if not to have it repealed.

"The assembly of Pennsylvania have this day chosen
a senator, Mr. James Ross, of Washington county, in
the place of Mr. Gallatin.

"A violent measure has been proposed in the House,
to sequester all debts due from American citizens to
British subjects. Such a motion will do no honor to
our country. Such laws are injurious to the debtor as
well as the creditor, for they cannot dissolve the contracts. It will not pass the House, and, if it did, it
would stop in the Senate.

"We are rejoiced that the civic feast in Boston succeeded no better. It is astonishing that Mr. A. should
ever have thought of implicating the government in so
indecent and hostile a frolic.* We have had an incessant struggle all the winter to restrain the intemperate

---

* This was a festival proposed to be held in Boston "to cele-
brate the successes of our French allies." The acting governor,
Samuel Adams, upon being applied to, consented to call out some
military corps to assist upon the occasion. But the citizens generally proved so lukewarm that the committee appointed to prepare it suspended their operations, assigning as a reason "the
uncertainty of our political situation and the distresses of our
trade."

ardor of the people out of doors and their too accurate representatives in both Houses. Too many of our good federalists are carried away at times by their passions and the popular torrent, to concur in motions and countenance sentiments inconsistent with our neutrality, and tending directly to war. But I hope we shall be able to make a stand against all fatal attempts.

"I long to be at home, but I dare not ask leave to go. The times are too critical for any man to quit his post without the most urgent necessity."

"7 April.

"We are still endeavoring to preserve peace. But one moves a series of commercial regulations; another, a sequestration of debts; a third, to prohibit all intercourse with Britain; a fourth, to issue letters of marque against Algerines; all tending to excite suspicions in Britain that we are hostile to her, and mean ultimately to join her enemies. One firebrand is scarcely quenched before another is thrown in; and if the sound part of the community is not uncommonly active and attentive to support us, we shall be drawn off from our neutral ground, and involved in incomprehensible evils. In danger of a war that will be unnecessary, if not unjust; that has no public object in view; that must be carried on with allies the most dangerous that ever existed, my situation is as disagreeable as any I ever knew. I should have no fear of an honest war; but a knavish one would fill me with disgust and abhorrence."

In the succeeding letter, the writer comments upon Mr. Clark's resolution to prohibit intercourse with

Great Britain, which was afterwards rejected by his casting vote.

"15 April.

"The House yesterday passed a resolution in committee of the whole, whose depth is to me unfathomable. The Senate will now be called upon to show their independence; and, perhaps, your friend to show his weakness or his strength. The majority of the House is certainly for mischief, and there is no doubt they represent the people in the Southern States and a large number in the Northern. *Vox populi, vox Dei,* they say, and so it is, sometimes. But it is sometimes the voice of Mahomet, of Cæsar, of Catiline, the Pope, and the Devil. Britain, however, has done much amiss, and deserves all that will fall thereon. Her insolence, which you and I have known and felt more than any other Americans, will lead her to ruin, and us half-way. We indeed are, in point of insolence, her very image and superscription; as true a game-cock as she, and I warrant you, shall become as great a scourge to mankind."

If Mr. Adams is correct in assigning the motive for the opposition to Mr. Jay, it is only adding one more to the large number of instances on record of political miscalculations. It can scarcely admit of a doubt that the treaty, which was the issue of his mission, roused an opposition which deterred the federalists from thinking of him as a candidate for the Presidency.

"19 April.

"Senate has been three days in debate upon the appointment of Mr. Jay to go to London. It has this day been determined in his favor, eighteen *versus* eight.

"You cannot imagine what horror some persons are in, lest peace should continue. The prospect of peace throws them into distress. Their countenances lengthen at the least opening of an appearance of it. Glancing gleams of joy beam from their faces whenever all possibility of it seems to be cut off. You can divine the secret source of these feelings as well as I. The opposition to Mr. Jay has been quickened by motives which will always influence every thing in an elective government. Pretexts are never wanting to ingenious men; but the views of all the principal parties are always directed to the election of the first magistrate. If Jay should succeed, it will recommend him to the choice of the people for President, as soon as a vacancy shall happen. This will weaken the hopes of the Southern States for Jefferson. This I believe to be the secret motive of the opposition to him, though other things were alleged as ostensible reasons: such as his monarchical principles, his indifference about the navigation of the Mississippi, his attachment to England, his aversion to France, none of which are well founded; and his holding the office of chief justice, etc.

"The day is a good omen. May the gentle zephyrs waft him to his destination, and the blessing of Heaven succeed his virtuous endeavors to preserve peace! I am so well satisfied with this measure that I shall run the venture to ask leave to go home, if congress determines to sit beyond the middle of May.

. . . .

"We are ill-treated by Britain, and you and I know

it is owing to a national insolence against us.   If they force us into a war, it is my firm faith they will be chastised for it a second time worse than the first.''

" 22 April.

"The President has appointed Mr. Jay to go to England as envoy extraordinary, in hopes that satisfaction may be obtained for the injuries done us in the capture of our vessels.   I have no very sanguine hopes of his success, but if any man can succeed, I presume he is as likely as any.   At least, he will give as much satisfaction to the American people as any man.''

" 5 May.

" I must remain here, because my friends say I must not go.   Those whose principles are the same with mine, whose views of public good coincide with mine, say that if we keep together, we shall succeed to the end of the session as we have hitherto done, in keeping off all the most pernicious projects.

"The ways and means before the House of Representatives is a very important and a very difficult system. While I confess the necessity of it, and see its importance in giving strength to our government at home and consideration to our country abroad, I lament the introduction of taxes and expenses which will accumulate a perpetual debt and lead to future revolutions.

"Mr. Jay is to immortalize himself over again by keeping peace.   This will depend on the valor of the French.   I begin to rejoice in their successes more than I did.   The English have treated us very ill.

"We must send a new minister to France, and

another to Holland. Mr. Fauchet begins to grace our democratic societies with his presence. This must not be carried very far. These assemblies are very criminal.

"O, that I were with you!"

" 10 May.

"We go on as usual, congress resolving one thing, and the democratical societies resolving the contrary; the President doing what is right, and clubs and mobs resolving it to be all wrong.

"We had in Senate, a few days ago, the greatest curiosity of all. The senators from Virginia moved, in consequence of an instruction from their constituents, that the execution of the fourth article of the treaty of peace, relative to *bona fide* debts, should be suspended until Britain should fulfil the seventh article. When the question was put, fourteen voted against it, two only, the Virginia delegates, for it; and all the rest, but one, ran out of the room to avoid voting at all. And that one excused himself.* This is the first instance of the kind.

"The motion disclosed the real object of all the wild projects and mad motions which have been made during the whole session. O, liberty! O, my country! O, debt! And, O, sin! These debtors are the persons

---

* Yeas, 2. Messrs. Monroe and Taylor.

Nays, 14. Messrs. Bradford, Cabot, Ellsworth, Foster, Frelinghuysen, Henry, Izard, King, Langdon, Livermore, Morris, Potts, Ross, and Strong.

Messrs. Hawkins, Jackson, and Martin appear to have been three of the persons who set the precedent, which has been often followed since, and by more distinguished public men. The usual attendance was about twenty-four.

who are continually declaiming against the corruption of congress. Impudence ! Thy front is brass.''

It is interesting to note the comment upon the introduction of the practice of voting with printed ballots, which has since become universal. The effect of it, in increasing the force of associated action, and diminishing the individual power of choice between candidates, has never yet been sufficiently set forth.

"17 May.

"Well ! Boston comes on. Mr. Morton is now to be its leader. How changed in reputation since 1788 ! I wonder not at the choice of well-born Winthrop. He might, I suppose, have been chosen at any time. His father was one of my best friends, and the son was a good son of liberty. I know of nothing to his disadvantage. The federalists committed an egregious blunder in a very unwarrantable and indecent attempt, I had almost said, upon the freedom of elections, at their previous meeting for the choice of governor. The opposite party, to be sure, practise arts nearly as unwarrantable in secret, and by sending agents with printed votes. But this is no justification, unless upon Cato's principle: *In corrupta civitate corruptio est licita.*''

A younger brother of Mr. Adams had been chosen at this election to represent the town of Quincy in the State legislature. In announcing it, Mrs. Adams had expressed to her husband her apprehension that he was too much inclined to hostilities with Great Britain.

The following comment contains the writer's system in
few words:

" 19 May.

" My brother will not vote for war, I hope, before it
is necessary as well as just.   Great is the guilt of unnecessary war !

" I have not a doubt but the farm has been well
governed.   I wish the State and the nation may be as
well conducted.

" The world is a riddle, which death, I hope, will
unravel.   Amidst all the trials I have gone ·through, I
have much to be grateful for: good parents, an excellent
wife, and promising children; tolerable health, upon
the whole, and competent fortune; success almost
without example in a dangerous, dreadful revolution,
and still hopes of better times."

This important session of congress expired, as has
been seen, without any marked proceeding.   But the
extent to which the sympathies of men had become
enlisted on one side or the other of the great struggle
going on in Europe can scarcely be understood at this
day without a familiar acquaintance with the newspapers
of the time.   The violent discussions that had been
held, and the close divisions upon all disputed questions
that followed, make a significant prelude to the furious
storm that raged during the remainder of the second
administration.

Previously to entering upon this, however, it may be
as well to close the correspondence of the season with
the following letter communicating a most interesting
fact to both the parties,—the entrance of their son,

John Quincy Adams, upon his diplomatic career. The Secretary of State alluded to was Edmund Randolph, who had succeeded to Mr. Jefferson at the beginning of the session.

"27 May.

"It is proper that I should apprise you, that the President has it in contemplation to send your son to Holland, that you may recollect yourself and prepare for the event. I make this communication to you, in confidence, at the desire of the President communicated to me yesterday by the Secretary of State. You must keep it an entire secret, until it shall be announced to the public in the journal of the Senate. But our son must hold himself in readiness to come to Philadelphia to converse with the President, Secretary of State, Secretary of the Treasury, etc., and receive his commissions and instructions, without loss of time. He will go to Providence in the stage, and thence to New York by water, and thence to Philadelphia in the stage. He will not set out, however, until he is informed of his appointment. Perhaps the Senate may negative him, and then his journey will be unnecessary."

The nomination was made two days after the date of this letter, and was confirmed by the Senate on the 30th. Ten days later that body dispersed.

Since the hour that the scales turned in favor of independence in Pennsylvania, that State has exerted a commanding influence over the internal politics of the United States. The manner in which that event was brought about, threw her into connections with New

England, which continued, with slight interruptions, down to the year 1794. At both of the elections, which had occurred since the organization of the new government, her electoral votes had been given in favor of Massachusetts, in the only case where there was a division, in marked contrast to the policy of New York; and the general character of her representation in both houses of congress had been friendly to the same power in the federal administration. But the causes which produced this state of things had been gradually wearing away, and others had been at work in the western section of the State, which heralded the change of policy that in time became decided. One great instrument to alienate the popular feeling was found in the law passed in 1791, laying a duty upon spirits distilled within the United States, which stimulated the discontent at once of the consumers and of those who found a market for their superfluous grain in the manufacture.

This law was one of the serious mistakes of the federal party. For the trifling revenue obtained proved by no means an equivalent for the irritation that, in the unsettled state of public affairs at the outset of a new government, ensued. Here is to be traced the rise of another individual, Albert Gallatin, not inferior to Hamilton in the powers of his mind, and much his superior in the shrewdness and discretion which he brought to the management of great public concerns. Excluded from the Senate by a constitutional obstacle, he had nevertheless succeeded in organizing the opposition of the western counties to such an extent as to render him a powerful coadjutor

in the policy of which Mr. Jefferson had become the
type. The zeal of the people in that region, however,
so far outran their discretion, that they broke out this
summer into open resistance to the authority of government. The civil officers were set at defiance, and
had to fly for their lives. And the duty devolved upon
the President of maintaining the supremacy of the
federal law by an armed force. Of this force, Mr.
Hamilton took the direction without having the nominal command. The mere appearance of it was sufficient to restore order, as none of the leading men in
that quarter had entertained any intention of pushing
matters to extremity. But the hostility to Mr. Hamilton, as a member of the cabinet, had become so bitter
in a large section of the Union, and his remaining in
it, after Jefferson's retirement, had been construed as
giving so decided a party complexion to the administration, that he deemed it best likewise to withdraw.
The next session of congress began in November, with
important changes to the country. Few of the elder
class of public men could be found willing to breast
the fury of the political elements. President Washington was obliged to select Oliver Wolcott, of Connecticut, whom Mr. Hamilton probably pointed out to
him, as the next secretary of the treasury, and Timothy
Pickering, of Massachusetts, to succeed General Knox,
who insisted upon retirement from the war department.
Both these appointments were from New England,
where the government was already sufficiently strong.
Neither of them gave any reinforcement to the popularity of the administration, which from this time
rested upon the name and character of the President

alone. Fortunate was it for the country that in the ordeal which ensued, such a support was reserved to carry it through in safety. For the events that occurred were of a nature to task even that strength to the utmost.

The short session of 1794–1795 passed away in a state of comparative calm. Although the opposition yet held a majority in the House of Representatives, its force had been weakened by the events of the summer, and both parties were willing, before engaging in a new trial of strength, to await the result of the negotiations which Mr. Jay was understood to be conducting with the British ministry. Only three days after the close of the session, the cabinet received the intelligence that the terms of a treaty had been agreed upon, and accordingly the President directed the Senate to be especially convoked in June for the purpose of passing upon its ratification. Mr. Adams's letters during this session are short, and being necessarily restrained by the obligation to secrecy, are very meagre. Yet they contain some hints.

"9 June, 1795.

" The Senate assembled yesterday, at eleven ; twenty-five members present. The new senators were sworn, and a committee waited on the President, who immediately sent a message with the treaty, which was read, together with a part of a volume of negotiations which accompanied it. Mr. Butler and Mr. Green arrived last night, as I hear, so that we shall be very full.

"Your curiosity, I doubt not, is all alive. But—mum—mum—mum."

Mrs. Adams was at this time in New York.   In the evening of the same day he wrote again, transmitting the pamphlet then just issued by Cobbett, called "A Bone to gnaw for the Democrats."

"The Senate are now in possession of the budget. It is a bone to gnaw for the aristocrats as well as the democrats; and while I am employed in attending the digestion of it, I send you inclosed an amusement which resembles it only in name.   I can form no judgment when the process will be over.   We must wait with patience.

"Be very careful, my dearest friend, of what you say in that circle and city.   The times are perilous."

The writer lived almost to the time to witness the feasibility of what he in the next letter manifestly regards as a very wild wish.

"11 June.

"If I could take a walk or a ride to New York in the evening and come here again in the morning, how clever it would be!

"Mr. Jay spent last evening with me, and let me into the history of the treaty and negotiation, explaining his views of its intent and operation.   I can say nothing upon it at present.

"I have read eight of Mr. A.'s dispatches; and fourteen remain to be read.   Government is much pleased with them.

"My love to all.   When I shall get away from this city, is uncertain.   But I have no hopes of being excused before the end of next week.   The treaty is of great extent and importance, and will not be rejected nor adopted without a thorough examination. I presume every member will wish for such an investigation as will enable him to render a reason for his vote, whether *pro* or *con.*"

During the absence of Mr. Jay, in England, he had been elected governor of the State of New York.

"18 June.

"Mr. Adet was presented to the President on Tuesday, and, accompanied by the Secretary of State, made me a visit immediately after his audience. I was not at home, but in Senate. On Wednesday morning I returned his visit at Oeller's hotel.

"He is not a friend to clubs—announced to the President the entire *annihilation of factions* in France, etc.

"His Excellency, Governor Jay, returned yesterday to New York. He has been very sociable and in fine spirits. His health is improving. We have no chief justice as yet nominated. It is happy that Mr. Jay's election was over before the treaty was published; for the parties against him would have quarrelled with the treaty, right or wrong, that they might give a color to their animosity against him."

"20 June.

"All the next week will be taken up, I suppose, in further investigations of the subject before Senate, and, indeed, I should be very glad to be insured that the decision will be as early as Saturday. If it should be

earlier, I shall be agreeably disappointed. I shall take
my departure as soon as the business is done.

"The day is at hand, when Governor Jay is to take
the reins in New York. May his administration be
easy to himself and happy for the people!"

The next letter contains an omen of the serious differences that occurred a few years later. Lansdowne
was the name of Mr. William Bingham's country-seat
near Philadelphia.

"21 June.

"The sun is so bright and augurs such heat that
I am doubtful whether I shall go out to Lansdowne to
dinner.

"I dined yesterday at Mr. Wolcott's, the Secretary
of the Treasury, with King, Ellsworth, and Cabot, and
a few others. The conversation turned upon old times.
One of the company expressed such inveteracy against
my old friend Gerry, that I could not help taking up his
vindication. The future election of a governor, in case
of an empty chair, excites a jealousy which I have long
perceived. These things will always be so. Gerry's
merit is inferior to that of no man in the Massachusetts,
except the present governor, according to my ideas and
judgment of merit. I wish he was more enlarged, however, and more correct in his views. He never was
one of the threads tied into the Essex knot, and was
never popular with that set."

"23 June.

"Some senators are confident we shall rise to-morrow or next day. If so I shall be with you on Sunday.
But these conjectures are always uncertain.

"Both the public dispatches and private letters of our dear boy are the delight of all who read them. No public minister has ever given greater satisfaction, than Mr. Adams* has hitherto. His prudence, caution, and penetration are as much approved as the elegance of his style is admired. Providence, I hope and pray, will make him a blessing to his country as well as to his parents.

"I went out to Lansdowne on Sunday, about half a mile on this side Judge Peters's, where you once dined. The place is very retired, but very beautiful—a splendid house, gravel-walks, shrubberies and clumps of trees in the English style—on the bank of the Schuylkill."

Mrs. Adams, whilst at New York, had been to see General Gates, and had written an account of his farming, in the vicinity of that place.

"24 June.

"The Senate advanced yesterday in their deliberations with so much diligence that it would be very easy to finish to-day; but it is not probable to me that they will. Whether to-morrow or next day, or the day after, I cannot determine.

"It would give me great pleasure to visit General Gates, and make my observations on his husbandry and gardening. I should hope to learn lessons and acquire experience in my favorite business and amusement, but the time will not permit. My affairs at home demand my immediate attention.

"I dine to-day with Colonel Pickering, and to-mor-

---

* His son, J. Q. Adams.

row with the President.   But if the Senate finishes to-day, I will make my apology.''

" 26 June.

" The Senate is to meet at ten this morning, and I hope will finish; but it is still uncertain.   I shall set out this afternoon, provided the Senate rises.

"I shall say nothing of public affairs, because the least said is soonest mended.''

The treaty barely received the necessary sanction of two-thirds of the Senate.   It certainly cannot be ranked as a triumph of American diplomacy, but it was a great deal better than war, which must have ensued without it.   The enemies of the administration, avoiding the responsibility of rejecting it, now flamed out in earnest opposition.   One of the senators from Virginia, violating his obligation of secrecy, communicated a copy of the instrument to a newspaper at Philadelphia, the effect of which was to precipitate a burst of indignation upon it from one end of the country to the other.   The first manifestation occurred in Boston, where, in a crowded assembly in Faneuil Hall, but a single individual ventured to interpose a word of objection to the universal cry of condemnation.   The same spirit was manifested in all the chief towns of the seaboard, and undoubtedly animated the population everywhere.   As is not uncommon, however, the very excess to which it was carried on the instant, led to a reaction in time.   Some hopes were entertained that the President might yet be induced, by earnest remonstrances, to withhold his signature. His answer to the people of Boston set that matter at rest. No more enduring memorial of a statesman's firmness is to be found in history. The effect of it was to rally around him all the leading friends of government, and to make the issue of the contest that raged during the subsequent session of congress far more doubtful than could have been possibly anticipated.

Neither the British nor the French government remained indifferent spectators of this warfare. The latter complained of the treaty not without show of reason, because it conceded in favor of her adversary a departure from the principles which had been agreed on between the two nations in the treaty of 1778, when the sanction of France was all-important to their establishment. This objection might have been decisive, but for the opportune exposure, through the agency of Mr. Hammond, the British minister, of a secret correspondence between M. Fauchet, the envoy of France, and Mr. Edmund Randolph, the Secretary of State, which seriously implicated the integrity of the latter. The precise extent of his misconduct has never been defined. He failed in his attempt to explain it. And the consequence was a rise in the popular feeling adverse to France, which was materially quickened by the intelligence now pouring in from Europe of the revolutionary excesses. Randolph was driven to a resignation. In this hour of distress, Washington looked over the wide surface of the land for efficient support. One after another of the best and strongest men was summoned to fill the vacant post. Not one of them had the courage to come. Under these circumstances, he was compelled to continue Colonel

Timothy Pickering in the office, to which he had, in
the beginning, transferred him only for the moment.
The acceptance of the place, when everybody else
shrank from it, was creditable to the manliness of Colonel Pickering, though the event proved big with the
fate of the administration that was to follow.

A memoir of this kind cannot, without exceeding
all reasonable limits, be expected to enter minutely
into the history of the period, however interesting it
may be.   It must necessarily confine itself to those
portions of it calculated to illustrate the life and character, the private feelings and the public action, of the
person to whom it relates.   Thus far, the troubles of
the times had not pressed heavily upon the mind of
Mr. Adams, because his situation, excepting upon rare
occasions, dictated inactivity, whilst it favored the
preservation of a serenity highly propitious to his
powers of observation.   It is this which gives so much
zest to the familiar correspondence with his wife, from
which extracts have been freely given.   They will now
be continued down to the moment when these feelings
begin to change.   The first symptom of this is to be
traced in the operation of the disturbed state of affairs
upon the mind of the President.   Deserted by the
leading men of his own section of country, and by
others to whom he had a right to look for assistance,
and compelled thus alone to breast the fury of an opposition growing more and more bitter towards himself, he grew more resolved upon positive retirement.
The rumors of his design, which now got abroad,
affected different interests very differently.   The federalists regarded it with dismay; the opposition with

faintly disguised satisfaction. The position of Mr. Adams was necessarily to be greatly affected by the event. Here his own speculations come in to describe it much better than any substitute could do.

"7 January, 1796.

"The President appears great in Randolph's vindication throughout, excepting that he wavered about signing the treaty, which he ought not to have done one moment. Happy is the country to be rid of Randolph; but where shall be found good men and true to fill the offices of government? There seems to be a necessity of distributing the offices about the States in some proportion to their numbers; but in the southern part of the Union, false politics have struck their roots so deep, that it is very difficult to find gentlemen who are willing to accept of public trusts, and at the same time capable of discharging them. The President offered the office of State to several gentlemen who declined: to Mr. Patterson, Mr. King, Mr. Henry, of Virginia, Mr. Charles Cotesworth Pinckney, of South Carolina, and three others whose names I do not recollect. He has not been able to find any one to accept the war office. The expenses of living at the seat of government are so exorbitant, so far beyond all proportion to the salaries, and the sure reward of integrity in the discharge of public functions is such obloquy, contempt, and insult, that no man of any feeling is willing to renounce his home, forsake his property and profession for the sake of removing to Philadelphia, where he is almost sure of disgrace and ruin.

"Where these things will end, I know not. In perfect secrecy between you and me, I must tell you that now I believe the President will retire. The consequence to me is very serious, and I am not able, as yet, to see what my duty will demand of me. I shall take my resolutions with cool deliberation. I shall watch the course of events with more critical attention than I have done for some time, and what Providence shall point out to be my duty, I shall pursue with patience and decision. It is no light thing to resolve upon retirement. My country has claims, my children have claims, and my own character has claims upon me; but all these claims forbid me to serve the public in disgrace. Whatever any one may think, I love my country too well to shrink from danger in her service, provided I have a reasonable prospect of being able to serve her to her honor and advantage. But if I have reason to think that I have either a want of abilities or of public confidence to such a degree as to be unable to support the government in a higher station, I ought to decline it. But in that case, I ought not to serve in my present place under another, especially if that other should entertain sentiments so opposite to mine as to endanger the peace of the nation. It will be a dangerous crisis in public affairs, if the President and Vice-President should be in opposite boxes.

"These lucubrations must be confined to your own bosom. But I think, upon the whole, the probability is strong that I shall make a voluntary retreat, and spend the rest of my days, in a very humble style, with you. Of one thing I am very sure—it would be to me the happiest portion of my whole life."

Parties were now very distinctly defined, and the great theatre of contention was the House of Representatives.

The first struggle took place upon an absolute demand upon the President for the papers connected with the negotiation of Jay's treaty. Here the opposition triumphed, and the President was driven to refuse them, in order to maintain the independence of the executive authority. The next contest was upon the measures necessary to carry the treaty into execution, and in that the administration finally prevailed. This is the occasion upon which Mr. Ames's speech earned him a reputation as an orator, which has survived his generation. The whole session was absorbed in these proceedings.

"20 January, 1796.

"This is one of my red-letter days. It is the anniversary of the signature of the declaration of an armistice between the United States and Great Britain, in 1783. There are several of these days in my calendar, which I recollect as they pass in review, but which nobody else remembers. And, indeed, it is no otherwise worth my while to remember them than to render an ejaculation of gratitude to Providence for the blessing.

"We are wasting our time in the most insipid manner, waiting for the treaty. Nothing of any consequence will be done till that arrives, and is mauled and abused, and then acquiesced in. For the anti's must be more numerous than I believe them, and made of sterner stuff than I conceive, if they dare hazard the surrender of the posts and the payment for spoliations, by any resolution of the House that shall render precarious the execution of the treaty on our part.

"I am, as you say, quite a favorite. I am to dine to-day again. I am heir-apparent, you know, and a succession is soon to take place. But whatever may be the wish or the judgment of the present occupant, the French and the demagogues intend, I presume, to set aside the descent. All these hints must be secrets. It is not a subject of conversation as yet. I have a pious and a philosophical resignation to the voice of the people in this case, which is the voice of God. I have no very ardent desire to be the butt of party malevolence. Having tasted of that cup, I find it bitter, nauseous, and unwholesome."

In no single particular has a greater change taken place in the political affairs of the United States than in the mode in which public questions are discussed. During the period now under consideration, the highest class of ability in the country was habitually enlisted in the production of elaborate dissertations for the newspapers upon the great topics of the day. These were commonly printed at all the central points, and being assiduously read by the people, exercised a strong influence upon their modes of thought and action. It may admit of question whether, with the enormous multiplication of local presses, established on a different plan, and the change of tastes and feelings that has happened, so useful a mode of keeping the public mind impressed with principles of importance has been preserved. The thirty-eight numbers of Camillus, alluded to in the next letter, which had a great effect in ultimately establishing Mr. Jay's treaty, would scarcely find a welcome among readers grown impatient of any thing beyond the meagre summary supplied by the magnetic telegraph.

"31 January, 1796.

"I have a secret to communicate to your prudence. The defence by Camillus was written in concert between Hamilton, King, and Jay. The writings on the first ten articles of the treaty were written by Hamilton; the rest by King, till they came to the question of the constitutionality of the treaty, which was discussed by Hamilton. Jay was to have written a concluding peroration; but being always a little lazy, and perhaps concluding, upon the whole, that it might be most politic to keep his name out of it; and perhaps finding that the work was already well done, he neglected it. This I have from King's own mouth. It is to pass, however, for Hamilton's. All three consulted together upon most, if not all the pieces.

"I read forever, and am determined to sacrifice my eyes, like John Milton, rather than give up the amusement without which I should despair.

"If I did not with you consider the universe as all one family, I would never stay another day here.

"I have read four thick octavo volumes of Tacitus, translated by Murphy, one thick volume of Homer's Iliad, translated by Cowper, besides a multitude of pamphlets and newspapers, since I have been here.

"I do not write enough. The habit of writing should not be lost as I lose it. Peter Pindar has it right:

> "'Search we the spot which mental power contains?
> Go where man gets his living by his brains.'

"If I had got my living by my brains for seven years past, I should have had more mental power. But brains have not only been useless, but even hurtful and pernicious in my course. Mine have been idle a long time till they are rusty."

The following frank and obviously sincere expression of the writer's feelings on the subject of official forms is in amusing contrast to the charges widely spread against him by the opposite party, and connived at by Mr. Jefferson himself, of excessive attachment to them:

"1 March, 1796.

"As to the subject of yours, of the 20th, I am quite at my ease. I never felt less anxiety when any considerable change lay before me. *Aut transit aut finit.* I transmigrate or come to an end. The question is between living at Philadelphia or at Quincy, between great cares and small cares. I have looked into myself, and see no meanness nor dishonesty there. I see weakness enough, but no timidity. I have no concern on your account but for your health. A woman *can* be silent when she will.

"After all, persuasion may overcome the inclination of the chief to retire. But if it should, it will shorten his days, I am convinced. His heart is set upon it, and the turpitude of the Jacobins touches him more nearly than he owns in words. All the studied efforts of the federalists to counterbalance abuse by compliment, do not answer the end.

"I suspect, but do not know, that Patrick Henry, Mr. Jefferson, Mr. Jay, and Mr. Hamilton will all be voted for. I ask no questions, but questions are forced upon me. I have had some conversations, purposely sought, in order, as I believe, indeed, as I know, to convince me that the federalists had no thought of overleaping the succession. The only question that labors in my mind is, whether I shall retire with my file-leader. I hate to live in Philadelphia in summer, and I hate still more to relinquish my farm. I hate speeches, messages, addresses and answers, proclamations, and such affected, studied, constrained things. I hate levees and drawing-rooms. I hate to speak to a thousand people to whom I have nothing to say. Yet all this I can do. But I am too old to continue more than one, or, at most, more than two heats; and that is scarcely time enough to form, conduct, and complete any very useful system.

"Electioneering enough we shall have. The inclosed scraps will show specimens."

The following is a good specimen of the writer's humor:

"13 March.

"I covet the harp of Amphion. What would I not give for the harp of Amphion?

"In my walks in the Cedar Grove, in Rocky Run, and on Penn's Hill, I should play upon my lyre, and the merry rocks would dance after me, and reel into walls. This would be to me a very pleasant and profitable private amusement. But there is another use I could make of my instrument in my public employment, more grateful to a benevolent heart, because more useful to mankind.   In no age of the world was it more wanted.

> "'Amphion thus bade wild dissension cease,
>   And softened mortals learned the arts of peace.
>   Amphion taught contending kings,
>   From various discords, to create
>   The music of a well-tuned state.
>   Nor slack, nor strain the tender strings
>   Those useful touches to impart
>   That strike the subject's answering heart,
>   And the soft, silent harmony that springs
>   From sacred union and consent of things.'

"Alas! I am not Amphion.   I have been thirty years singing and whistling among my rocks, and not one would ever move without money.   I have been twenty years saying, if not singing, preaching, if not playing:

> "'From various discords to create
>   The music of a well-tuned state,
>   And the soft, silent harmony that springs
>   From sacred union and consent of things,'

but an uncomplying world will not regard my uncouth discourses.   I cannot sing nor play.   If I had eloquence, or humor, or irony, or satire, or the harp or lyre of Amphion, how much good could I do to the world!

"What a mortification to my vanity!   What a humiliation to my self-love!   The rocks in the House of Representatives will not dance to my lyre.   They will not accord to 'a well-tuned state.'   They will not endure 'the harmony that springs from sacred union and consent of things.' They are for breaking all the instruments but that of the thorough bass, and then blowing you deaf and dumb. There are bold and daring strides making to demolish the President, Senate, and all but the House, which, as it seems to me, must be the effect of the measures that many are urging. Be not alarmed, however. They will not carry their point. The treaty will be executed, and that by the consent of the House.

"I am going to hear Dr. Priestley. His discourses are learned, ingenious, and useful. They will be printed, and, he says, dedicated to me. Don't tell this secret, though, for no other being knows it. It will get me the character of a heretic, I fear. I presume, however, that dedicating a book to a man will not imply that he approves every thing in it.

"The weather is so fine that I long to be upon my hills. Pray, since my harp cannot build walls, how do my friends go on who are obliged to employ their elbows in that laborious work?

"I sometimes think that if I were in the House of Representatives, and could make speeches there, I could throw some light upon these things. If Mr. Jefferson should be President, I believe I must put up as a candidate for the House. But this is my vanity. I feel sometimes as if I could speechify among them; but, alas, alas, I am too old! It would soon destroy my health. I declare, however, if I were in that House, I would drive out of it some demons that haunt it. There are false doctrines and false jealousies predominant there, at times, that it would be easy to exorcise."

The opposition demand for the papers, in the case of Mr. Jay's treaty, was carried, after a long and acrimonious discussion. This had inspired some doubts of their consent to appropriate money for carrying it into execution. Mr. Adams, in the next letter, alludes to this.

" 1 April.

" The newspapers will inform you of our interminable delays. The House have asked for papers, and the President has refused them, with reasons; and the House are about to record, in their journals, their reasons; meanwhile, the business is in suspense, and I have no clear prospect when I shall get home.

" It is the general opinion of those I converse with, that after they have passed the resolutions which they think will justify them to their constituents, seven or eight of the majority will vote for the appropriations necessary to carry the treaties into execution.

" Next Wednesday is assigned for the House to take the President's message into consideration. Two Massachusetts members, Leonard and Freeman, are gone home, and three more are among the most inveterate of the opposition, Dearborn, Varnum, and Lyman. Our people are almost as inconsistent in returning such men, as the Pennsylvanians are in returning adventurers from Geneva, Britain, and Ireland. If the constitution is to give way under these contending parties, we shall see it before long. If the House persevere in refusing to vote the appropriations, we shall sit here till next March, for what I know, and wait for the people to determine the question for us. One good effect of a persevering opposition in the House would be that we should preserve the President for another four years. For I presume he will have sufficient spirit to hold the helm till he has steered the ship through this storm, unless the people should remove him, which most certainly they will not.

"I will not sit here in summer, in all events. I would sooner resign my office. I will leave Philadelphia by the 6th or 7th of June, at farthest. Other gentlemen of the Senate and House are frequently asking leave of absence; but my attendance is perpetual, and will, if continued much longer, disorder my health, which hitherto has been very good. But I want my horse, my farm, my long walks, and, more than all, the bosom of my friend."

The retirement of President Washington removed the last check upon the fury of parties. Nobody else stood in the same relation to the whole people; and if even his name had latterly proved insufficient to silence obloquy, it very certainly followed that, for the future, no restraint could be expected in regard to any other. Of course, no expectation was entertained in any quarter that the person about to succeed him in office would be chosen by any general agreement. He was to be elected only upon the votes of one or the other of the parties into which the country was very equally divided. The question then narrowed itself down to a choice between the two men who might be brought forward, as the representatives of those parties, with the greatest prospect of success. The individual whom the opposition would sustain, with marked unanimity, was Thomas Jefferson. He had, from the day of leaving office, be-

come the very soul of the movement, and had succeeded
in inspiring its leading members with that species of
reliance upon him as its head, which, in all great enter-
prises involving the agency of numbers, is a necessary
element of victory.   The federalists, on the other hand,
enjoyed no such advantage.   A portion of them, embracing many of the active and intelligent leaders in
the Northern and Eastern States, reposed implicit confidence in Alexander Hamilton.   But they were reluctantly compelled to admit that that confidence was not
shared by the people at large, and that an attempt to
oppose him to Mr. Jefferson would be futile.   They
were therefore driven to turn their eyes from the true
object of their choice to others who might seem more
likely to prevail.

Of these there were but two persons particularly
prominent, John Jay and John Adams, both of them
strong in character, in talents, and in services, and
both meriting, to a great extent, the confidence of the
friends of the established government.   Both had been
conspicuous objects of attack by the opposition, and
both had suffered from it in their popularity.   Of the
two, however, Mr. Jay had been latterly the most
severely handled, on account of his agency in negotiating the treaty with Great Britain, which had so
narrowly escaped rejection.   And the issue of the
election, which had made him governor of his own
State, New York, before the substance of that treaty
had got abroad, was not so decisive as to dispel uneasiness at the idea of offering him immediately as a
candidate for a still higher office.   In addition to this,
Mr. Jay had little strength in the Southern States; nor

yet was he very firmly fixed in the affections of New England, a region the support of which was indispensable to the maintenance of the federal party. It was doubtful whether he could stem the popular feeling even in Massachusetts, which still gathered around Samuel Adams and Elbridge Gerry, in spite of their lukewarmness to the constitution and their later opposition. The only effective counterbalance was in John Adams, whose retirement would, it was feared, seriously endanger the federal predominance there. Such were the reasons which mainly contributed to the selection of him as the candidate for the succession, on the part of the federalists. Even the friends of Mr. Hamilton in Massachusetts, embracing the class of persons, already described in the analysis of parties which contributed to the establishment of the constitution of that State, who bore no good-will to Mr. Adams, either as a man or as a politician, were driven to adopt him, as under all circumstances the best instrument through whom at once to maintain their national policy and to fortify their influence at home.

Unfortunately, however, for this decision, one indispensable element to success in party struggles was overlooked. That element was perfect good faith. Had it been entirely preserved, the federalists would, even from their reduced vantage ground, have been able for some years longer to breast all opposition, however fierce. But it was not. The fact is now beyond dispute, that an indirect and clandestine effort was made at this election to set aside the person who had been openly accepted as the candidate of the federal party, in favor of another individual of whom nobody had thought in connection with the first office. This attempt was originated by Mr. Hamilton, and carried on through his particular friends in and out of New England. The mode selected was a perversion of the spirit, though not the letter, of the constitution, in that provision, as it was originally drawn, which regulated the form of voting in the Electoral Colleges. Every elector of President and Vice-President was directed to vote for two persons, without designating the office to which either was to be elevated. The consequence might easily follow, in a sharply-contested election, that, with a little collusion on the part of two or three electors, in scattering here and there a vote, the person really intended for the second office would be found to have more votes than he who had been selected to fill the first. The same result might also be obtained by securing a perfectly equal vote for both in one section of the Union, under the expectation that local preferences would make the desired difference in another. In such case, the effect would be to reverse their destination, and the former would become President, and the latter, Vice-President.

Thomas Pinckney, of South Carolina, the individual in whose favor this secret diversion was attempted, was so little known to the great body of federalists, as scarcely to be relied upon to be one of their number. He had never been seriously spoken of as a successor to Washington, so that, had he been actually advanced to that position by virtue of this device, his election could never have been regarded in any other light than as a shrewd trick, to be sanctioned only by its success. As it turned out, the scheme utterly failed. But even

the attempt was attended with the most fatal consequences to the federal party. It made the first spot on
their good name, and was ominous of the darker designs which were to follow. Mutual confidence ceased
to exist, and the first sign of disaster immediately appeared. A rumor of the project soon got abroad, and
spread distrust into every college of federal electors.
Those of them who meant to act in good faith to Mr.
Adams, determined, at all hazards, to cut off the possibility of such a result. As a consequence, eighteen,
in New England alone, who voted for him, gave their
second vote for some other person than Mr. Pinckney.
The end of it was, his failure to gain the second place,
for which he had been thought of. The aggregate
number of votes for him was only fifty-nine, whilst that
given for Mr. Jefferson, by the opposite party, reached
sixty-eight. Hence, under the operation of the constitution, Mr. Jefferson, though really the competitor
for the Presidency, yet as standing second on the list
of suffrages, became the Vice-President for four years.
The great opponent of the federalists was thus put in a
conspicuous place for the succession, by the very act of
those who entertained a dread amounting almost to
mania of the bare possibility of his elevation. Neither
is this the only instance furnished by the records of a
popular government, of the manner in which the keen-
est political contrivances are apt not only to baffle all
the expectations formed of them, but to precipitate the
very results against which they were designed most
sedulously to provide.

The election proved a very close one. Mr. Adams
received seventy-one votes, one more than the requisite

number.   But the quarter from which he obtained them,
betrayed changes adverse to the further ascendency of
the federalists.   Pennsylvania now, for the first time in
twenty years, deserted Massachusetts.   Her electors,
with one or two exceptions, voted for Mr. Jefferson,
and for Aaron Burr.   New York, on the other hand,
never cordial to New England, had given, for the first
time, her twelve votes to Mr. Adams, not without, however, associating with them exactly the same number
for Thomas Pinckney.   A single voice in Virginia and
one in North Carolina, prompted by the lingering
memory of revolutionary services, had turned the scale.
Had these been given to Mr. Jefferson instead, he
would have been President.   South Carolina, on the
other hand, steady to neither party, manifested the
same sectional bias which has ever since marked her
policy, by dividing her votes between Mr. Jefferson and
Mr. Pinckney.   Had thirteen of the afore-mentioned
eighteen New England electors voted for Pinckney, as
Mr. Hamilton desired, they would have made him
President.   Through all this confusion, one thing only
was clear, that the cohesion of principle, on the federal
side, was greatly weakened.   The land of William Penn
had at last cut loose from her revolutionary alliance,
and was henceforward to be regarded as the firmest support of the Virginia ascendency.   Neither could this
loss to Mr. Adams, who had done so much in originally
forming that union, be at all made up by the equivocal
fidelity offered by New York.   Of these two great
States, which exercise a paramount influence in determining the national policy, Pennsylvania, because the
most true to one system, has been far the most success-

ful in using her power with effect. No President, since 1796, has been chosen by the popular voice, whom she had not first designated by her wishes and her electoral votes.

Of all these various movements, Mr. Adams had not been an unobserving witness. He felt the insecurity of his position as a President of three votes, as he described himself, and those votes accidental tributes of personal esteem, not likely further to resist the engulfing tendencies of party passions. But these things did not disturb him, nor draw away his attention from the high nature of the responsibility to which he was called. He saw the country torn by dissensions, more or less connected with the fiery contest raging among the nations of Europe, and parties taking sides with zeal either for Great Britain or for France. So far as this had any tendency to affect the wholly neutral position of America, he was determined, at all hazards, to control it. He well knew the difficulties of the task before him, but they did not prevent his entertaining a sanguine hope of overcoming them. His spirit was of that kind which, lying perhaps too sluggish in days of calm, is fully called out only in the height of a tempest; which then glories in the occasion in proportion to the extent to which it tasks its power; which becomes calm and decided in action in the degree in which the disturbing elements seem to have the wildest play. He uttered no more than the truth, when, in writing to his wife at this time, he said: "John Adams must be an intrepid to encounter the open assaults of France, and the secret plots of England, in concert with all his treacherous friends and open enemies in his own country. Yet, I assure you, he never felt more serene in his life."

The minister of France had not permitted the election to pass without an effort to affect the result. He had caused the publication of a note, addressed to the Secretary of State, recapitulating all the grounds of complaint against the federal administration. This is alluded to by Mr. Adams in the following note to his wife, which is interesting on many accounts, but particularly as showing how the sentiments in some quarters which had become known to him, had affected him. It is proper to add that in a later note he expressed his own disbelief of the preference attributed to Mr. Jay.

"12 December, 1796.

"Adet's note has had some effect in Pennsylvania, and proved a terror to some Quakers; and that is all the ill effect it has had. Even the Southern States appear to resent it.

"If Colonel Hamilton's personal dislike of Jefferson does not obtain too much influence with Massachusetts electors, neither Jefferson will be President, nor Pinckney Vice-President.

"I am not enough of an Englishman, nor little enough of a Frenchman, for some people. These would be very willing that Pinckney should come in chief. But they will be disappointed.

"I find nobody here intimidated. Those who wish to say they are, dare not. There is a grand spirit in the Senate.

"Giles says, 'the point is settled. The V. P. will be

President. He is undoubtedly chosen. The old man will make a good President, too.' (There's for you.) 'But we shall have to *check* him a little now and then. That will be all.' Thus Mr. Giles.

"I am just now come from pronouncing a most affectionate address of the Senate to the President, in answer to his speech. I felt so much that I was afraid I should betray a weakness, but I did not. I thought I was very firm and cool; but the senators say that I pronounced it in so affecting a manner that I made them cry. The tears did certainly trickle. The President himself was affected more tenderly than ever I saw him in my life, in pronouncing his reply.

"The Southern gentlemen with whom I have conversed, have expressed more affection for me than they ever did before, since 1774. They certainly wish Adams elected rather than Pinckney. Perhaps it is because Hamilton and Jay are said to be for Pinckney.

.   .   .   .

"There have been manœuvres and combinations in this election that would surprise you. I may one day or other develop them to you.

"There is an active spirit, in the Union, who will fill it with his politics wherever he is. He must be attended to, and not suffered to do too much."

The day came when, as Vice-President, it was the official duty of Mr. Adams to declare the result of the election. The event was made the subject of a brief note, addressed to him by his wife, then at home in Quincy, which, for its simple beauty and truthful, womanly feeling, merits a place in this connection.

" QUINCY, 8 February, 1797.

" The sun is dressed in brightest beams
　To give thy honors to the day."

" And may it prove an auspicious prelude to each ensuing season. You have this day to declare yourself head of a nation. 'And now, O Lord, my God, thou hast made thy servant ruler over the people. Give unto him an understanding heart, that he may know how to go out and come in before this great people ; that he may discern between good and bad. For who is able to judge this thy so great a people?' were the words of a royal sovereign ; and not less applicable to him who is invested with the chief magistracy of a nation, though he wear not the crown, nor the robes of royalty.

" My thoughts and my meditations are with you, though personally absent ; and my petitions to Heaven are that ' the things which make for peace may not be hidden from your eyes.' My feelings are not those of pride or ostentation upon the occasion. They are solemnized by a sense of the obligations, the important trusts and numerous duties connected with it. That you may be enabled to discharge them with honor to yourself, with justice and impartiality to your country, and with satisfaction to this great people, shall be the daily prayer of your　　　　　　　　　　A. A."

With this official announcement, the relations which the Vice-President had for eight years continued to hold with the Senate, were felt by all to be changed, and it ceased to be expedient for him longer to preside over their deliberations. The time had not passed unpleasantly to him, for through the many vicissitudes of party conflicts he had succeeded in maintaining a cordial intercourse with the members, and in preserving an impartiality in the performance of his duties, which secured their good-will. Indeed, it may be doubted whether, on the whole, any period of his public life, of equal length, carried with it so many agreeable associations to his memory, and had so few of those drawbacks on enjoyment which must be found in the thorny paths of every statesman's career. Mr. Adams felt as if he could not vacate the chair he had been the first to occupy, and which he had held so long, without some manifestation of the sentiments that filled his breast. Accordingly, when, on the 15th of February, the Senate had accomplished its business for the day, and was about to adjourn, Mr. Adams rose, and, declaring his intention to avail himself of the leave of absence granted to him for the remainder of the session, seized the opportunity to add a few words of leave-taking. The speech which he made, and the answer subsequently returned on the part of the Senate, will be found in full in his collected works. It will be sufficient here to insert the passage which most nearly touches his personal relations to the individuals of the body. To them he said:

"I ought not to declare, for the last time, your adjournment, before I have presented to every senator present, and to every citizen who has ever been a senator of the United States, my thanks for the candor and favor invariably received from them all. It is a recollection of which nothing can ever deprive me; and it will be a source of comfort to me through the remainder of my life, that as, on the one hand, in a government constituted like ours, I have for eight years held the second situation under the constitution of the United States, in perfect and uninterrupted harmony with the first, without envy in one or jealousy in the other, so, on the other hand, I have never had the smallest misunderstanding with any member of the Senate. In all the abstruse questions, difficult conjunctures, dangerous emergencies, and animated debates upon the great interests of the country, which have so often and so deeply impressed all our minds, and interested the strongest feelings of the heart, I have experienced a uniform politeness and respect from every quarter of the house. When questions of no less importance than difficulty have produced a difference of sentiment (and differences of opinion will always be found in free assemblies of men, and probably the greatest diversities upon the greatest questions), when the senators have been equally divided, and my opinion has been demanded, according to the constitution, I have constantly found in that moiety of the senators from whose judgment I have been obliged to dissent, a disposition to allow me the same freedom of deliberation and independence of judgment which they asserted for themselves."

With a significant assurance of his hope, founded upon experience of this body, that no more permanent council would ever be necessary to defend the rights, liberties, and properties of the people against the executive, on the one hand, and the representatives, on the other, he terminated this address.

Thus ended the connection of Mr. Adams with the Senate. His life there had been calm, dignified, and prosperous, contrasting in all these particulars most strikingly with the stormy and perilous career upon which he was about to embark. The history of that time is now to be given; a history, the true materials for which have remained for more than half a century buried under the burden accumulated by the passionate conflicts and the bitter calumnies that swarmed in it. To this day, writers, and actors prominent in the United States, have sedulously shunned every allusion to the matter which might involve the necessity of expressing a judgment upon its merits. Even the necessary landmarks to guide the pioneer in his laborious and uncertain path have, until a comparatively recent period, been obscured from public view. Many are still wanting, and may never be supplied. Yet, with the imperfect means at hand, directed by a disposition to analyze with calmness and to observe with fidelity, it does not seem impossible to present a sketch bearing something like intrinsic evidence of its correctness. At all events, the task cannot be evaded in a biography of John Adams. Justice to his memory demands it. And however delicate the duty, involving, as it does, a necessity of exactly delineating the course of many leading actors of the time, as well as his own, it must be undertaken, subject to those restrictions without observing which no narrative of the kind can be of the smallest ultimate value. Nothing shall be set down in malice, nothing which is not believed to be fully supported by evidence open to the most rigid scrutiny, nothing which a Rhadamanthine judge of the most remote generation may not minutely weigh, in order to pronounce upon it that decree destined to remain indelibly graven upon the memory of mankind.

CHAPTER X.

THE obstacles which General Washington encountered in the attempt to reconstruct his cabinet during his second term of office have been already alluded to. After offering the chief post to five or six statesmen, always with the same ill success, he was compelled at last to settle down upon the individual as the permanent officer, whom he had at first selected merely for the moment. This person was Colonel Timothy Pickering, of Massachusetts. In like manner, the earlier retirement of Mr. Hamilton from the treasury had been followed by a similar embarrassment, out of which the President had been relieved only by advancing Oliver Wolcott, Jr., of Connecticut, from the post of comptroller, which he had held for several years. So, too, in the case of General Knox, who declined to remain Secretary of War, the President, after vain attempts to enlist abler men, had been forced to pitch upon James McHenry, of Maryland, as the only person who could be persuaded to serve. Mr. McHenry, it is true, was an estimable man, but Washington himself, when afterwards excusing the original appointment on the ground that he had had Hobson's choice, agreed with other federalists in admitting that the selection had by no means been such as to give real aid to an administration. The weakness of this combination, so long as the imposing presence of Washington was felt in the foreground, a representative of the whole people, was of comparatively little importance. But the moment that he retired from the field, giving place to a successor who had no similar basis of popular confidence to stand upon, and who had just come in upon a chance majority of three electoral votes, it became of the most serious consequence. Apart from all other considerations, the geographical distribution of the members was singularly unfortunate. The President, and two leading members of the cabinet, were drawn from the small territorial extent of New England, whilst neither New York nor Pennsylvania had any representative at all, and the whole wide region of country south and west of the Potomac saw only Mr. Charles Lee, the attorney-general, as the guardian of its interests in the executive department. No bright associations with the struggles of the Revolution clustered around these men, as had been the case with their predecessors in office; not a shadow of that confidence which leading abilities will always inspire when in place under a popular form of government, attended them. So far as moral influence over the mind and feelings of the country is to be considered, Mr. Adams, when he consented to continue the same gentlemen in office, might as well have attempted to go on alone.

Neither was this the most serious disadvantage under which he labored. Nor was it only that these persons owed their advancement to no preference of his, and therefore felt less obligation to defer to his authority, or to strain their energies to carry out his policy.

There was a source of weakness greater than all this. In point of fact, three of the four had been drawn from one section of the federal party, and that the one with which Mr. Adams had the least natural sympathy. Mr. Hamilton had been the effective agent through whom they had been promoted, and to him alone they looked as a guide for their own movements, as well as for directing those of the country. Their accession to office marked the epoch when his preponderance in General Washington's administration had become established, and they seemed to regard the substitution of a new President as in no way derogating from the liberty which they had taken of differing with and even sometimes of overruling the old one. Indeed, their construction of their official rights was far more latitudinarian than any since permitted, even in the liberal day of Mr. Jefferson. It resembled a joint claim upon the executive power, rather than the right to advise the President, and the duty ultimately to defer to his decision, however adverse to their opinion. Both the Secretary of State and the Secretary of the Treasury were naturally little prone to bend. They proved at times reluctant to respect even the great authority which encircled Washington. If so disposed towards him, how much less prepared were they to yield to the will of his successor. should he venture to insist upon a system of his own! There is no evidence that, at the outset, any one but Mr. Wolcott passed the formal compliment of offering to resign, in order to allow him a free choice of his advisers. But even had they all done so, no reason exists for presuming that he would have availed himself of the opportunity. He was disposed to place confidence in their co-operation and support. A change must have been attended with more or less of dissatisfaction in some quarters, and it was his desire to harmonize, rather than to distract public sentiment. His sanguine and self-reliant temperament led him to underrate difficulties. He thought he should bring his secretaries into his views, without a doubt. But not many days elapsed in his official career before he had reason to suspect that the task he had assumed would not prove so easy as he had imagined. The difference of opinion which then took place, most seriously compromising his prospect of free action as executive chief, was the premonition of the causes at work to bring on a rupture with and final dispersion of his transmitted council.

The most pressing danger, to avert which was the immediate duty of the new government, threatened from abroad. The mission of Mr. Jay to Great Britain, and the whole negotiation which followed, had been viewed with such unequivocal distrust by the French republicans and the party sympathizing with them in the United States, as to prompt a desire on the part of General Washington to neutralize its effects by an extraordinary manifestation of good-will to France. Conscious that the course of Gouverneur Morris had not been altogether such as the revolutionary party might have had a right to expect from an American envoy, he determined upon selecting, as a compensation, a successor from among the class known to be hearty well-wishers to them, even though he should be an opponent of his own administration, and dissenting from his policy. In this spirit he picked out James

Monroe, of Virginia, through whom he hoped to insure a hearty welcome to the national mission, and a useful channel for the restoration of a good understanding. But, however well intended this proceeding, it met with no corresponding success. Mr. Monroe proved either inefficient, or lukewarm, or unfortunate; and he satisfied his employer so little, that he finally decided on recalling him, and substituting in his place General Charles Cotesworth Pinckney, of South Carolina. Mr. Pinckney had been known at home as a federalist so moderate as to be classed by some as a neutral. But the French Directory, to whom Mr. Monroe seems to have made himself acceptable, not unwilling to strike some stroke in the domestic politics of the United States favorable to the ascendency of those they called their friends, determined upon visiting their resentment for his recall upon the head of his successor. To this end they instituted an imposing ceremony of leave-taking for Mr. Monroe, marked by a speech not a little offensive to the American government, and they utterly refused in any way to recognize Mr. Pinckney. They would not even permit him to remain within the limits of the French territory.

It was in the midst of these events that the change of administration occurred. Washington retired, not averse to an honorable discharge from the labor of unravelling this hard knot, and Mr. Adams came in, determined to make the attempt, but not without anxiety about the best mode of seizing the clue. He was a party man, and heartily agreed in the early views of the federalists; but his heart relucted at placing his administration at the outset upon any bottom less broad than that which had been laid by his predecessor. Neither could he see the wisdom of adopting a rule of exclusion from office, the effect of which would be to aggravate dissensions already too much weakening the spirit of resistance, instead of uniting the people better to counteract the insidious devices of the enemy from without.

In this spirit was the inaugural speech drawn up, with which he entered on his duties. Few efforts of the kind contain, within so narrow a compass, a more comprehensive view of a policy suitable for the chief magistrate of the United States, of any party. Not unaware of the rumors that had been sedulously spread against him, of his desire to alter the existing form of government, and to introduce something which had "an awful squinting to a monarchy," and not insensible of the importance of putting an end to them by a frank denial, he seized the opportunity to express his entire satisfaction with the constitution, as conformable to such a system of government as he had ever most esteemed, and in his own State had contributed to establish. Then, going to the root of these calumnies, he added the decisive words: "It was not then, nor has been since, any objection to it in my mind, that the Executive and Senate were not more permanent. Nor have I entertained a thought of promoting any alterations in it but such as the people themselves, in the course of their experience, should see and feel to be necessary or expedient, and, by their representatives in congress and the state legislatures, according to the constitution itself, adopt and ordain."

Having thus removed the obstacles heretofore put in

his way, he next declared the principles that should guide him for the future. With a high compliment to the administration as well as to the personal character of his predecessor, he proceeded to give, in one of the longest sentences in the language, his whole creed. Yet long as it is, perhaps none was ever constructed by a statesman with less redundance to convey the same amount of meaning. After alluding to the general satisfaction felt with the course taken by Washington as a model for the imitation of his successors, he added these words: "The occasion, I hope, will be admitted as an apology, if I venture to say, that, if a preference upon principle of a free republican government, formed upon long and serious reflection, after a diligent and impartial inquiry after truth; if an attachment to the constitution of the United States, and a conscientious determination to support it, until it shall be altered by the judgments and wishes of the people, expressed in the mode prescribed in it; if a respectful attention to the constitutions of the individual States, and a constant caution and delicacy towards the State governments; if an equal and impartial regard to the rights, interests, honor, and happiness of all the States in the Union, without preference or regard to a northern or southern, eastern or western position, their various political opinions on essential points, or their personal attachments; if a love of virtuous men of all parties and denominations; if a love of science and letters, and a wish to patronize every rational effort to encourage schools, colleges, universities, academies, and every institution for propagating knowledge, virtue, and religion among all classes of the people, not only for their benign influence on the happiness of life in all its stages and classes, and of society in all its forms, but as the only means of preserving our constitution from its natural enemies, the spirit of sophistry, the spirit of party, the spirit of intrigue, profligacy, and corruption, and the pestilence of foreign influence, which is the angel of destruction to elective governments; if a love of equal laws, of justice and humanity in the interior administration; if an inclination to improve agriculture, commerce, and manufactures for necessity, convenience, and defence; if a spirit of equity and humanity towards the aboriginal nations of America, and a disposition to meliorate their condition, by inclining them to be more friendly to us, and our citizens to be more friendly to them; if an inflexible determination to maintain peace and inviolable faith with all nations, and that system of neutrality and impartiality among the belligerent powers of Europe, which has been adopted by the government, and so solemnly sanctioned by both houses of congress, and applauded by the legislatures of the States and the public opinion, until it shall be otherwise ordained by congress; if a personal esteem for the French nation, formed in a residence of seven years, chiefly among them, and a sincere desire to preserve the friendship which has been so much for the honor and interest of both nations; if, while the conscious honor and integrity of the people of America and the internal sentiment of their own power and energies must be preserved, an earnest endeavor to investigate every just cause, and remove every colorable pretence, of complaint; if an intention to pursue, by amicable negotiation, a reparation for the injuries that have been committed on the commerce of our fellow-citizens, by whatever nation, and (if success cannot be obtained) to lay the facts before the legislature, that they may consider what further measures the honor and interest of the government and its constituents demand; if a resolution to do justice, as far as may depend upon me, at all times, and to all nations, and maintain peace, friendship, and benevolence with all the world; if an unshaken confidence in the honor, spirit, and resources of the American people, on which I have so often hazarded my all, and never been deceived; if elevated ideas of the high destinies of this country, and of my own duties towards it, founded on a knowledge of the moral principles and intellectual improvement of the people, deeply engraven on my mind in early life, and not obscured, but exalted by experience and age; and with humble reverence I feel it my duty to add, if a veneration for the religion of a people who profess and call themselves Christians, and a fixed resolution to consider a decent respect for Christianity among the best recommendations for the public service,—can enable me, in any degree, to comply with your wishes, it shall be my strenuous endeavor that this sagacious injunction of the two Houses shall not be without effect.''

When deeply stirred by internal emotion, Mr. Adams's manner became grave and very impressive. Nothing short of this could have made the delivery of so elaborate a paragraph at all effective before a large audience. The next day he wrote to his wife, in his most natural and candid manner:

"Your dearest friend never had a more trying day than yesterday. A solemn scene it was, indeed ; and it was made more affecting to me by the presence of the General, whose countenance was as serene and unclouded as the day. He seemed to me to enjoy a triumph over me. Methought I heard him say: 'Ay! I am fairly out, and you fairly in! See which of us will be happiest.'

"When the ceremony was over, he came and made me a visit, and cordially congratulated me, and wished my administration might be happy, successful, and honorable.

"In the chamber of the House of Representatives was a multitude as great as the space could contain, and I believe scarcely a dry eye but Washington's. The sight of the sun setting full-orbed, and another rising, though less splendid, was a novelty. Chief Justice Ellsworth administered the oath, and with great energy. Judges Cushing, Wilson, and Iredell were present. Many ladies. I had not slept well the night before, and did not sleep well the night after. I was unwell, and did not know whether I should get through or not. I did, however. How the business was received, I know not, only I have been told that Mason, the treaty publisher, said we should lose nothing by the change, for he never heard such a speech in public in his life.

"All agree that, taken altogether, it was the sublimest thing ever exhibited in America."

The fact is unquestionable, that this speech was very well received by the public at large. Even the members of the opposition declared themselves relieved by it from much anxiety, and disposed to await further developments of the executive policy. Mr. Jefferson, on taking his post as Vice-President, had gone so far as to declare that the high functions of the first office had been "justly confided" to Mr. Adams, and to deprecate any untoward event which should devolve the duties of it during his term of office upon himself. The only persons who manifested discontent were to be found among the federalists sympathizing with Mr. Hamilton. They lamented its tone as temporizing. Their party feeling would have prompted a thorough demarcation of the line between themselves and the opposition, by the delineation of a policy which every man should be obliged to notice, and by the acceptance or rejection of which his own position should be unmistakably defined. The avoidance of this course in the address was ominous to them of the accession to the chair of a man who would not meet their expectations; and this suspicion other events, which soon came to their knowledge, had a strong tendency to confirm.

The day before the inauguration, Mr. Adams had taken pains to seek out Mr. Jefferson, in order to propose to him to undertake the difficult experiment of reopening the avenues of negotiation with France. This was to be attempted by the establishment of a wholly new commission, formed on such principles of fair combination as to preclude every pretext for objection on the part of the French republic. And the first proof of this intention was to be found in the character and opinions of the Vice-President himself. Mr. Jefferson appears to have met this proposition with less cordiality than it merited at his hands. For though his reasons for declining to accept it himself were certainly valid, and were admitted to be so by Mr. Adams, there was no similar excuse for the lukewarmness visible in promoting the acceptance of the offer, when extended to Mr. Madison, and perhaps others of his friends. In the difficulties in which the administration was plunged, it was far more pleasant to dwell in the tents of opposition, than to be drawn out of them by a proposal of alliance in responsibilities which might cut off profitable complaint under failure, or divert elsewhere the advantages of success. Had this overture been accepted, important consequences might have followed at an early day, of which one might have been a reorganization of the cabinet. For it should be remarked that the first intimation of his idea, made by Mr. Adams, immediately after the inauguration, to Mr. Wolcott, then at the head of the treasury, was received by the latter with consternation, as a signal for his retirement. So far from favoring further advances to bring the opposition into a united effort to preserve peace with France, he had made up his mind that the effort itself was not worth repeating in any shape, until some opening should be made by her. Yet the alternative was embargo or war! For the depredations on American commerce, unblushing as they were unbounded, could only be checked by restraining navigation, or else defending it by arms. But an embargo was ruinous to trade, whilst war imperilled the finances. Mr. Adams had no inclination to assume responsibility for such consequences, so long as they could be honestly avoided. Yet finding that perseverance in his project might lead to an immediate difference with his cabinet, which he did not seek, whilst it met with no hearty response elsewhere, he at once abandoned all thoughts of Mr. Madison, and postponed, to a later moment, any decision upon the measure itself.

The chief members of the executive council, Colonel Pickering and Mr. Wolcott, had been long in the habit of looking outside of it for the general direction of the policy adopted within. This habit, formed from the time of their accession in Washington's administration, was now kept up without the smallest idea of any obligation on their part to apprise the new President of its existence. Of course, communications, more or less free, of what was said or done in the cabinet, were the consequence. In this way, Alexander Hamilton, the recipient of them, was become all-powerful in guiding the movements of the government. It had been so in the last days of Washington, and it was not likely to be less so after his dignified attitude ceased to inspire moderation, and when a much less popular chief was in his place. To the latter as the official incumbent, brought in without any hearty wish of theirs, they were, of course, bound outwardly to defer; but it is plain from their own admissions, that in all important questions they looked to Mr. Hamilton, and not to him, as the suitable guide of their action. As a consequence, it followed that unity in the executive policy became likely only when the President should happen, without knowing it, to fix upon the same measures which Mr. Hamilton suggested. And in all important cases of difference, the probability was strong that the President

would find his wishes either ineffectively seconded, or ultimately overruled.   Such, from small beginnings, grew
to be the settled practice under this administration.
Happily for the issue of the first measure, when revived
a few weeks later, Mr. Hamilton had thought of it too,
and had earnestly pressed it on his friends as one of the
first necessity.   He had even gone the length of proposing the selection of Mr. Jefferson, Mr. Madison, or
some equally marked representative of the opposition,
as one member of the joint commission.   These ideas
he had early directed some of his friends in congress to
lay before the President himself.   This unexpected reinforcement of Mr. Adams's wishes carried the day over
the repugnance of the secretaries.   But they yielded,
not without great misgivings.   Mr. Wolcott, especially,
saw in this concession some dangers, which scarcely
excited the observation of the others.   He then began
to conceive the possibility of failure in guiding the will
of Mr. Adams, and dimly to discern the results to which
it might lead.   Prudence was essential, or a change of
counsellors might be attended with a more or less complete ejection from the strongholds of power.

The intelligence received from France came in to
hasten the necessity of making a decision.   An act of
the Directory, of the 2d of March, had followed the
expulsion of Mr. Pinckney, which, in substance, an-
nulled the rule of *free ships, free goods*, ingrafted into
the treaty of 1778, and declared all Americans found
serving on board the vessels of Great Britain, pirates,
to be treated without mercy.   Under these circumstances, war would be justifiable.   The only question
was whether it would be expedient.   In order to

determine this point, the President requested the written answers of the members of his cabinet to a series of fourteen questions covering all the necessary points. This was on the 14th of April. A proclamation had already been issued, summoning congress to attend at Philadelphia at an extraordinary session, on the fifteenth day of May, there to receive the important communications which he was about to prepare out of these deliberations.

In answering the President's questions, not a single cabinet officer was found explicitly to recommend a declaration of war. All now acquiesced in the project of reviving negotiation by initiating a new and solemn commission, and some suggested means of facilitating a settlement. The commission having been determined upon, another step was, to designate the three commissioners. Mr. Adams still retained the wish to give one of the number to the opposition. He therefore suggested the union of his old friend of the Revolution, Elbridge Gerry, with General Pinckney and John Marshall. But this idea at once revived all the alarms of his advisers. Mr. Gerry had opposed the constitution, and had been ever since most obnoxious in Massachusetts to the particular class of federalists to which the secretaries belonged. Mr. Adams had casually dropped the name of another friend, Francis Dana. They strongly pressed to have him preferred; and, although this was giving to the commission a purely federal color, contrary to his original design, he cheerfully yielded to their desire. The very last fault that can be justly found with his course is that of a disposition to control their will. With the lights now furnished respecting their conduct, his error lay rather in conceding too much. But his nomination of Mr. Dana was of no avail, for that gentleman declined the trust, on the score of his health. And when the question came up anew, no second name was at hand to present, which could be made again to preponderate over the earlier selection; so Mr. Gerry received the nomination. The President's counsellors now felt that they were to struggle for their power. Mr. Adams might be bent to a certain point, but he could not be controlled. The expectations with which they entered on their places under him must be abandoned. And henceforth they were to retain them with a view, so far as might be, to rectify his deviations from their policy, and especially to keep the cabinet from going into the hands of other men.

A short time before the decision last mentioned, congress had assembled. The cabinet all cordially co-operated in preparing the opening speech, which must be conceded to be one of the most manly and dignified state papers that ever emanated from the American executive. Its simple recital of the offensive action of France at once rallied the spirit of the members to the support of their own government. Both Houses replied in warm approbation of the policy recommended, and the Senate soon afterwards ratified the nominations of the new commissioners. The federalists, fortified by the reaction everywhere springing up against France, on account of the excesses of her revolutionary era, showed a degree of strength to which they had for some time been strangers. Yet so fierce was the opposition that no attempt was made to press measures of an extreme character. The warmer friends of government complained of a want of vigor. Mr. Hamilton prepared for the use of the Secretary of the Treasury his views of the different objects of taxation, from which further sums might be obtained to the revenue in the present contingency. Of these, congress adopted only the ominous item of stamps, the very name of which did more disservice to government than all the sums collected from it could compensate for. They authorized a small loan of less than a million, and passed several acts, of which the chief were those against privateering, and the exportation of arms, for the further protection of the ports of the United States and for the increase of the naval armament. The time expended on these labors little exceeded three weeks, and both Houses adjourned in season to escape at Philadelphia all danger from the impending pestilence. Mr. Adams returned to his family at Quincy, having good reason to be satisfied with this outset. The commissioners were soon put on their way to the scene of their labors, and the whole country rested for a while, in earnest but quiet expectation of the intelligence which should announce the fate of the latest overtures to reconciliation.

Unluckily for the repose of the world, negotiations with France during the closing years of the last century had no fixed data upon which to calculate any probable issue. The men who held power, changed often; and the tone they took towards foreign nations, whilst they held it, depended less upon notions of equity and justice than upon the latest tidings from the armies of the republic. Unfortunate indeed is that country, the character of whose officers has no other recommendation than the single fact of the popular choice. None know better than the elect how soon that factitious value will vanish. As it happened, Messrs. Marshall, Pinckney, and Gerry reached Paris at a moment of extraordinary national intoxication. The young chief, who was about to astonish Europe with his deeds, and fill the world with his fame, was then beginning to make his employers sensible of the value of his energy. He had been cognizant of the *coup d'état*, under which the legislative and executive departments had been riven in twain, and the best part of the members exiled. And his victorious march in Italy was the sign under which the usurping section hoped to hold their power, maugre all resistance. The sport of fortune, the ordinary men who now held the reins, saw in their position no objects higher than the opportunity to enrich themselves. Napoleon's successes opened a paradise of jobs from army contractors, besides placing the Directory in a situation to dictate their own terms to weaker nations. Happy chance for such men as Barras, and Rewbell, and Merlin, just now turning up in their lives, soon to end, and never to return! But unhappy chance to all countries deemed weak in resources, which might be brought to deprecate the enmity of France, and pray for protection not to be had without a price! And particularly unfortunate chance to the United States, not yet strong enough to make their anger a cause of fear, whilst their commerce, which was growing to whiten every sea, presented a rich prey wherewith to fatten the officials of the hour!

It was to a government like this, that three single-hearted men, guiltless of a trick of diplomacy or a thought of venality, had been addressed, under the delusive notion that good sense, and truth, and justice might avail to procure an adjustment of every honest difference. The result may easily be conceived. They were met by arts against which they proved no match, by round-about contrivances to ascertain, before recognizing their position, what price they would offer for a treaty. And when the fact became certain that money was not to be made out of them, an adroit effort followed to dissociate the two impracticable commissioners from the third and more sympathizing one, in order to try the luck of an appeal to him alone. It was all in vain, however. Mr. Gerry, though he permitted the Directory to create an invidious and insulting distinction, gave them no opening for advantage over himself. Of his honesty and his patriotism, however it may have been disputed during the high party times that followed, no impartial person, at this day, will entertain a doubt. And whatever may have been his facility, it should be remembered that the same had been shown, in the same place, by no less a predecessor than Dr. Franklin. The Directory, foiled in their game, ceased to feel an interest in playing it further. Even before Mr. Gerry retired, inexorable to their solicitation to treat, signs appeared of their disposition not to press matters so far as to cut off every opportunity to retrace their steps.

This was a despicable species of adventure for such a noble country as France. Neither is it to be supposed that it would have been attempted in many other stages of its history. But it is in the nature of popular convulsions, when continued for a length of time, gradually to throw to the surface such dregs, that at last the whole community gasps in expectation of the bold hand which will at a single sweep skim them off from the sight. The hand that was ultimately to do this thing, was the very one yet interested to uphold the evil. To affront the United States irretrievably was the height of folly; for, admitting them to be of little positive weight in the scale of nations, they were yet not without power to harm, especially on the ocean, and if allied, as such treatment would inevitably drive them to be, with Great Britain, France's most dreaded foe, might prove formidable. Besides, the moral effect was exceedingly bad, in withering the sympathies of that large class of American citizens who had persisted, at every disadvantage, in upholding France at home. It was ungrateful, to say the least, towards those who had persevered, through all the odium incurred by their crimes, in glorying in the successes of their dear allies, as they loved to call them, to suffer them to be precipitated into the very jaws of the British lion. These considerations were disregarded a little too long. And when they began to be respected, the consequences were beyond the opportunity of recall.

For, in the mean time, the popular feeling in the United States was daily growing more adverse to France, and more friendly to the administration. The evidence of this became unequivocal upon the reassembly of the two Houses of congress at the regular session in November. No decisive tidings had then been received, so that the opening speech was confined to a simple reference to the difficulties, coupled with a recommendation, in any event, to provide suitable pro-

tection for national commerce. Allusion was briefly
made to the state of the relations with other powers,
but no suggestion of specific measures followed. It is
clear that the time for being explicit had not yet
arrived. But it was already far on its way. Mr.
Adams, so early as the 24th of January, 1798, in anticipation of the expected intelligence, deemed it prudent
to address to the members of his cabinet a letter, requesting their views of the course proper to be taken,
in case the commissioners should have failed in accom-
plishing the objects of their mission. Should a declaration of war be recommended? or an embargo?
Should any change be attempted, contingent upon
that event, in the nature of the relations held with
other European powers in general, and most particularly with Great Britain?

These were questions of the deepest importance.
The manner of putting them betrayed nothing of the
sentiments of the interrogator, beyond a marked disinclination to any approaches towards Great Britain.
It is not absolutely certain whether the secretaries of
state and of the treasury sent in any separate answers.
At all events, none are found among Mr. Adams's
papers. That the former wrote at this time to consult
Mr. Hamilton about the expediency of an alliance
offensive and defensive with Great Britain, and that
he received an answer, appears elsewhere. But there
is no trace of a suggestion of the kind to the President.
The only one of the cabinet who proposed a declaration of war, was the attorney-general, Mr. Lee. The
remaining member, Mr. McHenry, sent in an answer,
in which he dissuaded from a formal declaration, on

account of the aversion felt for it by a large portion of the people, but, at the same time, laid down a series of seven propositions to be recommended to congress, the effect of which, if adopted, would have been, if not to make war, at least to place the country on a footing to make it, both by sea and land. They were these:

1. Permission to merchant ships to arm.

2. The construction of twenty sloops of war.

3. The completion of the frigates already authorized.

4. Authority, in case of a rupture, to the President to provide, "*by such means as he may judge best*," ships of the line, not exceeding ten.

5. The suspension of the treaties with France.

6. An immediate army of sixteen thousand men, and a provisional one of twenty thousand more.

7. A loan, and an adequate system of taxation.

This paper is of the utmost importance to a clear conception of the internal movement of this administration; because there are the strongest reasons for presuming that, instead of being Mr. McHenry's simply, it contains the joint conclusions of Mr. Hamilton and the three secretaries under his influence. The recommendations are almost identically those which appear in Mr. Hamilton's private letters to Mr. Pickering. But in addition to this, the paper closed with some suggestions which show a coincidence even more marked with the peculiar policy which that gentleman was at the same time advocating in his correspondence.

Yet the place in which this appears the most striking, is in that portion of the answer which touches upon the relations to be observed with Great Britain.

Deprecating a formal alliance as inexpedient rather than as improper, it yet recommended that overtures should be made through Mr. King, to obtain a loan, the aid of convoys, and perhaps the transfer of ten ships of the line, *should congress give the authority to obtain so many;* and, what is most significant of all, it urged that, in case of rupture, a *co-operation* should be secured, by Great Britain's lodging ample powers of execution in the hands of her envoy to the United States, the object of which should be the conquest of the Floridas, Louisiana, and Spanish South America; all the territory on the east side of the Mississippi, together with the port of New Orleans, to be the share of the spoils allotted to the United States.*

---

* In order that there may be no doubt on this subject, an extract from Mr. McHenry's opinion is subjoined:

"As to England. Notwithstanding her naval victories and undisputed control of the ocean, her fate remains yet perhaps precarious, and must continue so, as long as invasion remains practicable or possible. This consideration may render it best to avoid entangling ourselves with an *alliance.* It may be said, besides, that the interest she has in our fate will command as much from her as a treaty; that, moreover, if she can maintain her own ground, she will not see us fall, and if she cannot, our help will not maintain her, and a treaty will not be observed. It may be said further; if we enter into an *alliance,* and France should endeavor to detach us from it, by offering advantageous terms of peace, it would be a difficult and dangerous task to the President to resist the popular cry for acceptance of her terms.

" Upon the whole, it would appear the safest course to avoid any *formal treaty,* and to do no more than to communicate through Mr. King the measures in train; to sound Great Britain as to a loan; as to convoys; and co-operation in case of open rupture,

A comparison of these views with the reputed capacity of the person claiming the paternity of them, as well as with those expressed by Mr. Hamilton to other persons, makes the inference irresistible that they were actually supplied by the latter, and that the knowledge of this fact was the reason why the other two cabinet officers felt themselves dispensed from the necessity of offering separate opinions.

All this had been done by way of preparation for probable events. When the news arrived which gave them a definite shape, and the details of the attempts upon the firmness of the commissioners, which had been instigated by the Directory, had been spread before the cabinet, Mr. Adams once more submitted

---

pointing the co-operation to the Floridas, Louisiana, and the South American possessions of Spain, if rupture, as is probable, should extend to her; to prevail on Britain to lodge in her minister here ample authority for all these purposes, as far as they can be managed by him, but to do all this without any formal engagement or commitment in the first instance. It might also be thrown out, in the event of co-operation, that we should expect all on this side the Mississippi, with New Orleans, to be ours. It would also appear expedient to direct a provisional negotiation to be opened for ten ships of the line, to be manned and commanded by us, to have effect, should congress give authority to the President, in case of open rupture, to provide so many. It would be best to charge with the instructions a confidential messenger."

Compare with this, Hamilton's letter to Pickering, printed in his *Works*, vol. vi. p. 278, and that to King, p. 348, and the later policy, as hereafter explained. The plan seems to have been communicated to the British government through Mr. King, but not as coming from the American government. This needs further explanations. *Hamilton's Works*, vol. vi. p. 368.

questions to his advisers. They were now reduced to two:

1. Should all the particulars be disclosed at once to congress?

2. Should the President recommend a declaration of war?

Again no answer came from the chief secretaries. Mr. McHenry contented himself with appealing to his former exposition of his views, to which he had nothing to add. And Mr. Lee, with a provident regard for the personal safety of the commissioners not yet known to be beyond the jurisdiction of France, only proposed a delay until that point should have been placed beyond a doubt.

With these views before him, Mr. Adams was now called upon to take a definite course. Of the source of the policy proposed to him by Mr. McHenry, he seems to have had no suspicion. But so far as it looked to more intimate connections with Great Britain, the argumentative form in which he put his questions sufficiently shows that it met with no favoring response in his bosom. It was at war with the whole theory of his life, and all the lessons of his experience. It is not unlikely that his conversation betrayed his opinions, for Mr. Pickering, very soon after this, communicated a significant hint to Mr. Hamilton, that the animosities engendered by the Revolution "*in some breasts*" would probably make the plan of co-operation impracticable. The fact is certain that no further direct effort was made to establish it through the agency of the President. Waiving all the recommendations that looked to such a result, he adopted the draft of a message prepared by Mr. Wolcott. But a single paragraph written by himself appears in this paper. It communicated his own intentions in the following terms:

"The present state of things is so essentially different from that in which instructions were given to collectors to restrain vessels of the United States from sailing in an armed condition, that the principle in which those orders were issued has ceased to exist. I therefore deem it proper to inform congress, that I no longer conceive myself justifiable in continuing them, unless in particular cases, where there may be reasonable ground of suspicion that such vessels are intended to be employed contrary to law."

This message was sent to both Houses on the 19th of March, 1798. It recommended no new measures, but repeated the exhortation to prepare for protection and defence made in former communications, as the result of a mature consideration of the dispatches. The dispatches themselves were, with a single exception, held back. That exception notified the government of a new act of hostility, forfeiting all neutral ships covering any productions of England, and shutting up France even to such as should, in their voyage, have barely touched at an English port. The message announced the failure of the mission, but gave no details of its proceedings. The papers had been reserved for the reasons suggested by the attorney-general. But with such a determination the impatience of neither party was content. Dignified and temperate as was the tone of the executive, Mr. Jefferson, fastening for a ground of complaint upon the single measure of self-defence, the withdrawal of the prohibition upon merchant ships to go armed, an act certainly not extravagant in the face of so violent a French decree, denominated this "an *insane* message;" whilst Mr. Hamilton, unsatisfied so long as no disclosure had been made of facts from which he clearly foresaw the advantages to inure to the party with which he was associated, set in motion, through a member of the House, a demand for the production of the documents withheld. This was adopted on the 2d of April, and the response returned in twenty-four hours. Thus came before the country a full disclosure of the tissue of intrigues, woven in France in order to extort money from the American commissioners. But out of superfluous consideration for the feelings of the three private individuals who had been prevailed upon to serve as go-betweens, Colonel Pickering, the Secretary of State, suppressed their names, and substituted for them the last three letters of the alphabet, X. Y. Z. Hence it happened that in popular parlance these dispatches came to be generally known as the X. Y. Z. correspondence.

Upon the arrival of General Marshall in the United States, the President sent another message to congress, bearing date 21st June, 1798, transmitting a dispatch from Mr. Gerry, who yet remained in Paris, which completed the series of papers belonging to the negotiation. At the end, he added these important words:

"I will never send another minister to France without assurances that he will be received, respected, and honored as the representative of a great, free, powerful, and independent nation.''

It is necessary to a right understanding of the events that followed, to bear the terms of this engagement clearly in mind. For in the different constructions given to it is to be found the ostensible cause of the division that took place in the ranks of the federal party.

The publication by congress of all the papers was like the falling of a spark into a powder magazine. Among the friends of France who had, down to this moment, with praiseworthy constancy, adhered to their allies, even through all the accumulated horrors of their revolutionary days, the news spread utter dismay, precluding them from defence or justification. Even the sanguine Jefferson beheld with consternation the peril to all his brightest anticipations from the huge rising wave of national feeling which promised to carry his federal opponents for a long way in triumph on its crest. The return of the commissioners only served to bring the popular enthusiasm to its height. There was but one voice to be heard, and that was in denunciation of the arrogance and profligacy of France, and in warm approbation of every measure calculated to uphold the dignity and the honor of the United States. The opportunity was a critical one to the individuals intrusted with power. Wisely improved, it would have insured the ascendency of their policy for years to come. Slighted or abused to gain equivocal ends, it might only prove the occasion of a more fatal overthrow. How it was actually used, it is one of the objects of the present narrative faithfully and impartially to disclose.

From what has been already described of the cabinet
action, the position of the President may now be pretty
distinctly perceived. Surrounded by advisers, three of
whom were proposing a system of measures prompted
by a gentleman not known by him to be in the secret
of his counsels, and not at all in harmony with his own
ideas, he seems to have declined the responsibility of
assuming the recommendation of it, and to have chosen
the safer course of devolving upon the two houses of
congress, as the proper arbiters, the task of determining
what it was best for the nation, under the circumstances,
to do. Down to this time he seems to have entertained
little distrust of Mr. Hamilton himself, and not the
slightest suspicion of the nature of the influences brought
to bear upon himself. It was only when his obvious
disinclination to the policy offered to his acceptance
had the effect of transferring the theatre for the exercise of them from the seclusion of his secret council to
the public arena of the two houses, that he could begin
to gather data upon which to form some notion of the
perils by which he was beset.

Among the younger and more active members of the
federal party in the north and east, Mr. Hamilton had
gradually become an idol. Without much hold upon
the judgment or the affections of the people at large, he
had yet, by the effect of his undisputed abilities and his
masculine will, gained great sway over the minds of the
intelligent merchants along the Atlantic border. His
previous doctrines, in unison with the feelings and interests of the most conservative class, had drawn to him
their particular confidence, whilst his position in the
first administration had facilitated the establishment by

him of a chain of influence, resting for its main support on his power over the mind of Washington himself, but carried equally through all the ramifications of the executive department. Thus it happened that even after he ceased to be personally present, his opinions continued to shape the policy of Washington's second administration and even that of his successor. But since the day of his retirement from the treasury he had thus far manifested no desire to re-enter public life, or to assume any direct share in the regulation of affairs. The prospect of a conflict with France seems to have been the first cause of a change of intention. He now showed signs of a wish not merely to devise the whole system of action, on the part of the government, but likewise to be in a position to direct its execution. He began to foresee a crisis worthy to call forth all his latent powers.

The President's voluntary act, by which the responsibility of initiating the desired system was transferred from the executive to the legislative department, was not unfavorable to the development of Mr. Hamilton's plans. His energetic dictation, seconded by the zealous co-operation of his able friends in both houses of congress, naturally gave the lead to opinion. Where the passions of men are heated to the pitch of enthusiasm in any cause, he who advises the most positive measures is generally likely to gain the earliest hearing. Thus it happened in this case. The federal policy proposed and adopted at this session of congress was largely the offspring of Mr. Hamilton's brain, though it fell far short of the extent of his conceptions. Whether for weal or woe, it is his name that should

be associated with it, and not that of the person then
filling the executive chair, whose opinions it very par
tially represented, and whose legitimate influence it
was designed to annihilate. Yet strange are sometimes the ways of Providence, which at one and the
same moment will not simply expose one man to responsibility for the plans and actions of another, but
will even make that other himself a medium through
which the censure attending them shall be the most
permanently visited on his memory.

The friends of Mr. Hamilton carried through congress some of the measures which had been proposed
in the cabinet, and one or two that were not in that
list. Without declaring war with France, they voted
the treaties with her to be null and void, and authorized hostilities equivalent to war. They sanctioned a
considerable augmentation of the actual army, with a
prospective organization of officers adapted to a much
more extended one, in case of invasion. They increased the navy by directing the construction or
purchase of new ships, and they placed the superin-
tendence of it in a distinct department of the government, over which they established a new cabinet officer. With the exception of this last change, all these
things had been under the consideration of the executive department. The case was different with some
other measures, and particularly those acts which have
ever since been known under the name of the Alien
and Sedition Laws; acts borrowed from the extravagant apprehensions entertained in Great Britain of the
spread of the revolutionary spirit, which proved of no
practical value whatever to America, whilst they fur-

nished an effective handle for attack against their authors. Lastly, congress enlarged the objects of taxation, and gave the necessary powers to obtain by loan a further sum of five millions of dollars. As has been said already, this was not all of the system of Mr. Hamilton, for that contemplated an offensive war, sustained by the ultimate establishment of a military organization of fifty thousand men; but it was in its principal features in unison with his views. To Mr. Adams, who seems scarcely to have been consulted by the active men, no part of it was particularly acceptable excepting that which organized the navy. His system was purely defensive, and his preference would have been to strengthen that arm as the main reliance in warfare, whilst the army should be only a means of deterring the enemy from the idea of invasion. Here is the origin of the difference of opinion in the federal party which in a short time led to the most important consequences.

And, indeed, if the reasons urged in favor of a great prospective army be calmly examined, they seem scarcely strong enough to justify the erection of so ponderous a system. The ostensible motive was the apprehension of invasion by France. But at that time France had not an inch of territory on the American continent. She was, moreover, deeply involved in hostilities with Great Britain and other powers, which tasked her strength quite severely enough in Europe. What was then the prospect of her inclination or ability to dispatch large armies to the United States, whilst so many fields of brilliant conquest remained unreaped close under her hand? Neither had she, in point of fact, shown by any act of hers the remotest disposition towards an expedition of any sort. The naval preponderance of her island neighbor presented too formidable an obstacle, even if there had been no other. So long as the danger apprehended was only contingent, it seemed to require no more than a provisional extension of the established force, to be resorted to when necessary, and to be discontinued with the cessation of the necessity. But the plan of Mr. Hamilton was not limited to this. It had every aspect of a solid establishment, of greater or less extent, it might be, but of permanent duration. It very clearly contemplated other contingencies than that which was immediately before the public, and prepared for a different class of necessities. What the precise nature of them was, has never been fully laid open. But as some notion of them is of the very first necessity to a true conception of the difficulties of Mr. Adams in his Presidency, an attempt will now be made, from the materials which have found their way to the light within the last few years, to furnish such an explanation as they appear to justify.

It may be recollected that in the elaborate plan presented by Mr. McHenry, which has been already described, the herald of that part of Mr. Hamilton's system which appeared afterwards in congress, some stress was laid on another measure not proposed in that body. This was, the expediency of sounding Great Britain, touching a loan of ten of her ships of the line, and what was called a *co-operation*, in case of rupture, for the conquest of the Floridas, Louisiana, and the South American possessions of Spain. But inasmuch as Spain had not at this time made herself a stumbling-block of offence, it seems as if no special occasion had occurred for contemplating a plan to attack her American possessions, especially in conjunction with Great Britain, at the very time when the quarrel of the United States was only with France, and the way of providing for that was the single topic proposed for consideration. The mystery is not explicable unless the clue can be supplied from elsewhere. It can only be accounted for by knowing the fact that at this very time Mr. Hamilton had become a party to a grand project of revolution in South America, conceived years before in the fertile brain of Francisco de Miranda, but now taking the form of a political combination, the details of which are found singularly to correspond with this feature of the plan submitted to the President by Mr. McHenry.* At the date of McHenry's paper, Miranda was in London, anxiously awaiting the decision of the prime minister, Mr. Pitt, upon the extent to which Great Britain would undertake to assist him. And he had the best reasons for believing that that minister's favorable answer depended upon the prospect of co-operation held out by the American government. According to Miranda's plan, Great Britain was to supply ships not exceeding twenty, money and men, but the United States were to furnish not less than seven thousand men, two thousand to be cavalry, and that not at first

---

* The original project, signed by persons calling themselves deputies of South America, may be found in the appendix to the first volume of the collected works of John Adams.

only, but throughout the war that might ensue, no matter how long. As a compensation for this engagement, the allotment of conquered territory, in case of success, was that which was pointed out in Mr. McHenry's paper, and perhaps the West Indies besides, excepting only Cuba. It is therefore difficult to resist the conviction that the same person who drew the plan offered to Mr. Adams, was at the time fully apprised of Miranda's projects, and was desirous so to shape the policy of the American government as to bring it into co-operation with them. For the rest, these facts are certain: that Mr. Hamilton was, during this period, in confidential communication with Miranda; that he suggested a change of the scheme, so far as to supply all the troops from the United States, instead of a part, which was accepted; and that the command of the troops so supplied had been conceded to his wishes. Possessed of the knowledge of all these facts, it becomes easy to understand the reasons for an organization of the military force more extensive than would be needed merely for defence. That Mr. Hamilton contemplated heading an expedition to act for a greater or less period outside of the limits of the Union, and against the possessions of another nation than France, is beyond the possibility of doubt. It was, therefore, very natural that he should be active to promote the establishment of a larger force than would appear necessary to those who had not been let into the secret of the uses to which a part of it was to be put.

Neither is this the only or the most serious consideration attending this remarkable project. The proposed co-operation with Great Britain, at a moment when she was deeply engaged in a war with the French, by a joint attack upon the dependencies of a power in close alliance with them, could scarcely fail to involve the most momentous results to the futurity of the United States. It was, first of all, about to render them dependent upon Great Britain for ships and money, to execute the object immediately in view. But granting that this could be gained at once, and with a small expenditure of the joint resources of the two nations, a thing by no means certain, the long train of consequences which victory involved, only then begins to be perceptible. The regions of South America, which were thus to be torn away from the control of Spain, were to be established as independent "under a moderate government, *with the joint guarantee of the co-operating powers,* stipulating equal privileges in commerce."* Such is the language used by Mr. Hamilton himself. But a joint guarantee, given in time of war, to the dependencies of one of the belligerent nations, to secure, against its consent, certain terms to them at all events, could not have been maintained without converting all those engaged into parties to the war, so long as it should last, and until the restoration of peace by some new form of negotiation. The effect of such

---

* Hamilton to King, *Hamilton's Works*, vol. vi. p. 347. This letter is deserving of the closest attention by all who desire to understand the history of this period. Mr. King's public and private papers, not yet before the world, must throw a flood of light on these transactions. See also Hamilton to Miranda in the same volume, p. 348.

a necessity could not fail to be a drawing closer of the alliance of the co-operating powers, and an entanglement in all the fortunes of the general struggle. An alliance was assumed to be inevitable in the South American project. It is not to be doubted that, though not advocated at the outset, it was distinctly contemplated by Mr. Hamilton, as an ultimate consequence of the execution of that scheme. But it is obvious that such an event could not have taken place without a complete abandonment of the neutrality which had been declared a cardinal point of the federal policy under General Washington's administration.

But apart from all views of foreign service, temporary or permanent, for the contemplated army, there were considerations growing out of the state of things at home, which greatly weighed on the mind of Mr. Hamilton to make him favor a permanent military organization. His tendencies were never to popular ideas. At the outset of the Revolution, even the fresh enthusiasm of his youth had much of early bias to struggle with before adopting the American cause. Neither by birth, education, taste nor habits of life entertaining faith in theoretical democracy, his later observation had only confirmed his profound distrust of everything which savored of the profession of it. His honorable and successful labors to effect the establishment of the federal constitution, were guided not so much by his confidence in the intrinsic excellence of that instrument, as by his anxiety to escape the danger of something worse. And his confidence in the permanency of that, never great, had been seriously impaired by the trials to which it had been subjected, and by the visible accumulation of elements regarded by him as sooner or later threatening its subversion. To his mind, the future presented, as he grew older, no other vision than that of a great crisis, threatening the very foundations of the social system, from which there could be no escape, and which it was important to be in the best situation to meet. Confident of his own powers, he very naturally looked within himself for the agency adequate to cope with the danger. And foreseeing that this danger would inevitably entail civil commotion, he found it not difficult to convince himself that to his genius was allotted the control of the physical means necessary to restore order out of chaos. The first and most immediate duty was to be in a condition to act with effect in support of the government. And if this could not be done without resort to force, force must be at hand to use whenever the occasion should require it. Neither was his system one of aspirations purely selfish. Strong minds seldom fail to associate with dreams of their own glory the modes of exercising power for the good of their fellow-men. Considering their happiness as mainly dependent upon a sense of security from domestic convulsions, his first aim would have been to gain that end at any rate, even should it be done at some expense of their liberties. But, this fundamental point once well settled, those liberties might be freely enjoyed up to the very limits of that necessity.

This seems to be somewhat the transcript of the mind of Hamilton during the last years of his life, as it can be gathered from a close observation of his principles, his language, and his action. He had been some time waiting for the occasion that might call out

the capacities which he felt that he possessed. His
great aspiration was for military lead.   And it is by no
means unlikely that in this estimate of his powers he
was not mistaken.   Some of the elements that insure
command he certainly had.   The time had now arrived
when the field was opening to him abroad as well as at
home.   Hence his earnest advocacy of a permanent
army as a consequence of the difficulty that had occurred with France.   Hence his still more earnest
labors to pave the way to the command of that army
for himself.

An army was raised—not such as he had contemplated, but enough to begin with.   The next point was
the command ; and the nomination to that was vested
in the President.   Nothing but an extraordinary stretch
of his favor could bring Mr. Hamilton within reach of
it, for, in point of rank and former services, his claims
fell far below those of many prominent officers of the
Revolution still on the stage.   But of the favor of Mr.
Adams, at least to so great an extent as was now required, Mr. Hamilton had his own reasons to feel very
uncertain.   Not oblivious of the secret efforts to set
him aside at the time of his election, and too proud to
run the risk of a refusal, he addressed himself to the
task of attaining his end through an intermediate
agency.   This was by appealing to a power, with whose
wishes, if once expressed, the President would deem it
too dangerous to contend.   Such a power existed in
the person of General Washington, to whom the whole
country looked as the individual to be called to the
chief command, in case of exigency.   And Mr. Hamilton too well knew the confidence entertained in his

abilities by Washington, not to be sure that he should himself be relied upon as one of his most useful assistants. So far every thing turned out according to his expectation. The President nominated Washington to be Lieutenant-general of the forces. And the latter accepted, but not without adding two conditions: one, that he should not be called into active service until it should be indispensable ; the other, that he should have the right of selecting the officers of his staff. In anticipation of the second condition, Mr. Hamilton had already opened the way to consultations with Washington, and had pointed out the only post in which he would consent to serve. It was that of inspector-general, with the rank of a major-general. These demands were readily assented to on all sides, and the lists of the organization were accordingly made out.

But although things had thus far gone according to expectation, the most important point, the designation of the second in command, had not yet been settled, or, if to be so regarded, it had not been settled auspiciously to the hopes of Mr. Hamilton. In the list of officers of the second rank, presented by Washington, nominated by the President, and ratified by the Senate on the same day, were three names, Hamilton, Knox, C. C. Pinckney. The question of priority among them had not been started, even though Mr. Pickering and Mr. McHenry directly, and Mr. Hamilton indirectly, had invoked the interposition of Washington to determine it at once. Such a decision involved considerations of delicacy towards the other two officers, which neither the President nor General Washington felt at liberty to overlook. According to all received

ideas, the elevation of Hamilton could not be regarded
otherwise than as offensive to them. Knox and Pinckney were both greatly his seniors in the revolutionary
army. The former had been at the head of the department of war both before and after the adoption of
the constitution. The latter was a brigadier-general in
1783. If the law established in the Revolution were
to be regarded as unrepealed, both would be entitled
to the precedence as a matter of course. Mr. Adams
saw no occasion to justify his going out of the path to
set it aside. General Washington, for reasons having
a particular relation to the quarter in which attack was
most apprehended, inclined to prefer Mr. Pinckney.
And, though partial to Hamilton, he was very reluctant
to wound the feelings of General Knox.

In the midst of these doubts, Mr. Pickering and Mr.
McHenry, in conjunction with other friends of Mr.
Hamilton, set in motion the most extraordinary influences to bring about the result they desired. To General Washington, in retirement at Mount Vernon, they
represented that the federalists in congress and in the
country demanded the elevation of Hamilton. To the
Senate, at Philadelphia, they urged that this was the
cherished wish of Washington. These movements
were successful so far as to make the accidental order
of the names, as ratified, appear to convey an intention
to determine the rank; but this was not enough of
itself to counteract the legal force of the precedents
setting the other way. Some direct act of the President would be necessary, after all, or the design would
fail of accomplishment. It was at last obtained, by
operating upon the strong prejudices of General Wash-

ington. In the casual conversations in the cabinet upon the organization of the army, Mr. Adams had let drop some intimations of a wish to give a share of the commissions to leading military men of the opposition. Among the names mentioned by him of suitable persons, were those of Aaron Burr, and Peter Muhlenberg, of Pennsylvania. Knowing the strong dislike of the first entertained by Washington, intimations were soon given to him of the tendencies of the President, and of the possibility that he might, if he he did not anticipate the danger by a firm demand of the list of nominations exactly in the order presented by himself, be liable to have Burr forced upon him as quartermaster-general, or in some other confidential post. These representations wrought upon Washington so far as to bring forth the desired peremptory request, attended with a menace of resignation in failure of immediate compliance, an act so little in consonance with the general spirit of Washington's life and relations to the President, as at once to imply the existence of some unusual influence to produce it. The contrivers of this measure were not mistaken in their calculations of its success. Mr. Adams gave way. He referred the decision to the pleasure of General Washington, who promoted Hamilton. General Knox refused to accept his commission in consequence. General Pinckney, on the contrary, acquiesced.

Every thing seemed at last to settle down according to the wishes of the cabinet. The first actual conflict between them and their nominal chief had ended in their triumph. They began to think their power established. Washington's place, they foresaw, would be but a pageant; and that the virtual command of the new army, carrying with it the direction, in conjunction with them, of the future policy of the nation, would henceforth centre in the hands of their real leader, Alexander Hamilton. It was, indeed, a great victory; but it was of that class which is the forerunner of greater defeats. Mr. Adams opened his eyes to the nature of the situation to which it was about to reduce him. He keenly felt the circumstances of *duresse* under which this result had been brought upon him, and he foresaw, in the motives that prompted the act, that it was only a prelude to worse things. From this time may be dated the beginning of his distrust of his ministers and of his determination to resist their control.

Whilst these things were passing in the interior of the cabinet, Mr. Adams, with the earnest eloquence of his nature, was responding to innumerable addresses poured in upon him from all quarters of the land, and, in his turn, animating his countrymen to stand by their rulers in the trial to which the follies of a foreign government were subjecting them. The effect of the grand burst of enthusiasm that had been elicited, lost none of its imposing character in the distance at which it was seen from the other side of the ocean. The Directory perceived that a mistake had been made, which had had the effect of exposing them to ridicule in Europe, and of annihilating their influence in America. They at once disavowed the agents who had appeared so industrious to effect their designs upon the pockets of the nation by working on the fears of the commissioners, and quietly set in motion new means of recovering lost ground. The evidences of this change in their policy reached the President long after he had retired for the summer to his farm at Quincy. The gradual effect which the reception of them, from time to time, produced upon his mind, it is of the utmost importance to a clear knowledge of the subsequent events, to trace with some minuteness.

It was one of the most gloomy seasons in Mr. Adams's life. His house was not, as he had generally known it, a refuge from harassing cares, a resource against public anxieties, a fountain at once of vivacity and of affectionate sympathy, a treasury of judicious and faithful counsels. Mrs. Adams lay stretched on the bed of illness, for a long time flickering between life and death; and even when issuing from the trial, but slowly dispelling the uneasiness her frail condition could not but awaken. In the midst of his domestic sadness came up the serious consideration of his public situation. For the first time, in connection with the movements of Mr. Hamilton and his friends, he now understood the dangers which impended over him. Although not by any means acquainted with the whole truth, he saw enough to understand the nature of the expedients resorted to for the purpose of controlling his will. He had had more than one occasion to feel that his cabinet officers were effective instruments to this end, and that he could place little reliance upon them for the execution of his own wishes. Yet he was to be exposed to the world and to posterity as the responsible instrument to execute a policy, in framing which no discretion was to be allowed him. Already the outline, so far as it had been developed, alarmed him. It involved demands on the public purse which he saw no means of supplying, without risk of convulsions, and the establishment of a permanent military organization, the necessity for which he could not understand. Above all, his instincts warned him, in no dubious tones, that the extraordinary management resorted to for the purpose of placing Mr. Hamilton at the head of this great power, was designed certainly to give to him, and in certain contingencies, perhaps, to the country itself, A MASTER.

Whilst agitated by these doubts, letters from Francisco de Miranda arrived. They were skilfully drawn to have an effect. They set forth the project, which had been listened to by Great Britain, and solicited the co-operation of the American government in its execution. They held out the idea, not likely to be inoperative on the supposed weak points of Mr. Adams, that the institutions to be given to the South American States, in case of success, were to be formed after the model which he had labored so strenuously in his writings to recommend. And they closed by representing the arrangements to be now so far perfected, that upon his answer to the present application would the execution depend. Of the deep and intimate connection of this scheme with the system of Mr. Hamilton, Mr. Adams then had no suspicion. He knew, indeed, that by the same channel which conveyed this dispatch, letters had been received both by Generals Hamilton and Knox; but he had no idea of the extent to which they might be enlisted in carrying it out. There can now be no doubt that Colonel Pickering, Mr. Wolcott, and Mr. McHenry knew more about it than they cared to disclose; and that the main features of the plan were familiar to Mr. Hamilton's friends in both houses of congress. Why was it that, under these circumstances, this important operation had no issue? The answer is to be found in the situation of Mr. Adams. No one of the parties engaged was willing to take the risk of communicating to him the whole truth. Under these circumstances, he acted upon the application in the most simple and summary way possible. "We are friends with Spain," said he, in a letter to the Secretary of State. "If we were enemies, would the project be useful to us? It will not be in character for me to answer the letter. Will any notice of it, in any manner, be proper?" The Secretary never ventured to answer the questions; and the grand plan thus perished by inanition. Indeed, other events were approaching which soon put all notion of prosecuting it with the consent of Mr. Adams utterly out of the question.

On the 1st of October, 1798, Elbridge Gerry arrived in Boston, on his return from the unfortunate mission to France. Although by no means satisfied with the course which he had thought it proper to take, in remaining after his colleagues left Paris, Mr. Adams had in no degree suffered his confidence in the integrity of his old friend to be impaired. He therefore welcomed him home cordially as ever, and showed himself prepared to listen with a favoring ear to any arguments he might have to offer in his justification. It proved the less difficult for Mr. Gerry to relieve himself from censure that he was able to communicate to him good reasons for believing that his stay had not been without its measure of utility. He narrated the last movements of Talleyrand, his earnestness to retain him for the sake of commencing a negotiation, and his professions of regret at his determination to depart, all furnishing to him symptoms of a softening on the part of the French Directory, and of a wish, at least in part, to retrace their steps. These communications were received by the President in a friendly spirit to the maker, but with a very natural distrust of the grounds upon which they had been based.

Not a week elapsed, however, before intelligence came from a new and a wholly different quarter, to make upon him a deeper and much more abiding impression. This was received from Mr. Murray, the minister of the United States in Holland. It disclosed clearly enough the uneasiness of France at the danger of an approximation of her opponents in other countries towards Great Britain, her most formidable enemy. Here was visible a new motive for the sudden change of intentions which Mr. Gerry thought he had perceived before his departure, and a sufficient reason for waiting to learn more. These dispatches of Mr. Murray, though sent through the Department of State, were not to be deposited there, as they involved the names and characters of persons in Holland, whose safety might be seriously implicated by exposure. This is a material fact in the narrative, and its bearing will appear presently. The contents of them were, however, well known to Colonel Pickering, and perhaps to other members of the cabinet.

Revolving these various communications in his mind during his retirement at Quincy, Mr. Adams could not resist the belief that a possibility yet existed of averting the calamity of war. In this spir.t, he addressed a letter, on the 20th of October, to Colonel Pickering, the Secretary of State. Reminding him of the approach of the session of congress, he proceeded to lay before him some thoughts which, in his opinion, deserved to be maturely considered, and upon which he requested early efforts to obtain the advice of the other cabinet officers. They were comprised in two propositions, as follows:

The first, whether it would be expedient for the President to recommend a declaration of war.

The second, whether any further proposals of negotiation could be made with safety, or *any new envoy named,* prepared to embark, *in case assurances should be given that he would be received.*

The symptoms of hesitation, visible in the second question, and still more so in the reasoning of the letter, seem to have burst like a clap of thunder over the heads of the cabinet officers. No answer to either question, or sign of recognition of its existence, was ever returned. The experiment of overruling the President, which had succeeded so well in the case of Mr. Hamilton, was now changed into a fixed policy. Of their system, war was an essential part. In his message to congress of the 21st of June, Mr. Adams had pledged himself "that he would never send another minister to France, without assurances that he would be received." To that pledge, in its most rigid sense, they resolved to hold him; and, warned by this signal, they set themselves at once to prepare such a form of words for his adoption at the opening of the

session, as should leave him no loophole for retreat.
Some of them had fixed their minds on a declaration
of war. To act with more force, they called together
a council of their leading friends, including the military generals happening to be assembled at Philadelphia, Washington,* Hamilton, and Pinckney, where
they matured the language of a draft intended for the
use of Mr. Adams in his opening speech, the duty of
offering which was devolved upon the person then supposed to be personally most agreeable to him, Mr.
Oliver Wolcott.

There is no reason to suppose that when Mr. Adams
arrived† at Philadelphia in the last days of November,
1798, he had the smallest suspicion of what was awaiting him, or of the severity of the trial to which his
firmness was to be put. He had seen in the newspapers, on his way, indications of a disposition in some
quarters to push for a declaration of war, but he had
not regarded them as proving any settled purpose. In
this spirit he met the members of his cabinet. The two
questions presented in his letter of the 20th of October,
of which no notice had been taken, were now formally
brought forward by him. No one ventured to suggest
an immediate declaration of war, as the President not
only did not propose it, but his opinion was clearly

---

* There is no evidence yet before the world, that General
Washington actually took part in the consultation.

† In writing to his wife, on his arrival, he says: " For once I
have accomplished a journey from Quincy to High Street without
one escorting man or horse. This was done by invention, as I
will explain some other time." Yet this was the person charged
by his opponents with a great fondness for forms and ceremonies.

seen to be adverse; some of the members were themselves not ready for it; so it was tacitly agreed to leave all notice of the subject out of the speech. The great struggle was upon the other question: to wit, whether any circumstances would justify a renewal of negotiations by the United States. Mr. Adams leaned to the affirmative. He required, however, the manifestation of the strongest evidence of sincerity on the part of France as a preliminary condition. The paragraph which he prepared, expressive of his sentiment, yet remains among his papers. Whether it was offered at this cabinet meeting is not positively known, though altogether probable. There is evidence that the Secretary of State, at least, had had it communicated to him. It explicitly declared the President's disposition to send a minister to France or to receive one from there, whenever the assurances required in his former message of the 21st of June should be forthcoming. If it was submitted at this meeting, the fact that it was not adopted, shows that there was no inclination in the President to be tenacious about terms. On the other hand, the draft which had been prepared in the council already mentioned, and presented by Mr. Wolcott for his acceptance, proved generally satisfactory to him. He concurred in its recommendations, and consented to adopt it, but with the exception of a single passage, to the language of which he demurred. That passage stood thus:

"In demonstrating by our conduct that we do not fear war in the necessary protection of our rights and honor, we shall give no room to infer that we abandon the desire of peace.   This has been wisely and perseveringly cultivated, and as between us and France, harmony may be re-established at her option.

"*But the sending another minister to make a new attempt at negotiation would, in my opinion, be an act of humiliation to which the United States ought not to submit without extreme necessity.   No such necessity exists.* It must, therefore, be left with France, if she be indeed desirous of accommodation, to take the requisite steps. The United States adhere to the maxims by which they have been governed.   They will sacredly respect the rights of embassy.   Their magnanimity discards the policy of retaliating insult in bar of the avenues to peace, *and if France shall send a minister to negotiate, he will be received with honor and treated with candor.*"

The purport of this language could not be mistaken. It was intended to put an opinion in the mouth of the President which would cut him off from the possibility of initiating a mission, no matter what might be the change of disposition in France.   And it proposed to require the government of that country to originate the measure, which there was very little probability that it would do, in the attitude in which it then stood towards Europe.   It was the United States who were mainly suffering by the continuance of the misunderstanding.   Their commerce was the prey of France, who, in return, had no assailable equivalent exposed to reprisal.   To require such a condition, was therefore little short of insisting upon an indefinite duration of their own grievances, and a war on a mere point of form into the bargain.   The President declined to commit himself to any such extent. The first open struggle of his administration took place. His advisers insisted upon the adoption of the passage, some of them with great warmth and pertinacity. This moment was to decide whether Mr. Adams was yet to stand in history the same man who had determined to defend Captain Preston, the same man who had been avoided in the streets of Philadelphia for urging independence, the same man who in Holland and in France had set aside the dictation of Count de Vergennes, or a mere cipher in the most critical period and the most responsible position known in the annals of the nation. The course he took may be readily conjectured, if this narrative thus far has been anywise successful in tracing the outlines of his character. He persevered in requiring a modification, small in extent, it is true, but significant enough to answer the purpose. His version, as it stands in the speech actually pronounced, reads as follows:

"But in demonstrating by our conduct that we do not fear war in the necessary protection of our rights and honor, we shall give no room to infer that we abandon the desire of peace. An efficient preparation for war can alone insure peace. It is peace that we have uniformly and perseveringly cultivated; and harmony between us and France may be restored at her option. But to send another minister without more determinate assurances that he would be received, would be an act of humiliation to which the United States ought not to submit. It must, therefore, be left to France, if she is indeed desirous of accommodation, to take the requisite steps.

" The United States will steadily observe the maxims by which they have hitherto been governed. They will respect the sacred rights of embassy. And with a sincere disposition on the part of France to desist from hostility, to make reparation for the injuries heretofore inflicted on our commerce, and to do justice in future, there will be no obstacle to the restoration of a friendly intercourse. In making to you this declaration, I give a pledge to France and to the world that the executive authority of this country still adheres to the humane and pacific policy which has invariably governed its proceedings, in conformity with the wishes of the other branches of the government, and of the people of the United States. But considering the late manifestations of her policy towards foreign nations, I deem it a duty deliberately and solemnly to declare my opinion, that, whether we negotiate with her or not, vigorous preparations for war will be alike indispensable. These alone will give us an equal treaty and insure its observance."

A comparison of the two passages will show the significance of Mr. Adams's alteration to consist more in what he expunges than what he inserts. The clause, exacting from France the initiation of a new mission as a preliminary step to peace, wholly disappears, and there remains only a requirement of acts to prove a pacific disposition, the withdrawal of hostility, and the readiness to do justice both for the past and for the future. Negotiation was therefore made to depend upon the actual return of good faith in France, and not upon any particular mode of showing it. And although preparation for war was still strenuously insisted upon, the duration of it was made contingent only upon her persistence in refusing the most equitable propositions. Unobjectionable as this statement of a national position seems to the eye of reason and of Christian charity, it was received by the cabinet officers with the most gloomy forebodings. Mournfully did they retire from the conference, under a conviction that their plan had failed, and that their official, meant to be likewise their real President, after all.

The speech was made to congress on the 8th of December, 1798, in presence of Generals Washington, Hamilton, and Pinckney, then assembled at Philadelphia for the work of organizing the army, and of all the principal officers of the government. It was brief and manly in its terms, reviewing the state of the relations with the powers of Europe, and inculcating the necessity of energy and union under the embarrassments with which the nation had to contend. The only important recommendation was one touching the extension of the navy. This, which was Mr. Adams's favorite policy, he proposed to develop to a size sufficient to guard the coast, and protect the trade of the country, as well as to facilitate the safe transportation of troops and stores from any one point of the seaboard to every other. Upon this issue, the opposition chose to take the broadest ground of resistance; so that the navy became one of the chief topics of dissension during this administration. And here, Mr. Adams's individual opinions were in perfect harmony with all sections of the party he represented.

But in other points, where no such agreement existed, the failure to control the executive in regard to

the possible renewal of negotiations with France, precipitated matters to an issue.   No longer sure of overbearing Mr. Adams, through his cabinet, the friends of
Mr. Hamilton immediately turned their eyes to congress, in the expectation that an appeal to them might
avail, and that a majority could be persuaded to dictate
to him their policy as the sentiment of the whole party.
A meeting was accordingly summoned ; and the members, now largely preponderating in both Houses, very
generally attended it.   Here the expediency of making a declaration of war was urged, and warmly and
perseveringly pressed.   But although many of the most
brilliant orators appeared to favor it, their eloquence
could not avail to effect the object.   A small majority
decided the point against them.   The result was defeat ; and a consciousness on the part of Mr. Hamilton's adherents, that, from this time, they must consider themselves as not possessed of the ascendant in
the party counsels, and that the future course was not
to be one exclusively of their suggesting.

Of course it followed, according to all recognized
notions in political associations, that the minority,
having been fairly outvoted, was bound to do one of
two things, either to acquiesce or to secede.   And if
the case was not deemed important enough to justify
the latter step, then it was no more than just to adopt
the former cheerfully.   Since war was put out of the
question, it seemed the part of wisdom to unite, so far
as practicable, in the intermediate policy.   To this,
however, the friends of Mr. Hamilton manifested but
little inclination.   On the contrary, their failure was
rather the signal for laying aside further reserve towards

him whom they considered as the cause of it. In this course the Secretary of State took the lead. Far from respecting the confidential nature of his post, he had never hesitated, when he pleased, to exert his influence secretly to counteract the President's wishes. This had been strikingly exemplified in the case of Colonel William Stephens Smith, Mr. Adams's son-in-law, whom General Washington had placed in his list of general officers, and whom the President had nominated to the Senate for an appointment. Taking advantage of his confidential knowledge of the President's intention, Colonel Pickering hastened to the Senate, privately to rouse, in advance, the necessary opposition to defeat it. The same vindictiveness was repeated at a later period, without, however, being then attended with the same success. It now flamed forth, in a vehement manner, against Mr. Elbridge Gerry. Not satisfied with preparing an official report upon his dispatches, so harsh in its character as to call forth the positive interposition of Mr. Adams requiring a modification of its language, he extended his annoyance to the point of disputing the petty items of his pecuniary accounts. Towards Mr. Adams himself he continued only the forms of civility, which did not restrain him from disregarding his wishes, neglecting his injunctions, and, among his circle of intimates, disparaging both his acts and his conversation. Thus it was that, when officially requested, on the 15th of January, 1799, to prepare the draft of a project of a treaty and a consular convention, such as the United States might accept, if proposed by France, Colonel Pickering seems to have passed it over without notice. Thus it was that the reflections in his report, bearing upon Mr. Gerry, were not modified without stubborn resistance. The same state of things, though in a far less degree, prevailed in Mr. Adams's relations with the secretaries of the treasury and of war. His familiar talk, never sufficiently guarded, was watched only to be reported for the purpose of fastening inconsistency upon his public action. His wishes were liable to become known abroad, and neutralized by anticipation, if never openly resisted in words. Mutual confidence could not long survive such a state of things. Although not fully alive to the extent of the combination in his cabinet with a power outside of it, such as it has been but very lately disclosed, he yet instinctively felt that he was no longer among friends. Hence that, if any public act should be absolutely demanded on his part, the execution of it would depend only upon the degree in which he could make his unaided individual energies overbear all opposition.

It has been remarked that the policy of the federalists of the Hamilton school was war; that of a portion of them, aggressive war. The motives to it were twofold. 1. The preponderance which an appeal to the patriotic feeling of the people was giving to the party. 2. The great military organization which it was throwing into their hands. With the aid of these forces, they trusted to procure modifications in the laws, and even in the constitution itself,* so to fortify their posi-

---

* This seems the unavoidable construction to be put upon the language of Mr. Hamilton, when he speaks of "surrounding the constitution with more ramparts," and of "the erection of addi-

tion in the government as in time to render it inexpugnable by the opposition. A calm examination of this whole theory, and a comparison of it with the temper of the American people, can scarcely fail at this day to convince any one how visionary, not to say indiscreet, such ideas really were. They were never even remotely shared by Mr. Adams. He roused the country to war, solely as a measure of defence, and to deter France from further persevering in her aggressions. The first appearance of relaxation on her part, far from being hailed by him with misgivings and aversion, was watched with interest, though naturally not unmingled with distrust. At the opening of the session, nothing had occurred to justify in his mind any change of his position taken in June preceding. On the other hand, enough had appeared to forbid the propriety of going one step further, and cutting off even a chance of reconciliation.

In this state things remained during a considerable portion of the session of 1798–1799. Mr. Adams, in the mean time, continued to receive communications of a very interesting nature from Mr. Murray, all of them tending to prove a real change in the French policy. On the 21st of January, the terms of the Directory's answer to the Dutch offer of mediation reached his hands. They declared that the disposition of the French to reconciliation had been already unmistakably made known at Philadelphia, and they imposed upon

----

tional buttresses to the constitution, a fabric which can hardly be stationary, and which will retrograde, if it cannot be made to advance."—*Works*, vol. vi. pp. 384, 416.

the government of the United States the responsibility
of the consequences, if it should persist in misconstruing
or repulsing it. This paper, decisive enough, had it
emanated from any government of unimpaired character, was yet worthy of some consideration, if viewed
simply as a stroke of crafty diplomacy. It threw the
burden of perpetuating a quarrel from the French upon
the American side. Nothing sustained the administration of Mr. Adams so firmly as the popular conviction
that the blame lay wholly with France, and that no
measures of hostility had been resorted to until every
hope of peace had been exhausted. The knowledge
that France had made specific offers to modify her
offensive policy, and that the offers had met with no
attention, would soon be spread abroad by her friends,*
and would scarcely fail to renew the strength of opposition. These were strong considerations for at least
listening to the proposals. Yet they were not decisive;
for they could not be said to contain such assurances as
would warrant a departure from the memorable pledge
given by the President in his message of the 21st of June.

Ten days later, however, something came of a much
more positive character. A letter from Mr. Murray
was received, in which he narrated the particulars of
his interviews with M. Pichon, the French agent at the
Hague, respecting the nature of the assurances required
by the terms of that message. Difficulties of form were
interposed. But they had been at last somewhat skilfully surmounted by the preparation, on the part of M.

---

* The notes of M. Talleyrand to M. Pichon were actually
printed in a newspaper in Virginia in the summer of 1799.

Talleyrand, of a dispatch, addressed to M. Pichon, in which, whilst reiterating the professions of a desire to come to a good understanding with America, he managed to introduce a promise, in the very words that had been used by the President, to wit, that a new envoy, if sent, would be "received as the representative of a great, free, powerful, and independent nation." This dispatch, thus prepared, was placed in the hands of M. Pichon to be by him delivered to Mr. Murray, and by him, in turn, transmitted to the government of the United States.

The receipt of this paper filled up the measure of Mr. Adams's responsibility to his country. The question, and an immensely important one, both to his fellow-citizens and to himself, was how it should be met. Should he refuse to do any thing? In that case the burden of all the evil consequences to the country would fall upon himself alone. He might have averted them, had he only acted. Such an idea would ever recur to poison the quiet of his remaining life, and to spoil the remembrance of past sacrifices and services. No! He could not stand still. Clearly, something was to be done.

Then the question followed, what he should do.

Should he call his cabinet into consultation, and prepare them for the adoption of a new measure of negotiation?

If he did take this, which was obviously, under common circumstances, the proper course, there were strong grounds for believing that all his efforts would be defeated, and come to nothing. Of Colonel Pickering's views and feelings, even with the full knowledge of Mr.

Murray's communications, he had every reason to be sure beforehand. Experience had already warned him of the fate which the slightest intimation of an offer to revive a mission to France was likely to meet. The presentation of it in the cabinet would lead to a warm protest, and to the necessity of either persevering against an opposition profiting by the tactics of delay to become concerted in the Senate, or of abandoning the measure altogether. Judging from subsequent events, there can be little doubt that in these views of probabilities Mr. Adams's foresight was correct. Party passions had reached such a 'height, that if he had pursued any ordinary course, it is nearly certain his decision would have been overruled, and his influence ever afterwards annihilated.

No greater trial has befallen a chief magistrate of the United States. None greater ever befell Mr. Adams, and yet this narrative has shown that he had not been without severe ones. But his convictions of duty were never more clear. War impended over the country, and a chance was yet left to avert it. He was bound not to permit that chance, however slight, to escape. He meditated the means in his own secret heart. There was but one way. He ought to send to the Senate a communication nominating a minister to go to France; and the person must be the individual through whom the overtures for accommodation had been transmitted, William Vans Murray, now minister at the Hague. On the 18th of February, accordingly, the members of the Senate, not one of whom had a suspicion of what was coming, were astounded by the reception of a message from the President, covering the dispatch of Talleyrand to M. Pichon, as the motive to his decision to nominate Mr. Murray. The terms used by him were most carefully guarded in every particular, assuming no risk in trusting too readily the professions of M. Talleyrand, and providing that no advance should be made beyond the appointment, until further assurances, the most unequivocal, should be publicly and officially given by France that the minister now nominated would be honorably received.

It would be difficult, were it within the proper limits of this work, fully to describe the mixed and opposite emotions with which this proceeding was received by the members of the Senate. A large majority of them were now federalists, the greater part, devoted friends of Mr. Hamilton. But Mr. Jefferson, the chief of the opposition, was its presiding officer, and under him yet rallied the small band of his friends who had survived the political tornado of the preceding year. All were equally astonished. The letters of Mr. Murray to the President had been, for the sake of the persons compromised in Holland, kept within the knowledge of very few. And even some of those few had their own reasons for not aiding to give them publicity. They knew and feared the tendency of the President's mind, and had been endeavoring to counteract it by efforts to commit him, so far as they could, before the public, to their own views. Hence it happened that, in the absence of all acquaintance with the true grounds of the nomination, the wildest conjectures were let loose. "Is Mr. Adams mad?" asked a federal senator of Colonel Pickering, the Secretary of State, who affected greater ignorance than he really had. On the one hand, Mr. Jefferson, the Vice-President, was full of poor suspicions that the President had kept back Talleyrand's letter for months, in order to let the war measures go on; and that, finding himself compelled to disclose it at last, he had done so only to let the Senate reject it. Whilst the Secretary of State, on the other, exultingly vindictive, informed General Washington, three days after the event, "that the President was suffering the torments of the damned at the consequences of his nomination."

By way of set-off against these opposite speculations, and to show how Mr. Adams actually felt, it may be as well here to introduce two private letters of his, written to his wife at the very time these gentlemen were penning their epistles. Intermixed with some comments upon matters of no public interest, are these remarks upon the memorable act.

"22 February.

"I have no idea that I shall be chosen President a second time; though this is not to be talked of. The business of the office is so oppressive that I shall hardly support it two years longer.

"To-night I must go to the ball; where I suppose I shall get a cold, and have to eat gruel for breakfast for a week afterwards. This will be no punishment.

"Since my nomination of Murray I have been advised by some to name my son John and Mr. King, with Mr. Murray. But I answer that the nomination of either Mr. King or Mr. Adams would probably defeat the whole measure. Rivalries have been irritated to madness, and federalists have merited the Sedition Law, and Cobbett the Alien Bill. But I will not take revenge. I do not remember that I was ever vindictive in my life, though I have often been very wroth. I am not very angry now, nor much vexed or fretted. The mission came across the views of many, and stirred the passions of more. This I knew was unavoidable. The reasons which determined me are too long to be written.''

Of his anxieties he writes in these words:

"Your sickness last summer, fall, and winter has been to me the severest trial I ever endured. Not that I am at this moment without other trials, enough for one man. I may adopt the words of a celebrated statesman, whom, however, I should not wish to resemble in many things. 'And now, good judge,' says he, 'let me ask you, whether you believe that my situation in the world is perfectly as I could wish it; whether you imagine that I meet with no shock from my superiors, no perverseness from my equals, no impertinence from my inferiors. If you fancy me in such a state of bliss, you are wide from the mark!' ''

The following thoughts were called out by private matters, but they equally elucidate the state of his mind.

"25 February.

"Frederick, Franklin, and other *soi-disant* philosophers insist that nature contrives these things, with others, to reconcile men to the thought of quitting the world. If my philosophy was theirs, I should believe that nature cared nothing for men, nor their follies, nor their miseries, nor for herself. She is a mighty stupid wretch, according to them; a kind of French woman, sometimes beautiful and clever, but very often diabolical; a kind of French republic, cunning and terrible, but cruel as the grave, and unjust as the tempter and tormentor.

"I believe nothing like this of nature, which to me is a machine whose author and conductor is wise, kind, and mighty. Believing this, I can acquiesce in what is unpleasant, expecting that it will work out a greater degree of good. If it were possible that I should be mistaken, I at least shall not be worse off than these profound philosophers. I shall be in the same case hereafter, and a little, a great deal better here."

Among other modes of binding the President to a policy he was thought not to favor, one had been resorted to by the Secretary of State, which has already been mentioned in another connection. This was to draw up an official report, embracing a summary of the negotiations with France, into which the severe strictures upon the conduct of Mr. Gerry, that roused objections on the part of Mr. Adams, were introduced. The incidental matter had occupied so much of his attention, and the effort to modify it had become so exclusively an object, that he seems to have suffered the other portions of the document to pass almost without notice. Construing this as approbation of every thing that he did not censure, Colonel Pickering afterwards labored to fix upon Mr. Adams a charge of inconsistency between his action at that time and his nomination of Mr. Murray a month later. Feeble as the reasoning is, to justify so violent a presumption, the following letter, written at the moment, sufficiently disposes of it, by showing three things: first, that he saw no necessity for the paper at all; secondly, that his approbation of it, when prepared, was quite dubious even after the required changes had been made in it; and, lastly, that even that share which he gave, had been modified by the reception, soon afterwards, of evidence impairing its positions. Thus he deals with the subject, in the letter just quoted. Mrs. Adams had been quite sick.

"The report was not at last as it should have been. But it is very different from the report made to me. I scratched out a little. I wanted no report. In short, it is one of those things that I may talk of when I see you. After I sent that report to congress, I received a letter, which has favored Mr. Gerry's opinion and made against the report.

"I have instituted a new mission, which is kept in the dark, but when it comes to be understood, it will be approved. O! how they lament Mrs. Adams's absence! She is a good counsellor! If she had been here, Murray would never have been named, nor his mission instituted!

"This ought to gratify your vanity enough to cure you!"

These letters illustrate the difficulties under which Mr. Adams labored within his cabinet, in the effort to maintain his own views of policy and duty. The majority of the Senate was not disinclined to arrogate a share of

control over him.   After two days of delay, the nomination of Mr. Murray was referred to a committee of
five persons, all of them federalists.   Of this committee,
Mr. Theodore Sedgwick was chairman, who had already
sent off to Mr. Hamilton a request for instructions what
to do.   In the mean time its members determined on
the extraordinary step of personally visiting the President, to learn the reasons, if he had any, for the measure,
and to obtain alterations equivalent to an entire abandonment of it.   Such was the temper of the impetuous
class.   Perpetually indulging the hope of overruling the
judgment of their chief, they fancied that a display of
senatorial authority might be sufficiently imposing to
prompt a voluntary withdrawal of his act, and save them
the necessity of voting upon it.   The chief agent, who
records this, was likewise the person who but eight
years before had warmly commended, for his "unconquerable intrepidity," the very man upon whom he was
about to try this crucial experiment.

Mr. Adams met this proceeding with far more moderation than it merited.*   He very properly protested
against it as an attempt to dictate to a co-ordinate
department, but upon assurances being given that no
official shape should attach to the results of the conference, he consented to a free conversation with the
gentlemen.   The result did not, however, correspond
with their expectations.   Mr. Adams proved quite
impracticable.   "I have, on mature reflection," said
he to them, "made up my mind, and I will neither

---

* Mr. Sedgwick admits that it was "an infraction of correct
principles," but, as usual with party men, he lays the blame of it
on necessity. *Works of Hamilton*, vol. v. p. 217.

withdraw nor modify the nomination." Yet perceiving them disposed to transfer their objections from the mission itself to the person named by him to fill it, he did nevertheless make a corresponding change in his position. Should the Senate think proper to decide against Mr. Murray, he suggested the possibility that he might then propose to join with him in a commission two other individuals, who should be sent from the United States whenever the requisite assurances should be obtained that they would be favorably received. This step Mr. Stoddert, his Secretary of the Navy, in a letter written to Mr. Adams some years afterwards, characterized as wise, but, in his opinion, as derogating from his personal dignity. But it is not easy to understand how any proposal that is truly wise is likely to be wanting in dignity. In this case, it would seem rather to have been a very just discrimination between firmness and obstinacy, between adherence to the substance and concession in the form. The very fact that his visitors consented to enter into the second question, raised the strongest implication of their surrender of opposition to the first.

In point of fact, the objections to Mr. Murray were such as senators might legitimately entertain, and as were not without intrinsic weight. The President's reasons for selecting him are obvious enough. He was already in Europe, where he had been resorted to by the French government as a medium of opening their communications with America. Of course they would be precluded from raising objections to further negotiations with the person of their voluntary choice, or, if they did, his testimony as to what had already passed

would furnish to the world the strongest evidence of
their bad faith.   Yet reasonable as were these grounds,
and unexceptionable as was Mr. Murray himself, it
cannot be denied that his position in the United States
had not been so prominent as to justify laying exclusively upon his shoulders so heavy a responsibility.   In
proposing to join him with two other men of great
weight of character, Mr. Adams did exactly what the
country would have required of him, and rendered all
further opposition to his policy impossible.   The
committee retired, having gained nothing but the opportunity to reject Mr. Murray, without taking the responsibility of defeating the mission.   A meeting of the
federal senators was held at the house of Mr. Bingham,
at which this step was finally resolved upon.   But even
this poor satisfaction was denied to them.   For the
President, learning the result of their consultations in
season, and construing it as a decisive expression of
opinion, anticipated their formal action, by sending a
new message early the next morning, joining Oliver
Ellsworth, chief justice of the supreme court, and Patrick Henry, of Virginia, in the commission with Mr.
Murray, and attaching the conditions which he had
mentioned in his conference with the committee.   This
act was decisive.   The reluctant senators had in the
mean time received an answer from Mr. Hamilton,
warning them that a rejection of the measure was utterly
out of the question, and proposing no amendment beyond an enlargement of the commission, such as was
now voluntarily offered.   Every objection was thus removed, and nothing was left to the remonstrants but to
ratify with the best grace they could.   Yet, singularly

enough, as if the judgment of Mr. Adams was ever to stand approved before posterity, the only one of the three nominations which appears on the record as unanimously confirmed, is exactly that which had been objected to, that of William Vans Murray.

Such is the history of this, the most noted event of Mr. Adams's administration. The news of it spread rapidly over the nation. People received it with various and opposite feelings. Some rejoiced, not because they hoped the country might be benefited, but rather that the opposition would be helped. Some mourned, not because the country would, in their opinion, suffer from it, so much as for fear lest the federalists should be shaken by the appearance of dissension. Mr. Jefferson exulted in the idea that "the nomination silenced all arguments against the sincerity of France, and rendered desperate every further effort towards war," neither of which propositions would have been true, had France persevered, instead of changing her policy. Mr. Hamilton and his friends, on the other hand, inveighed against the act as a fatal and dishonest desertion of a settled policy, which required war at least until the time when the French should publicly sue for peace. Neither was this true, the moment after France ceased to show a disposition to provoke a war. Between these hypotheses lay the narrow path which Mr. Adams had marked out for himself. Ready for war, if France continued faithless, he was not less ready for peace the moment she showed signs of returning reason.

Great, indeed, was the responsibility of the course he took, and heavily would his name have been burdened in after-ages, had the event failed to correspond to his expectations. As it actually turned out, there can be no question that the country was rescued from a false step, the consequences of which, in the view of the long wars that afflicted the Christian world, the imagination is baffled in attempting to define. In determining his course, Mr. Adams could confidently count upon no support, unless it was from that inert conscience of the quiet and moderate classes, which never approves but with reserve, or commends without qualification; a conscience, the voice of which, most loud when there is the least necessity for its exercise, is too apt to be frightened into silence in the noise and bustle of factions, when it might do the most good. But even that voice could not now be immediately commanded, since the materials for judgment were not yet before the people. As they gradually made their way, the effects became visible. The moderate federalism of the Middle and Southern States first came up to his support. The only two members of his cabinet who represented it, now ranged themselves decidedly with the President, and in opposition to their colleagues. Patrick Henry applauded the act, although obliged for personal reasons to decline his place in the new embassy. It was equally sustained by the person substituted, Governor Davie, of North Carolina. John Marshall, the leading mind of the rejected mission, as well as the pillar of his party in Virginia, signified his decided approbation. Jay was startled into doubts by the vehemence of the condemnations passed by his friends, whilst Knox, and Lincoln, and Dexter, and many others, less known but equally decided repre-

sentatives of federal opinions, rallied in his defence.
The consequence was, that in a short time all direct
attacks upon Mr. Adams for originating a negotiation
became futile. The efforts to defeat it were not, however, pretermitted. They now took the indirect shape
of procrastination, in the hope, by that means, of bringing it ultimately to nothing. And so well were they
concerted, that a will less determined than that of Mr.
Adams would scarcely have availed to prevent their
success.

And here it must be conceded that a great error was
committed by the President. Weary with the conflicts of the session, and anxious to return to the only
spot in which he really took delight, his home and his
farm, he waited at Philadelphia just long enough to
mature with his cabinet the points fixed as *ultimata*, in
case the negotiations with France should be renewed,
and to prepare the papers required to meet a popular
outbreak against the direct tax, in one or two counties
of Pennsylvania, before he took his departure for the
summer. General Washington had been in the habit
of doing the same thing, it is true; but Mr. Adams
would have done well to remember that his authority,
when absent, was not at all to be compared with his
predecessor's, and that, great as it was, even that had
not always been respected by some of the cabinet.
And if this had happened with Washington, when
there was no want of general unison in his counsels,
how much more likely was it to occur now that marked
lines of difference were drawn! In truth, this would
have been the time to come at once to an understanding with his counsellors, as to the footing upon which

they were to stand with him for the future. He had a
right to demand from them, what a later incumbent in
the same office, General Jackson, did from his cabinet,
with energy and success, that is, either a hearty general co-operation in one policy, or an opportunity to
replace them with persons who would promise it. Had
he known the true state of things, there is no reason to
doubt that he would have now done what he did after
he partially discovered it. But as yet he retained some
confidence in the good faith of his ministers. He knew
their sentiments, and understood the nature of their
connections, but he saw nothing in all this to prevent
them from joining, with good-will, in executing his
wishes. Too much trust in the honesty of others was
the source of the mistakes which did the most to injure
his reputation in his lifetime. It gave repeated opportunities for acts of treachery on the part of correspond-
ents, to whom, in the confidence of friendship, he had
written unguarded letters ; and it at this time presented
to his confidential officers an irresistible temptation to
wield, without stint, the power in their hands, for the
express purpose of controlling his plans and defeating
his policy.

It will be recollected that notwithstanding Talleyrand's assurances given in the letter to M. Pichon, the
messages to the Senate, nominating the ministers, contained a further provision, guarding against a repetition
of the treatment experienced by the former commission. They were not to go to France until direct
pledges, from the French minister of foreign relations,
that they would be received and treated with in character, should have been transmitted. Of course, this

interposed months of delay. On the 6th of March, the Secretary of State was instructed to inform Mr. Murray that a literal execution of this condition must be insisted upon; that no indirect or unofficial communication of any kind would be permitted, and no variation of the designated policy listened to, with a single exception, in case the Directory should themselves prefer to send out a minister to Philadelphia. Mr. Murray did not receive his instructions until May. On the 5th of that month, he addressed to M. Talleyrand a note giving the substance of them. Talleyrand replied on the 12th, by explicitly repeating the assurances which had been required, and somewhat querulously complaining of the delays, which, as nobody knew better than he, the bad spirit betrayed in previous transactions had been the only reason for interposing. Mr. Murray at once forwarded this paper; but owing to the slow transmission across the water customary in those days, his dispatches did not arrive in America until the 30th of July.

The next day, the Secretary of State sent M. Talleyrand's note to the President at Quincy, with a comment, which overlooked the substantial concession it contained, to dwell on the language that might be construed as offensive. The President, on the other hand, saw in it only a change of policy, no matter what the motive that prompted it, and disregarded every thing else. His reply to Mr. Pickering contains these words, which comprehensively define his whole line of policy:

" Still they (the French) shall find, as long as I am

in office, candor, integrity, and, as far as there can be any confidence or safety, a pacific and friendly disposition. If the spirit of exterminating vengeance ever arises, it shall be conjured up by them, not me. In this spirit I shall pursue the negotiation, and I expect the co-operation of the heads of departments.

"Our operations and preparations by sea and land are not to be relaxed in the smallest degree. On the contrary, I wish them to be animated with fresh energy. St. Domingo and the Isle of France, and all other parts of the French dominions, are to be treated in the same manner as if no negotiation was going on. These preliminaries recollected, I pray you to lose no time in conveying to Governor Davie his commission, and to the chief justice and his excellency" (Ellsworth) "copies of these letters from Mr. Murray and Talleyrand, with a request that, laying aside all other employments, they make immediate preparations for embarking. . . . . . Although I have little confidence in the issue of this business, I wish to delay nothing, to omit nothing.

"The principal points, indeed all the points, of the negotiation were so minutely considered and approved by me and all the heads of department, before I left Philadelphia, that nothing remains but to put them into form and dress. This service I pray you to perform as promptly as possible. Lay your draft before the heads of department, receive their corrections, if they shall judge any to be necessary, and send them to me as soon as possible."

The three points, alluded to as agreed upon before the President left Philadelphia, were extremely simple.

1. Indemnity for spoliations committed upon American commerce. 2. The exclusion, as a question of negotiation, of all doubt of the wrongfulness of the seizure of American vessels for want of the paper called a *rôle d'équipage;* and, 3. A refusal to continue the treaty guarantee of the French West Indies. With these landmarks, settled upon as *ultimata* the 11th of March, it would seem as if, in anticipation of the opening of negotiations, the leisure before the return of letters from Europe could have been advantageously used to bring the necessary instructions to a state requiring no further delay. Colonel Pickering seems, however, to have given them little attention, until compelled to do so; and it was six weeks from the receipt of the answer from France, before they had reached a state to be submitted to the approval of the President. A few days of this delay had been caused by the necessity of removing the public offices to Trenton, on account of the ravages of the yellow fever in Philadelphia. But a much stronger reason existed for it, a hint of which now, for the first time, reached the President, in a letter from Mr. Stoddert, the Secretary of the Navy. That gentleman intimated, in cautious but significant terms, that Mr. Adams's presence was absolutely necessary at Trenton. Simultaneously with the draft of instructions, a letter arrived, signed by Colonel Pickering, but understood to be concurred in by the other heads of department, suggesting the propriety of suspending the mission, at least for some time. Next came a letter from Chief Justice Ellsworth, assigning unusual demands upon his time in his official circuit, as a reason for asking early notice, in case the President should

determine to postpone the mission. The coincidence
was remarkable, to say the least of it. But it seems at
that time to have roused in Mr. Adams no suspicion of
the truth. It decided him, however, to take the advice
of Mr. Stoddert, to go to Trenton ; and to pay a visit
to Judge Ellsworth, at his residence in Middletown, on
the way.

The repugnance which the friends of Mr. Hamilton
entertained to this mission had not been diminished by
time. They felt that its success would be disastrous to
the war policy, the plan of the army, and of co-operation with Britain, and fatal to the hardly won elevation
of their chief. Hence the want of alacrity manifested
in accelerating it, the anxious watch for something
which might embarrass it, and the eagerness to seize
the opportunity when it was thought at last to have
happened. This occurred about the 26th of August,
when the public officers removed to Trenton, at which
time the Secretary of State received a private letter
from Mr. Murray, announcing a new revolution in the
Directory, with strong symptoms of the restoration of
the Jacobins to power, and the resignation of most
of the ministers, including Talleyrand himself. This
letter was immediately submitted to the other heads of
department, and a consultation held, upon the propriety
of making it a basis for transmitting to the President,
contemporaneously with the form of instructions to the
commissioners then nearly ready, a joint remonstrance
against the prosecution of the mission. It was so determined ; and Colonel Pickering, with his customary
activity when his heart was in the work, in forwarding
another copy of the instructions to Chief Justice Ells-

worth, apprised him likewise of the conclusion to which the cabinet had come, hinting, as there is reason to believe, at the expediency of his reinforcing this application to Mr. Adams, by sending another from himself, as if from an independent source. This produced the letter of the chief justice which has already been mentioned. Altogether the combination was formidable enough. It had members and well-wishers far and wide among the class peculiarly enlisted in the views of Mr. Hamilton, all of whom seem to have waited, with their expectations raised to the highest pitch, the issue of one more attempt to overrule the impracticable President.

The manner in which Mr. Adams met this assault seems to have entirely deceived its projectors. Apparently unconscious of what was going on, he looked at the papers submitted to him, with a single eye to the merits of the question offered to his consideration, and expressed the simple and natural conclusion to which they led. In a suspension of the mission for a few weeks, if events in Europe should seem to demand it, he signified no unwillingness to acquiesce. This is the substance of his replies to both the secretaries, Messrs. Pickering and Stoddert, and to Judge Ellsworth, each of whom had written to him. He even went so far as to designate the latter part of October as the limit of the delay, promising in the mean while to be himself at Trenton by the 15th, then and there to judge what it was best, from a view of all the circumstances, to decide. His own opinion, in favor of the prosecution of the mission at the end of the period designated, from a fair comparison of all these papers, can scarcely be mistaken. Yet the hopes which they excited in the persons to whom they were addressed went very much further. Judge Ellsworth construed his letter as suspending the voyage. And the secretaries augured from theirs an increased probability of victory, through the means which a closer approximation with Mr. Adams would furnish. In order the better to concert their measures, Judge Ellsworth was requested to come from Hartford, whilst General Hamilton himself remained at Newark, within call. Colonel Pickering, in the mean time, had so entirely dropped all reserve, in his mode of speaking of the President, as to create in the minds of at least two of the cabinet a conviction that he ought at once to be removed.

This was the end of the fourth and last, as it was the greatest trial in the public life of Mr. Adams. And looking back upon the details of it, as given by all the various parties concerned, the wonder is, that he went through with it in the manner which they describe. With his quick and inflammable temperament it would have occasioned no surprise, had he, at the expense of violent and long-continued altercations with the resolute men around him, perhaps with some loss of personal dignity, painfully succeeded in maintaining his authority. That such a contest had been expected and provided for, there is every reason to believe. Possibly it might have been arranged to make a combined or separate protest against his perseverance, which should drive him to the necessity either of removing his counsellors at once, or of going on in the face of their declared disapprobation. Whatever may have been these calculations, they were destined to be signally disappointed. For he sustained himself without the shadow of a conflict. Mr. Adams paid a brief visit to Chief Justice Ellsworth, at Windsor, on the 3d of October, in which he appears to have expressed the same sentiments to be found in his letters. Judge Ellsworth construed them as he wished; yet some doubts must have sprung up, which drove him to accept Mr. Pickering's invitation to Trenton. The President arrived at that place on the 10th, quite unwell with a severe cold taken on the journey. He met the members of the cabinet with cordiality. Yet one of the number perceived a difference in his treatment of them, especially of the New England members. Mr. Hamilton was soon on the spot also. All awaited the moment for a trial of strength.

At last it seemed really to have arrived, and under circumstances singularly favorable to the success of the combination. For the news had just come of the only successes of the British expedition under the Duke of York, in Holland, and of the victorious progress of the Russians under Suwarrow in Switzerland. Grant a delay of but a few days, and the next ships might announce Louis the Eighteenth established on the throne of the Bourbons. Such was the cry. The excitement was at its height, and the eagerness to gain a postponement could scarcely be kept within control. Mr. Adams watched the tone of the conversations, and wrote privately to his wife an expression of his amazement at the scene. The vehemence he found in others had the effect of making him perfectly calm. He had no faith in the predictions, and he penetrated the motives of those who were making use of them. He saw it was not a delay merely, but a defeat of the mission, that was anticipated. He foresaw the possibility of a general peace which might insulate America, and in this he proved correct. Whether he had any warning of what his ministers had in store for him, or whether his own sagacity sufficed to comprehend it, is not disclosed. At all events, he was calm and perfectly prepared when, on the evening of the 15th of October, he summoned the cabinet to a meeting. They came, filled with expectation. He began the conference by laying before them the draft of instructions to the commissioners, prepared by the Secretary of State, and sent for his approbation to Quincy, but not yet adopted, on some points of which he still desired their advice. It was accordingly discussed, amended, and finally met their unanimous approval. But this process consumed much time. It had got to be eleven o'clock, too late to begin upon a new discussion. The President started no further propositions, and the members felt that it was no more than proper to disperse. They did so without reluctance, considering the struggle as only put off, perhaps until morning. Great, indeed, must their amazement have been, when, instead of a new summons, two of them received, before breakfast, a laconic direction from the President, in writing, that the papers agreed upon for the use of the commissioners should be forthwith made out, and that the frigate United States should be put in readiness to receive them, and set sail for France on or before the 1st of the coming month.

At this remote period, the tone used by the cabinet officers in complaining of the issue of this contest, appears not a little extravagant. They treat the President as if he had wilfully set a trap for them ; as if he had deceived and cheated them out of all chance of opposing his wishes; as if they were the aggrieved persons, because he had not consented to run into the snare which they had set to entangle him. They now imputed to him a sudden fit of caprice, just as they had done in November, when he refused to adopt their draft of a speech, and just as they had done in February, when Mr. Murray was first nominated. And they labored to make out of their studied efforts to fasten upon him some previous marks of acquiescence in their own opinions, the evidence to establish the charge. A calm survey of his course confutes all this. Indeed, the admissions which here and there occur in their own letters, of their fears of his disposition towards their policy, sufficiently prove their distrust of all these attributions. Else what need of the elaborate combinations made to overrule his will, beginning in November of the preceding year, and steadily kept up until now? Did these not sufficiently show the sense entertained of the strength and energy of character which it was indispensable to overcome? Yet, the favorite charge against Mr. Adams, with which they succeeded in making some impression against him on the public mind, was wavering and inconsistency! This seems like assuming that wavering and inconsistency, in the face of a combination so powerful as this, could effect about as much in executing a consistent policy as the most persevering firmness. Up to this time, whatever else had been said of Mr. Adams, not one of these persons, or any others, had ever disputed his decision and his energy. These were the characteristics which had been the most fully developed in the course of his career, and made the basis of his reputation as a public man. Surely, at this late stage, there is no likelihood that he would begin to develop symptoms of a wholly different and opposite character. Those symptoms might, indeed, have been perceptible, had he acted in any other manner than he did ; had he given way upon any essential point, or prayed for any intermediate concession from his opponents. They are not deducible from any fair construction of the whole tenor of his language and action during these months of trial. His purpose was plain at the outset, and the measures which he took to execute it were simple, easily to be understood, and surely calculated to reach their end. No doubt or delay was interposed by himself, although his hopes of success seem never to have been very sanguine. From first to last, the ruling motive was to rescue, with credit to the country, the imperilled principle of neutrality in the wars of Europe, to which he had all his life been devoted. Neither is it to be questioned that he viewed with alarm the permanent military organization, which others, under his official sanction, were seeking to fasten on the country. He was still essentially the same man that he was when he distrusted in the Revolution the dictatorial powers conferred even on Washington. Hence when the moment came, in which there was ground for supposing peace might be restored, he did not suffer it to pass away unused. The result was that peace was actually made. The clouds rolled away from the political sky. And however evere the trials through which he passed to attain it, however deeply his name was loaded with obloquy by both the contending parties, he might justly have said of this action, as he did to his wife in the memorable case of Independence : "I can see that the end is more than worth all the means. And that posterity will triumph, even though we should rue."

On the 5th of November, the commissioners sailed for their destination.

In view of the probable consequences had Mr. Adams permitted himself to be overruled, this independent act appears fully to justify the terms he subsequently used in defending it, as "the wisest, the most resolute and disinterested action of his life."

Satisfied with the accomplishment of his object, the President retained no appearance of ill-will to his recalcitrating counsellors. Only two days after his decision on the embassy, he drew up his customary call upon the heads of department, for their views of the topics proper to be presented to the consideration of congress in his opening speech. This call was as freely answered as in former cases; and Mr. Adams used the materials thus supplied him as he had always done. One little variation, however, may deserve to be noted. The drafts presented by the Secretaries of State and of the Treasury, were not adopted to the same extent as heretofore, and greater recourse was had to that furnished by the Secretary of the Navy. As a whole, the speech is far more the emanation of his own mind than either of its predecessors. The main question which had agitated all parties, the mission to France, was dispatched in a few words, so ordered that all might assent to them. Allusion was particularly made to the differences which had occurred among the commissioners appointed under two articles of the treaty with

Great Britain, and which had put a stop to the proceedings. A revision of the judicial system was recommended; and, in conclusion, an earnest exhortation was given to a perseverance in defensive measures pending the negotiations. The speech is quite short, but in dignity and simplicity it holds its rank with all the other public papers of this administration. It was coldly responded to by the Senate, in which Mr. Hamilton's friends preponderated; and warmly by the House of Representatives under the guidance of John Marshall, who this year commenced that career at home which shed its lustre on some of the highest posts in the government during a prolonged life. He was the exponent of the moderate section of federalists, representing the Southern and Middle States, whom the earlier events in this administration had returned to congress in unusual numbers, and who now gave a tone to the proceedings by no means satisfactory to the more extreme division. For the most part they approved of the policy of Mr. Adams, and favored a retreat from the violent measures of the last year. As a consequence, all efforts to develop the policy of a large army were abandoned; loans or taxes were authorized to as small an extent as possible, and a considerable number showed symptoms of a desire even to repeal the Sedition Law.

Indeed, it must be now conceded that the greatest and most fatal error of the federal party is to be found in the enactment of this law. The other measure, touching the relations of aliens, especially in time of war, which was made equally the burden of complaint by the opposition, although it vested extraordinary powers in the hands of the President, does not, on the whole, seem indefensible, under the general right of self-protection which inheres in every form of social organization, and which no process of reasoning will succeed in practically doing away. But it cannot be denied that the attempt to punish individuals for mere expressions of opinion of public measures and public men, to subject them perhaps to fine and imprisonment, and certainly to heavy and burdensome charges in their defence, for exercising a latitude of speech, however extreme, in the heat and excitement attending the political conflicts of a free country, verged too closely upon an abridgment of the liberty of speech and of the press to be quite reconcilable to the theory of free institutions. It furnished a very strong ground of concentration to the opponents of the administration, of which they eagerly availed themselves under the guidance of Mr. Jefferson, moderated and softened by the more balanced judgment of Mr. Madison. Hence sprang up the celebrated resolutions of Virginia and Kentucky, which furnish internal evidence of the sources from which they respectively emanated. These resolutions have been made, more or less, the basis of theories and movements in the United States ever since; but nevertheless, if they should ever be pushed to their practical consequences, it is certain that they must make a national government impossible. Thus it is and ever has been in the conflicts of men, that collision itself produces extremes of opinion, which invariably show themselves in the simultaneous development of opposite errors. And the change which time brings about between parties, reverses the doctrines less than it does the persons who proclaim them. No government can afford to relax the powers which it is called to wield, to the extent that its enemies will be likely to demand. If the federalists encroached upon freedom, their opponents equally bordered upon license; if the former tended to make rigid the muscles of the law, the latter strove to unstring the nerves of liberty. Government prospers only as it stands equidistant from these extremes, alike insensible to menace and incapable of wrong.

The origin of these laws, which have become a word of fear to the popular ear in the United States, it is not material here to investigate, excepting so far as Mr. Adams can be supposed to have been concerned. That he had no hand in suggesting them is very certain. That he declined to insert in his speeches recommendations, submitted by his officers, to restrict the rights of aliens and of naturalization, is likewise certain. Yet when they had been once passed upon by the two houses of congress, he had no such constitutional doubts as would justify his declining to affix his official signature to them, nor any scruples about putting them in execution, in an emergency. On the other hand, he had no confidence in their value as effective measures, and very little inclination to attempt experiments. It was this well-understood state of his mind that caused great dissatisfaction among those federalists who had favored their adoption. The traces are frequently visible in such of their letters as have come to light. There was in this respect a radical difference of opinion between these persons and Mr. Adams, which shows itself incidentally in other acts of his administration.

His disposition was naturally affectionate and his feelings tender, so that when not stirred by any unusual and positive emotion, there was a constant tendency to be lenient in deciding upon conduct. This may best be illustrated in the various sentences by courts-martial which came up for his approval; in almost all of which he is found averse to the confirmation of harsh judgments. It is perceptible in the sluggishness with which he moved under the instigations of his cabinet to execute the laws now in question. And it becomes striking in the proceedings attending the condemnations for treason, a more particular account of which will presently be given. From all these circumstances, joined to the fact of an almost total absence of allusion to them in his private correspondence, it is fair to infer that Mr. Adams's participation in the Alien and Sedition Laws was confined to his official act of signature. So far as this goes, he is responsible for them, but no further. Yet his name has been associated with them ever since, as much as if he had been the sole contriver of the arbitrary policy which they have been supposed to symbolize. In this respect more unfortunate than his predecessor, General Washington, who is ever associated with all the most brilliant aspirations for human freedom, and yet of whom nothing is more certain than that he actually approved and defended these obnoxious statutes, and that, had he been in the executive chair at the time of their passage, they would equally have received from him a cheerful signature.

That great luminary was, at the moment reached in the present narrative, just setting on the horizon. Never more active in the mere operations of political canvasses than during the preceding year, his death removed the last tie which bound the federal party together, and saved him the painful necessity, to which some indiscreet friends were driving him, of deciding whether to enter once more the arena of contention in person or not.   Early in the summer of 1799, the idea had been thrown out by individuals, the friends of Mr. Hamilton, of effecting the displacement of Mr. Adams by appealing to Washington to come forth and consent to fill the President's chair for the third time.   The plan had been submitted in secret to the members of the cabinet, who had connived at rather than promoted it, up to the time when the final struggle for predominance took place at Trenton.   That once over, no further restraint seems to have bound them.   Consultations took place in the New England States, the result of which was that Gouverneur Morris of New York was commissioned to address a formal supplication to the venerable chief to consent to help the country in this hour of its distress.

Without venturing to question the motives that prompted this movement, it may be permitted here to venture a doubt whether its authors had sufficiently considered the state of the times, or foreseen the embarrassments into which they were about to plunge the person to whom they probably wished nothing but good.   So bitter had party feelings become, and so sanguine the opposition under Mr. Jefferson's lead, that even Washington could no longer hope to stand as the type of the sentiments of a whole people.   But any thing less than unanimity would have thrown a cloud over the closing splendor of his day.   Neither is

there any reason to suppose that he ever thought differently. At all events, he was never called to express
an opinion. The letter of Gouverneur Morris, which
would have forced him to it, found him on his death-
bed, preparing for other scenes than those disturbed
by the stormy passions of men. As he passed away,
the effect was for the moment to calm those passions
into silence. Persons of all shades of opinion united
to do honor to his memory. Probably Mr. Adams had
not been made aware of the secret movements alluded
to. He had not been insensible to the use that had
been made of the influence of Washington to restrain
the freedom of his own action, but it had inspired no
suspicion of the motives of that hero, and it in no way
diminished the regrets he felt at his decease. Among
the various tributes paid to his excellence, that given
by the President in his reply to the address of the
Senate on the occasion is remarkable for its feeling.
Two passages of it may serve as an illustration:

"In the multitude of my thoughts and recollections on
this melancholy event, you will permit me only to say,
that I have seen him in the days of adversity, in some
of the scenes of his deepest distress and most trying
perplexities; I have also attended him in his highest
elevation and most prosperous felicity; with uniform
admiration of his wisdom, moderation, and constancy.

"The life of our Washington cannot suffer by a
comparison with those, of other countries, who have
been most celebrated and exalted by fame. The attributes and decorations of royalty could have only
served to eclipse the majesty of those virtues which

made him, from being a modest citizen, a more re-
splendent luminary. Misfortune, had he lived, could
hereafter have sullied his glory only with those superficial minds, who, believing that characters and actions
are marked by success alone, rarely deserve to enjoy it.
Malice could never blast his honor, and envy made
him a singular exception to her universal rule. For
himself he had lived long enough to life and to glory.
For his fellow-citizens, if their prayers could have been
answered, he would have been immortal. For me, his
departure is at a most unfortunate moment. Trusting,
however, in the wise and righteous dominion of Providence over the passions of men and the results of their
counsels and actions, as well as over their lives, nothing
remains for me but humble resignation."

With this melancholy event faded the last hope of
preserving harmony in the counsels of the federalists.
Mr. Hamilton, in losing the hold he had obtained
upon the confidence of General Washington, was compelled to surrender all further expectations of controlling their policy. He foresaw that the command of
the army, which he virtually held already, would not
be conferred upon him in terms. Many of the induce-
ments which had tempted him to aspire to it, had
already been weakened by the unexpected turn affairs
had taken both abroad and at home. The policy which
he had originated was in ruins, and he only looked to
save detached portions of it. But the resentment which
he felt against the individual whose action had most
contributed to destroy it, had taken the place of other
emotions. It showed itself most decisively throughout

the attempts that were from this time made to bring about some sort of co-operation between the sections of the party. Of these, the largest in numbers sided with the President, whilst the minority made up in talents and activity for that deficiency. All were, however, equally sensible of the pressure of the united opposition, and nearly all were disinclined to forget the risk of a common discomfiture, and perhaps a lasting dispersion, in a mere conflict of personal ascendency. In their minds, the danger of the success of Mr. Jefferson was imminent, and the salvation of the country from that peril, a vital question. In order to escape it, all the federalists in congress were summoned to meet together, for the purpose of devising some means of establishing concert in their future action. The immediate question related to the candidates to be presented at the election for the Presidency and Vice-Presidency soon to come on, which involved the necessity of determining the position of Mr. Adams. The minority warmly and earnestly demanded that he should be set aside. But when urged to name a substitute, they had none to present with the smallest prospect of success. It was generally felt that the retirement of Mr. Adams would only open the way to the accession of Mr. Jefferson.

Sensible of the truth of this, especially in New England, from whence many of the minority came, they found themselves at last compelled to offer a compromise. They consented to accept Mr. Adams as one candidate, provided that General Charles Cotesworth Pinckney, the same gentleman who had the year before so cheerfully submitted to the military precedence of Mr. Hamilton, could be adopted as the other, and no understanding made of the intent in filling the respective places. But even this concession was more than it was possible to obtain. The overruling objection was that the suspicion it would raise of bad faith would inevitably elect Mr. Jefferson. Hence, the best that could be done was to agree that the two persons named should be equally supported by all the federalists throughout the country; it being, however, understood, that Mr. Adams, though designed to fill the first office, was subject to those chances of a different result which the peculiar operation of the constitutional provision might naturally present. Such are the terms of this compact as explained by persons belonging to the minority. Mr. Hamilton seems to have been dissatisfied with them, though his friends acquiesced. Mr. Adams had no agency direct or indirect in producing them. The age of personal solicitation for high office had not arrived.

In the mean time, however, two events occurred of great importance. The first was, the election of the legislature which would determine the political character of New York at the presidential election. Here the influence of Mr. Hamilton had been exerted in furtherance of the design he now avowed, to set aside Mr. Adams in favor of Mr. Pinckney. Upon that pivot the selection of the federal candidates in the city had been made to turn just as it did at the election four years before. The consequence was that the moderate class of men were neglected, from a fear that they might lean to Mr. Adams. Mr. Burr, who saw the error, immediately adapted his policy to the contingency, and succeeded in connecting them with the opposition. In this way, General Gates, always friendly to Mr. Adams, George Clinton, and the Livingstons, were drawn into a combination with which they had little affinity beyond a common enmity to Mr. Hamilton, and which, by attracting the doubtful voters in the city, effected the final return of the State to its old revolutionary associations, against New England, and with the adverse influence of Virginia.

The other event was the execution of the design the President had for some time entertained of changing the members of his cabinet. With Mr. McHenry he had never been entirely satisfied, on the score of his incompetency to the laborious office to which he had been assigned. Complaints of him had abounded ever since the commencement of the administration, but they had grown more and more loud after his duties were increased by the difficulties with France. The traces of this are visible in the correspondence of General Washington, of Hamilton, of Wolcott, and many other leading men. They reach even to a manifestation of impatience with the President for not acting with more energy in removing him. But Mr. Adams, as has been already remarked, entered upon his post with no disposition to make changes in the administration, and least of all in the case of Mr. McHenry, for whom, in his personal intercourse, he had learned to cherish some regard. There can be little doubt that the intentions of that officer were of the best; but as little, that his capacity and energy were by no means corresponding. The consequence was, that he became insensibly dependent upon the abilities of Mr. Hamilton for aid in conducting the details of his department, subject, however, to vacillation and change under the disturbing force applied from time to time by the will of the President himself. The effect was to present to the world an appearance of irregularity and uncertainty, which materially contributed to shake confidence in the system of the administration. These symptoms grew more perceptible as the difference between the President and Mr. Hamilton became more wide. To the latter Mr. McHenry habitually deferred, as the director of his official administration. To him he looked, and not to Mr. Adams, as the guide of his political system. Hence his deference to the wishes of the latter became cold, reluctant, and dilatory, as the breach with Mr. Hamilton grew more positive.

But Mr. Adams had now reached a point when he foresaw that a necessity might occur for the co-operation of some one in the reduction of the military system who sympathized more closely with his own views. Washington was no longer the nominal commander-in-chief. His decease would involve the necessity of deciding upon the position of Mr. Hamilton as the next in command, on which he had made up his mind beforehand. And he knew Mr. McHenry's relations too well, and had experienced too much of his opposition in his cabinet, not to comprehend the necessity of his removal, if he desired to make sure of the execution of his own policy. Yet there is no knowing how long he might have delayed his action, but for an accidental conversation which terminated in an open variance. Of this conversation, Mr. McHenry afterwards furnished to Mr. Hamilton his own version. It is fair to infer from it at least this, that Mr. Adams lost his temper, a failing for which Mr. Hamilton afterwards made him pay a severe penalty, and for which he sometimes reproached himself. He was thus led on to say many unguarded, and some harsh things, that might have been better omitted, at least in presence of an enemy on the watch to take advantage of them. So far as they wounded the feelings of Mr. McHenry, Mr. Adams afterwards regretted them, for no man ever bore less malice in his composition. But he did not regret the step to which they brought him. McHenry's resignation was no sooner offered than accepted, to take effect in three weeks.

The case of Colonel Pickering came next. Falling into his office rather by accident, he had manifested in the performance of its duties great industry, punctuality, courage, and qualifications, if not of the first class, certainly far from discreditable to himself or to the country which he had been called to represent. His public papers have the merit of clearness, directness, and simplicity. Had he contented himself with an exclusive devotion to his duties, and a faithful co-operation with the objects of his chief, there never could have been a question of his removal. But herein was his great mistake. Never much used to the control of his vehement impulses, he construed his position as permitting him the right not only to dispute in private, but to counteract both in public and private, such portions of the measures of the President as he happened to disapprove. Neither was this all. He did not hesitate to use the information which he obtained by virtue of his confidential relation, the more effectually to promote his views.

The acts and the language of Mr. Adams were noted
and reported, not less than the details of his official
policy, for the sake of either controlling or defeating it,
and at any rate of discrediting him. No similar practice has occurred since that period. Of the extent to
which it was carried, Mr. Adams was never made fully
aware. If he had known what has since been disclosed,
it is impossible to suppose that Colonel Pickering could
have remained in his cabinet a day after the 6th of
July, 1798. Why he knew no more than he did, might
cause a little wonder, considering that Colonel Pickering was not a man of concealments, if all history did not
show that people around a ruler, whose evidence is really
worth having, are seldom forward to acquaint him with
unpleasant truth. He did know enough, however, from
the revelations made at the time of Mr. Murray's nomination, and still more at Trenton, during the memorable struggle six months later, to become convinced
that his duty to himself required the presence of an adviser in the State department in whose fidelity he could
have full confidence. Accordingly, he seized the opportunity now presented by the resignation of Mr.
McHenry, to extend to Colonel Pickering the offer of
retiring in the same manner. This was done in a
perfectly unexceptionable form, although no room was
left to doubt the alternative in case of his refusal. The
reply of Colonel Pickering is not in his customary style.
It is not direct, nor logical in adapting the premises to
his conclusion. It dwells upon his poverty in a manner
that, if it meant anything, seems to deprecate the stroke
which his own conduct, as he could not fail to know,
had deprived him of the right to resent. For his col-

leagues, who had been best acquainted with it, manifested no surprise at the sentence. Some of them had expected it would happen earlier. If then he felt it to be inevitable, it would have been more dignified not to plead in mitigation of it. Especially as he was full of schemes of vengeance, which he communicated at once to Mr. Hamilton, offering to supply him with many facts which his official station had put in his power, to make up what he called "a frank and bold exposure of Mr. Adams."*

This intimation met with a favorable reception from the person to whom it was addressed. The nominations of John Marshall, of Virginia, as Secretary of State, in the place of Colonel Pickering, and of Samuel Dexter, of Massachusetts, as Secretary of War, instead of Mr. McHenry, sufficiently indicated the intentions of the President. They had been received with satisfaction by the moderate federalists, whilst they were viewed by the others as precluding all further insinuations of bargaining with the opposite party, in which they had largely indulged, and, at the same time, a sure presage of the downfall of their own influence. Anxious to ascertain, by personal observation, the probability of averting this calamity by the substitution of General Pinckney for Mr. Adams as the President for the next term, Mr. Hamilton undertook a journey through Massachusetts, New Hampshire, and Rhode Island, the States where the people were supposed to be the most likely to make difficulties, on account of their attachment to the latter. This was

---

* *Hamilton's Works*, vol. vi. p. 443.

executed in the month of June, 1800. The issue was
not favorable to his hopes. He found "the leaders of
the first class generally right, but the leaders of the
second class were too much disposed to favor Mr.
Adams." The remedy was an exposure of the sort
which Colonel Pickering had proposed. Of course,
he and McHenry could be relied upon for aid in supplying the materials. But that was not enough. Recourse must be had to another person still in place, and
able to betray all the movements of the cabinet down
to the last moment. That person was Oliver Wolcott,
Secretary of the Treasury, whose fidelity Mr. Adams
never for an instant suspected; who had always so carefully regulated his external deportment, that no one
could suppose him likely to become the secret channel
through which all the most confidential details of the
administration, of which he was a part, should be furnished, with the intent to destroy its head.* Yet such
is the fact which history now most unequivocally dis-
closes. Instead of being too suspicious, as the enemies
of his own household chose to describe him, the President had, in the excess of his confidence, retained in
his bosom the most subtle and venomous serpent of
them all.

The session of congress had been marked by a more
decided preponderance of the federalists in both
branches than had been the case for years. But in the
House the accessions had not been of the more violent
class. The effect of this was visible in the legislation,
the character of which was moderate, creditable, and

---

* Wolcott to Hamilton. *Works*, vol. vi. p. 444.

judicious. All thoughts of the great military organization which had been contemplated, were at once abandoned. The plans of expenditure which threatened severely to burden the growing energies of the people were reduced; whilst measures were continued to enforce and confirm the system of naval defences, and to persevere in the interdict of all commercial intercourse with France. Several important laws were enacted of a purely domestic character, calculated to quiet past difficulties, or to develop the resources of the country. The dulness of ordinary legislation was now and then relieved by eloquent debates. The most important of these related to an instance of extradition of a seaman charged with crimes committed on board of a British frigate. It was the case of Thomas Nash, or, according to the opposition, who insisted that he was an American and improperly surrendered, of Jonathan Robbins. This discussion elicited a display of the abilities of the House on both sides, and terminated in a speech from John Marshall, which at once settled the question, and established his own reputation as the first man of the assembly. Taken all in all, there are few portions of the legislative history of the country, to which the historian can look back with more pride and satisfaction than to the details of this session. The Lower House was yet a deliberative assembly, confining itself to the objects before it, and discussing them in a business-like and yet a comprehensive spirit; and the Senate was a select council of statesmen, true to their duties, not ambitious of logomachy, and not making their honorable station subsidiary to other objects with which it has no natural or legitimate connection. If the federalists have sins to answer for, that of letting down the dignity of the government is not among them. The result of their action at this period was greatly calculated to increase the public confidence in the wisdom and discretion which they brought to the direction of affairs. That such would have been the effect, had it not been for the untoward nature of the events that followed, there is strong reason to believe.

Previously to entering upon these, it is necessary to explain one other circumstance which contributed to keep open the breach now made in the ranks of the federal party. Some time in the spring of 1798, there had taken place in Northampton County, in Pennsylvania, as has already been mentioned, an armed resistance to the levy of the direct tax, which spread into two or three of the neighboring counties, and for a few days assumed an appearance so alarming as to justify the President's proclamation and orders to equip a military force to put it down. The mere apparition of this force proved sufficient to effect the object. The men who had taken the lead in the disorders, being deserted by their fellows, were made prisoners, and handed over for trial to the courts. The principal one was a person by name John Fries, who was found with arms in his hands, acting as a chief, although he seems to have possessed few qualities to recommend him for any such elevation. His associates, generally from among the German population of the State, proved to be of a low order of intelligence, utterly unequal to devising any scheme of concerted resistance to rightful authority. At the next term of the United States circuit court, which took place in a few weeks, Fries was put upon his trial, on the charge of treason, and, after nine days spent in the proceedings, was found guilty by the verdict of a jury. The result was immediately communicated to Mr. Adams, at Quincy, by Colonel Pickering and by Mr. Wolcott, in separate letters, expressive of their satisfaction. The latter incidentally mentioned that Mr. Lewis, of counsel for the prisoner, had on all occasions during the trial insisted that the offence committed did not amount to treason. He likewise reported the remark as coming from Fries, that persons of greater consequence had been at the bottom of the business.

Both these suggestions seem to have had much weight in the mind of Mr. Adams. He deeply felt the responsibility imposed upon him. To Colonel Pickering he replied in these words:

"The issue of this investigation has opened a train of very serious contemplations to me, which will require the closest attention of my best understanding, and will prove a severe trial to my heart."

To the attorney-general, Mr. Lee, he sent a request to obtain a sight of Mr. Lewis's reasons for his opinion, whilst to Mr. Wolcott he wrote for information as to the character of Fries, the nature and extent of the combination of which he appeared to be the head, and the truth of his intimation, that others of greater importance were behind the scenes. He ended with these words:

"It highly concerns the people of the United States, and especially the federal government, that, in the whole progress and ultimate conclusion of this affair, neither humanity be unnecessarily afflicted, nor public justice be essentially violated, nor the public safety endangered."

These letters were received by the persons to whom they were addressed, with some dismay. They did not understand why the President should entertain his own views of the law, after the proper court had adjudicated upon it, and they honestly thought that the public safety required an immediate example to be made of Fries. "Painful as is the idea of taking the life of a man," said Pickering, "I feel a calm and solid satisfaction that an opportunity is now presented, in executing the just sentence of the law, to crush that spirit, which, if not overthrown and destroyed, may proceed in its career, and overturn the government."

Obviously two different views of duty are here presented, both conscientiously held, but having their source in radical differences of natural character. A conflict between them was, for the time, postponed by the decision of the court that condemned Fries, which granted a new trial, on the ground that one of the jury was proved to have prejudged the case. Another long and very elaborate hearing followed, Judge Chase now presiding instead of Judge Iredell, the issue of which was the same as before, the condemnation of Fries. This involved the fate of two other persons dependent upon the views taken of the same general testimony. Once more the question of ordering their

execution came up for the consideration of the President. It was just at the moment when the change was
taking place in his cabinet officers, and whilst but three
persons remained to advise him. To those three he
therefore submitted, on the 20th of May, a series of
thirteen questions, the drift of which sufficiently shows
the state of his own mind.* The answer, given on the
same day, showed a division of opinion among the
three; Mr. Wolcott remaining unshaken in his belief
that the execution of all three was demanded in order
"to inspire the well-disposed with confidence in the
government, and the malevolent with terror;" the
other two believing that the execution of Fries would
"be enough to show the power of the laws to punish."
But even they inclined to the execution of the three,
rather than to have all three released.

In this case the cabinet could not complain that they
had not been consulted at every step. But that seems
to have made no difference in the feeling with which
at least one of the disaffected viewed the direction of
the President, given the next day, that a pardon should
be made out for all the offenders. As usual, an effort
was made to prove inconsistency, and from thence to
deduce a personal motive for the act. It was a "fatal
concession to his enemies." The act was "popular
in Pennsylvania." Such was the tone of the disappointed federalists, who saw in it, and, so far, very
correctly, another divergency from the policy which

---

* The view of treason opened in this case there is no room
here to consider. It must infallibly come up for revision at some
time or other in the courts of the United States.

they would have introduced into the federal government. In truth, there is no need of searching deep to find causes for the opposite opinions generated by this event. They lie thickly spread upon the surface of the correspondence during this administration, much of which is laid before the world in the present work. They are the legitimate offspring of the division of opinion into three forms, which has been distinctly developed in the action of all the administrations in America since the first, and which must ever show itself in nations enjoying free institutions, wherever they may be found.

This is the period when the administration of Mr. Adams for the first time appears as a consistent whole. His cabinet was now substantially in harmony with him. Only one member of it remained to repine at the policy indicated, secretly to wish it defeated, to disparage the acts and motives of his chief and his colleagues, and to betray all the proceedings to their enemy.* Henceforth there is no room for details, as the administration pursued the even tenor of its way, laboring to smooth off the external difficulties with which it had to contend. In this task it was eminently successful. Mr. Marshall, the new Secretary of State, set in motion a negotiation which put an end to the irritations that had followed the inability of the two different commissions under Mr. Jay's treaty with Great

---

* " If I can escape from the toils without loss of character, I will take care not to expose myself to such *risques* as I have of late encountered." Such is Mr. Wolcott's confession of his state of mind at the time of his resignation.

Britain to come to an understanding. And out of the obscurity the signs of peace began to dawn even on the continent of France. Napoleon had at last stepped in to the place which he had long kept in his eye, pushing down, on the one hand, the relics of the old *régime*, and, on the other, the crumbling columns of the revolutionary temple. To him a quarrel with America seemed purely preposterous. It followed, as a natural consequence, that peace became only a question of terms. He who was busy in holding in his vigorous grasp the reins of Europe, was not likely to have his attention long turned aside by the complaints from the United States of an anterior policy for which he himself had no respect. Yet the conqueror of Marengo could not be expected to consent to have concessions dictated to him by any power which had not ready means at hand to enforce them at the point of the bayonet. The American commissioners, fully conscious of the delicacy of their situation, accommodated themselves to it with dexterity and judgment. The treaty, which was the result, like many other instruments of the same sort before and since, touched but lightly on the causes of grievance between the two countries, and seemed to grant little redress to the wrongs of which America justly complained. But it gained what was of more worth to them ; and that was, a termination of all further danger of war, and a prevention of the causes of future difficulties. And even what it lost of redress was the consequence not so much of the treaty itself as of the temper of the Senate, which caused one of the articles to be expunged as a condition of its ratification. The nature and consequences of this amendment will be explained presently. It is sufficient now to say that these measures had the effect of re-establishing the neutral policy of the United States, which had been for years in imminent peril, and of smoothing the way to the period of great prosperity which followed. It is difficult to imagine any other result of the turmoil and conflict of opinions that had so long prevailed, which, on the whole, deserved to insure a better return of gratitude to its authors, from the great body of citizens most deeply interested in the country's welfare.

Yet, strange as it may seem, from that day to this, an award of merit for such a successful termination of the difficult task of this administration has been entirely withheld. The causes of this must now be explained, however painful may be the task. The federal party could have easily borne the trial of the appeal to arms against France and of a direct tax. It might have gone safely through the fire of the Alien and Sedition Laws, and its corollaries of the Virginia and Kentucky resolutions. Possibly it would have breasted the odium of an army needlessly large, and organized for other than its ostensible objects. But it could not be expected to endure the cross of *bad faith*. The moment when an active minority determined to adopt a line of conduct marked by indirectness of purpose even to treachery, was the moment when wise and patriotic citizens had reason to foresee that shipwreck must inevitably ensue.

Although the truce which had been agreed upon by the two divisions of the party, at the close of the session of 1800, had been predicated upon a concession of a fair and equal support of Mr. Adams and Charles Cotesworth Pinckney, as candidates for the highest office, the designation of Mr. Adams for the preference being rather understood than avowed, it very soon became known that Mr. Hamilton and his friends felt at liberty to exert themselves to the utmost, in secretly decrying the character and conduct of one of the persons, for the sake of creating an ultimate preponderance for the other. The word was confidentially given out that Mr. Adams must be sacrificed. To this end information was to be privately furnished of the defects in his character, which were relied upon as a justification for this extraordinary course. As yet but a very small por tion of the correspondence, through which this plan was attempted, has found its way to the light. To dwell on its unpleasant details is no part of the present purpose. It bears on its face the verdict which posterity will not fail to pass upon it. All the prominent actors betray their sense of its character so clearly as to make forbearance to expose it no virtue. The letters of Oliver Wolcott, of Fisher Ames, of George Cabot, of James McHenry, of Benjamin Goodhue, all equally plead guilty to the tortuous expedients of political rancor. Yet nobody will charge them with deliberate malice or dishonesty. They were servants of a will stronger than their own; of a spirit that could never brook a superior nor abide an equal; of one whose disappointment had been as great as his aspirations, and whose self-restraint yielded under the temptation of wreaking his vengeance upon the person who had occasioned it. Mr. Hamilton's rivalries, whether with Jefferson, with John Adams, or with Aaron Burr, were never kept within the limits of defensive or moderate warfare; and to this cause it was that he owed his premature and inglorious downfall.

Mr. Adams on his side was not of a spirit to be daunted by denunciation, or to permit himself to be sacrificed without a murmur. He had formed his own opinions of the policy of Mr. Hamilton and his friends, which had impaired his confidence in them, not less than theirs had become impaired in him. The measure which they had first proposed to him under the name of *co-operation* with Great Britain, he now fully believed to have been intended only as a preliminary to an alliance, offensive and defensive, which would have shut out all prospect of further preserving a neutrality in the wars of Europe.* And indeed, it is difficult at this distance of time to resist the conviction, that such must have been the consequence of their system, even conceding that they may not themselves have foreseen it. But such an admission can be made only at a heavy expense to their sagacity, so that the inference from the testimony on record is rather that they acted from design. At all events their course had so far committed them, as to render great prudence advisable in avoiding to give cause for an exposure of these differences. Such prudence they unfortunately did not exercise. Intelligence of their endeavors to destroy his character and reputation

---

* Mr. Gibbs, whose admissions must be taken as superseding the necessity of further citation of authorities, so far as they relate to the policy of this section of the federalists, concedes that "an alliance *might* have taken place;" but he says, "it would have been for common defence." Vol. ii. p. 219. Mr. Hamilton, however, expressly declares that he contemplated offensive operations. *Works,* vol. v. p. 184.

soon reached the ears of Mr. Adams, as it could scarcely fail to do, however secretly they might labor. In this crisis he was not likely to confine himself to defence. Cool and collected when summoned to act in public on any emergency, he was seldom in the habit of resisting his natural impetuosity in the less guarded hours of private intercourse and familiar conversation. Then it was, that he would give to his language the full impress of his vehement will. He spoke out his thought with the force which only indignation gives. This must be confessed to have been his greatest disqualification for success in public life, which requires, above all things, an open countenance with closed lips, the offspring of an impassible heart. Mr. Adams had nothing of this. His nature, though placable, was ardent, and it occasionally impelled him to say more than he really meant, which he sometimes himself described as rodomontade, and to express even what he did mean much too sharply. These were errors, it is true, but at least they sprang from qualities thoroughly honest. The consequence was, that his language excited a greater degree of sensibility in the objects of his attack from its unsparing directness. He charged the hostility waged by Mr. Hamilton and his friends against himself to their disappointment in failing to establish through his aid the desired connection with Great Britain, against France. And his statement may now be affirmed to have been in substance correct, without the necessity of implying the existence of wrong motives in them. Yet such a charge could not fail at that time to strike deeply at the influence of those at whom it was levelled. The evidence how much they felt it, is visible in their secret letters.

The danger was great that even the relatively small popular force they could command, would dwindle away, and leave nothing but leaders.   It was plain, too, that their plan of setting aside Mr. Adams by obtaining an equal vote for General Pinckney, was breaking down. There were those in New England, who, when they learned the object of the scheme, could not be induced to sacrifice Mr. Adams.   Mr. Hamilton had become convinced of it by personal observation.   The consequence was inevitable, that the success of the federal party would make Mr. Adams President.   And to this, involving, as he foresaw it must, the loss of all power over the next administration, he was not prepared to bring his mind to submit.   He proceeded to take his measures, in order to prevent it.

It has already been mentioned that Mr. Hamilton, immediately upon his return from New England, applied to the Secretary of the Treasury for details of confidential transactions in the cabinet, to be used by him "among discreet persons," to destroy their faith in Mr. Adams. But this was not the only object he had in view; for in the same letter he added an intimation of a design to write to Mr. Adams, touching certain reports in circulation of allusions made by him, in conversation, to the existence of a British faction, of which he, Hamilton, was named as one, and to demand an explanation.   He added these words: "Mr. Adams's friends are industrious in propagating the idea, to defeat the efforts to unite for Pinckney.   The inquiry I propose, may furnish an antidote and vindicate character.   What think you of this idea?   For my part, I can set malice at defiance."

From this language it would seem clear, that the project of calling upon Mr. Adams had its source in other motives, than a quick sense of personal injury. It was a politic movement designed to neutralize the labors of Mr. Adams's friends to defeat the success of Mr. Pinckney. The effect of calumny upon himself, he professed not to apprehend.

Mr. Wolcott replied to this letter on the 7th of July. He evidently understood Mr. Hamilton in the sense just given. He cheerfully agreed to furnish the requisite information, so soon as he could arrange his papers, much disturbed by his late official removal to the new seat of government, because he thought "it would be a disgrace to the federal party, to permit the re-election of Mr. Adams." And he closed by saying, "You may rely upon my co-operation in every reasonable measure for effecting the election of General Pinckney."

On the 1st of August the call upon Mr. Adams was accordingly prepared. As addressed to a person then holding the office of President of the United States, and endeavoring to make him responsible not only for reports of his own conversations, but also for the supposed language of his political adherents, it is very obvious, that Mr. Hamilton could not have expected any reply. Very certainly, propriety demanded that none should be made. Mr. Hamilton in point of fact, did not anticipate a reply. For only two days afterwards, and seven days before his note reached Mr. Cabot, through whom it was forwarded to Mr. Adams, he wrote again to Mr. Wolcott, expressing impatience at the delay of the promised statement, and announcing an intention to proceed at once to a publication of his opinion of Mr. Adams, as "best suited to the plain dealing of his character." Then, with the singular inconsistency which marks almost every step of these proceedings, he went on to show how little he felt that he was acting up to the honest character which he claimed for himself. The words are too remarkable to be omitted.

"There are, however," he says, "reasons against it. And a very strong one is, that some of the principal causes of my disapprobation proceed from yourself, and other members of the administration, who would be understood to be the sources of my information, *whatever cover I might give the thing.*

"What say you to this measure? I could predicate it on the fact, that I am abused by the friends of Mr. Adams, who ascribe my opposition to pique and disappointment; *and could give it the shape of a defence of myself.*"

Surely this language will scarcely answer to any definition of the term *plain dealing.* It sufficiently shows that the demand of an explanation was a mere cover to an attack which Mr. Hamilton had for some time designed to make, out of the materials with which his confederates of the cabinet had been steadily supplying him during the whole period of the administration. And that he was withheld from it only by the fear of betraying the sources from which he had got his information. This difficulty pressed hardly not on him alone, but upon the confidential friends to whom he communicated his intentions. George Cabot, Fisher Ames, and Oliver Wolcott himself grew pale at the idea of an open assault upon the President. They all wrote letters of remonstrance, dwelling upon the imputation of breach of faith to which it exposed them with their own friends, if the design of destroying Mr. Adams should be avowed, and upon the absurdity of the other position, of continuing to uphold as a candidate a person whom the argument was intended to prove wholly unfit for the office. These three letters supply a curious but painful picture of the moral difficulties, into which honorable men sometimes allow themselves, in the heat of party passions, to get entangled. But a deeper shadow falls upon it, when the fact is perceived that the concluding advice of all three is, not to withhold the attack, but only to withhold the name of the assailant. It would be safer to make it anonymously. This proposal to skulk in ambush could not have fallen pleasantly on the feelings of Hamilton, even when under the unnatural tension to which they were now subjected. Neither would the stroke be nearly so effective. He concluded to prosecute his purpose, regardless equally of their good and bad advice; and on the 26th of September he transmitted to Mr. Wolcott the draft which he had prepared, with a request that he would "note exceptionable ideas or phrases." "Some of the most delicate of the facts stated," he added, "I hold from the three ministers, yourself particularly; and I do not think myself at liberty to take the step without your consent. *I never mean to bring proof,* but to stand upon the credit of my veracity."

The reply of Mr. Wolcott is long. It corrects many statements in the draft, and dissuades the publication of others. But its most remarkable admissions appear in the conclusion. He says:

"As to the measure itself, I can give no opinion. My feelings and individual judgment are in favor of it. I never liked the half-way plan which has been pursued. It appears to me, that federal men are in danger of losing character in the delicate point of sincerity. Nevertheless, when I consider the degree of support which Mr. Adams has already received; that our friends in Massachusetts say that they still *prefer* the election of Mr. Adams; that the country is so divided and agitated as to be in some danger of civil commotions, I cannot but feel doubts as to any measure, which can possibly increase our divisions. You can judge of the state of public opinion in the eastern States better than I can. If the popular sentiment is strong in favor of Mr. Adams,—if the people in general approve of his late public conduct, or if there is a want of confidence, for any reason, in General Pinckney, I should think the publication ought to be suppressed; on the contrary, if the publication would increase the votes for General Pinckney, and procure support to him in case he should be elected, it would certainly be beneficial. Notwithstanding your impressions to the contrary, I am not convinced that Mr. Adams can seriously injure your character."

It should be recollected that the professed object of Mr. Hamilton's paper was the defence of character. How little stress Mr. Wolcott laid upon it, is shown plainly enough in this extract. What he considered to be the true object, is likewise clear. If the attack could be the means of politically destroying Mr. Adams, or of establishing General Pinckney, it was worth

making. If, on the other hand, Mr. Adams was likely
to maintain his ground in the affections of the people of
Massachusetts, the publication which was to prove his
unfitness for their confidence was to be suppressed.
Surely no more can be necessary to prove that he
viewed the thing as a pure electioneering device. Not
so with Mr. Hamilton, however. He went on to print,
without giving his friends any assurances of the mode in
which he meant ultimately to use his paper. Perhaps
he had not made up his own mind, down to the moment when an accident is supposed to have settled it
for him. His arch-enemy, Aaron Burr, by some means
not yet fully explained, got access to the sheets whilst
passing through the press, and caused extracts to be published in the opposition newspapers far and wide. The
partial use thus made of the attack, was assigned as a reason for authorizing a complete publication. So it came
out, under the title of a " Letter from Alexander Hamilton, concerning the Public Conduct and Character of
John Adams, Esq., President of the United States."
This was in the very last week of October, but a short
time before the choice of electors in the different States.
If the single purpose had been to defeat Mr. Adams at
all hazards, no more propitious moment could have
been thought of. Yet, with the singular fatality of retribution, which more than once attended the acts of
Mr. Hamilton, the sequel showed that, at the instant of
this publication, he was striking the first spade into
what was ere long to be to him a duellist's grave.
Whilst on the other hand, the object of his vindictive
assault, outliving the days of bitter trial, which it prepared for him, was destined at last to close his eyes

with the acclamation of millions uniting to do unexampled honors to his name.

A publication, having for its object the destruction of the public character of a man who had spent twenty-five years of his life in stations of the highest responsibility, in some of which he had acquitted himself so honorably as to have extorted even from its author both praise and support, needed the most convincing proof of very grave offences against the public good in order to make it justifiable before the world. Especially was this true, when a consequence was liable to ensue, that was esteemed by the assailant, and at least one-half of the nation, to be fraught with extreme peril to the state. That such a consequence did not actually follow, is not material to this view of the case. The only question is, what Mr. Hamilton himself anticipated. In magnifying, as he habitually did, the dangers certain to attend the triumph of Mr. Jefferson and his friends, he in the same degree magnified his own responsibilities, if by any act of his that triumph were to be secured. Neither could he release himself from them, excepting by the offer of the most irresistible evidence to show such incompetency or malfeasance in office on the part of the individual relied upon by his own party as the only formidable competitor for the public favor, as to render it probable that the country would suffer even greater evils from his success. So soon as the news of Mr. Hamilton's pamphlet went abroad, men of all parties naturally expected disclosures of the gravest offences, involving the moral and political integrity of the President. What was their surprise, then, to discover, in the course of thirty printed pages, that the proofs relied upon to show Mr. Adams utterly unfit to be Presidnt, were not deemed by the author himself sufficient to prevent his advising his friends not to withhold from the object of his invective one single vote!

Of course the charges could not fail to correspond to the monstrous logical solecism, with which they concluded. The gravest of them were founded upon the determination of Mr. Adams to initiate the mission of Mr. Murray to France without consulting his cabinet; upon his perseverance in afterwards dispatching Messrs. Ellsworth and Davie, in opposition to the better judgment of Mr. Hamilton and his friends; and upon his pardon of John Fries, who according to them should rather have been hanged. Neither of these acts, even if admitted to be an error, was shown to have vitally injured the government, or to involve any censure of the author beyond a defect of judgment. At this day, neither of them stands in need of justification even on that score. The facts have already been submitted in the present chapter. They are supported by all the original documents connected with them, as found spread forth at large for the first time in the collected works of Mr. Adams. Upon these materials it will be for impartial posterity to decide with whom the errors really rested, whether upon the accused or his accuser; and, even should it be possible to attach the slightest censure to the former, for doing what he firmly believed to be his duty, against the judgment of his nominal friends, whether such errors, followed by such fortunate consequences in the restoration of peace abroad and of quiet at home, were of so mischievous a kind as to establish the charge of unfitness for high station, which was the ostensible purpose of the attack.

As to the general imputation upon Mr. Adams of an impracticable spirit, which led him to act without the advice of his cabinet, and to rely solely on himself, as the caprice of the moment, rather than any fixed opinions, might dictate, its utter groundlessness is sufficiently shown by the publication now made of the secret papers and correspondence of his administration. By these it will appear, not only that he consulted the members of his cabinet constantly, and called for their written opinions upon almost every important question, but that he often adopted their conclusions in the very language which they proposed, in many cases, even at the sacrifice of his own. The few exceptions that occurred were those in which a concerted attempt was making by his ministers to overrule his known convictions upon matters of the most serious importance. In these instances he certainly did decline to call for opinions of which he knew the nature too well already, and he did take such a course as to defeat their efforts at counteraction, and to provide for the full execution of his own policy. The very fact that he acted with such consistency in reaching the desired results, is a sufficient answer to all the efforts to stigmatize him as wavering and uncertain. These charges originated rather in the hopes that he would fluctuate, gathered from the concessions the authors of them could wring out of his casual and unguarded conversation, and in the disappointment at discovering in his action no traces of the vacillation upon which they had counted. There is no doubt that, when not stirred by any emotion, Mr. Adams's disposition was easy and inclined to yield. If he committed any mistake, it was in conceding too much rather than too little to his ministers. The effect was to lead them on to attempts upon his independence, which they would scarcely have ventured on a character more outwardly stern, and from which it was too late to retreat when they found him fully roused to their nature and to the necessity of defeating them. Thus it twice happened that the very moment when they felt the most sure of their success in controlling him, was exactly that when a single exercise of his will, to their great mortification, demolished their straw-built castles at a blow.

If any further answer were necessary to this charge, it might be found in the perfect harmony and efficiency of his cabinet after he had succeeded in organizing it to suit himself. With such men as John Marshall and Samuel Dexter for his counsellors, his system went on vigorously, partaking of the valuable fruits of the reflections of all, and jarred by no discord whatever. The motive for contention had been removed. Indulging in no wild dreams of overruling their chief for special purposes of their own, nothing remained to contend about, excepting which should most effectively serve the common cause. The effects are made visible in the steadiness of the policy pursued during the rest of the administration; and the nature of the intercourse appears in the private correspondence which has been published elsewhere.

With regard to the minor causes of complaint in Mr.

Hamilton's pamphlet, which resolve themselves into natural imperfections of temper, and personal foibles, such as men of every grade in life are liable to, if it were conceded that the charges, instead of being greatly exaggerated, were just, to the full extent alleged, the fact would scarcely avail as an argument in the pending controversy, unless it could be proved that the consequences showed out in public conduct of a pernicious or shameful character. The great measures actually adduced, whether in their inception or in their execution, prove nothing of the kind. Even the calm Washington was not free from occasional bursts of violent passion, as nobody claimed more fully to know than Mr. Hamilton himself. For he is reported as authority for the statement, that so great had been the General's asperity of temper towards the close of the war, as very much to impair his popularity in the army. That Mr. Adams was subject to the same infirmity, in a much greater degree, and with less power of self-control, is unquestionable. But the traces of it are nowhere visible in the public acts of his life, in the records of his administration, or in his correspondence with his ministers. However warm his conversation may at times have been, in his action he never failed to be cool. One proof of this is that the issue of his measures so seldom failed to correspond to his calculations. And certainly neither the nomination of the commissioners to France nor the pardon of Fries can be said to form exceptions to this remark. Yet these two acts form the substance of Mr. Hamilton's charge of incapacity. Well will it be for any future chief magistrate, and well for the republic itself, if, during his term of office, nothing more dishonorable should ever be proved against him.

Neither is it essential, in this connection, to go into any elaborate defence of Mr. Adams from the other imputation, of inordinate vanity. Even conceding it to be true to the extent affirmed, it yet remained to prove how the manifestation of it had done any injury to the public. For of public action only was there, in this case, any question. Vanity is a foible which may unpleasantly affect the relations of men with each other in social life, but there are plenty of cases in history to show that it is not incompatible with the possession of the very highest qualities of character and the noblest attributes of statesmanship. Nobody at this day will dispute the fact that Cicero, in his writings, shows himself, in this particular, among the weakest of men. Yet it is quite as undeniable that he will forever rank in the very first class of orators and statesmen, of thinkers and writers and actors, among men.* Neither is it necessary to go further for an illustration than to the very case of Mr. Hamilton himself. Singularly enough, one of his most devoted friends has left on record his testimony as well of his own sense, as of that of many others at the time, of Hamilton's betrayal, in this very publication, of the same fault which he was so prompt to charge upon Mr. Adams.† Yet

---

* The remarks of the historian Niebuhr upon this trait of Cicero's character are of universal application, and are well deserving of consideration by generous minds. *Lectures on the History of Rome,* edited by Dr. Schmitz, vol. iii. pp. 24, 25.

† *Works of Hamilton,* vol. vi. p. 482.

nobody will be disposed to question, on that account, Mr. Hamilton's abilities to play a great part in public affairs. To dwell more at large on this branch of the attack, seems to be superfluous. For were it all exactly as is affirmed, instead of being much exaggerated, the whole would not go very far to establish the fact that Mr. Adams could not, nevertheless, be, at the same time, a wise, an energetic, an independent, and an honest President.

This publication was not received with approbation by the public or by the federalists. The press teemed with replies, all written with more or less vigor, and some not unfelt by Mr. Hamilton himself. His most ardent friends, McHenry, Ames, and Cabot, reported to him, the last-named so candidly and faithfully that he anticipated the loss of his friendship from it, the nature of the censure he had incurred. All felt that if he had succeeded in pulling down Mr. Adams from his eminence, it had been done only by bringing in ruins with him the pillars of the federal structure. If this consideration filled the members of one party with grief, it correspondingly exalted their opponents. So fluctuating had been their confidence in their power to overthrow Mr. Adams, that even their sanguine chief had more than once entertained the notion of abandoning opposition to him, and directing the strength of his party to the question of the succession. But this pamphlet did more to invigorate them than all their own efforts. A curious admission of this fact, made under his own hand, by one of the most active partisans in the struggle, has recently found its way back from the other side of the Atlantic. In transmitting a copy to his friend, General Collot, who had fled to Paris from a threatened application of the Alien Law, not without justice in his case, the editor of the Philadelphia *Aurora*, the most efficient press in the service of the opposition, wrote the following note, on the 3d of November:

"CITIZEN GENERAL,—This pamphlet has done more mischief to the parties concerned than all the labors of the *Aurora*.

"WILLIAM DUANE."

Not yet was it among the least singular of the consequences attending this strange history, that the pamphlet should have been fatal to the prospects of the very person whom it was originally designed to aid, and should have elevated the author's most bitter and deadly enemy in his place. As in the case of Thomas Pinckney, who lost the Vice-Presidency by Mr. Hamilton's interference at the preceding election, so Charles Cotesworth Pinckney, on the present occasion, was cut off, in the same way, from the opportunity of arriving fairly at one of the two highest stations. Without possessing abilities of the first class, General Pinckney had owed the respect which followed him in life quite as much to his integrity and nice sense of personal honor, as to the creditable manner in which he acquitted himself of his duties. This might have secured for him from the legislature of his native State, a repetition of the experiment which had been made in favor of his brother at the preceding election, a union of his name with that of Mr. Jefferson as the choice of

the two candidates of the Electoral College. Had
such a union been actually made, the effect would have
been his elevation certainly to the second office, and
perhaps even to the first. That it was not made, was
very much owing to the decision of General Pinckney
himself. Unwilling to subject himself to the remotest
suspicion of bad faith, after the reception of Mr. Hamilton's pamphlet admitted of a possible inference of
collusion, he insisted upon standing or falling upon the
same ticket inseparably with Mr. Adams. The consequence was that the federalists would enter into no coalition, and Thomas Jefferson was enabled to secure
seven votes to Aaron Burr, the ubiquitous evil genius
of the author of the pamphlet himself.

Under the circumstances in which the parties went
into the election, with the federalists divided among
themselves, and with little heart or hope, the cause of
surprise is that they should have come so near success as
they did. The loss of the election in the city of New
York, in the month of May preceding, had determined
the votes in the legislature of that State for Mr. Jefferson.
But even this would not have turned the scale, had
South Carolina, which hung in suspense, proved true.
Both results were arrived at through the cool astuteness
of Aaron Burr, profiting by the excessive self-reliance
of Mr. Hamilton. In truth, the latter was no match
for his opponent in the game to which he had lent himself. With abilities beyond comparison higher, and aspirations the magnitude of which alone gave him far
superior dignity, he only failed in sufficiently measuring
the descent he was making when he entered upon the
arena of partisan intrigue on the same level with his

arch-enemy. The source of this error is to be traced to a deficiency in early moral foundations, the effects of which, here and there, make themselves visible, breaking out of the folds of a noble nature throughout his career, but especially towards its close. It was this which substituted the false idol of honor, as worshipped in the society of his day, for the eternal law of God; which impelled him to justify himself against a charge of peculation of the public money at the expense of a public confession of what to him seemed the more venial offence of aiding to corrupt an immortal soul; which led him into the clandestine relations with the cabinet officers of Mr. Adams, and the ultimate breach of confidence he made such awkward attempts to hide; which prompted that application to the upright John Jay, marked by the latter with so significant a condemnation;* and, lastly, which, in the vain idea of the importance in his ulterior schemes, of retaining the regards of superficial men, drove him, against his most solemn convictions of duty, to the act that presented him unannealed for the final sentence of his Maker.

In the election, the event which one section of the federalists had anxiously desired, an equality of the votes between Mr. Adams and Mr. Pinckney, did not happen, by reason of the refusal of Arthur Fenner, of Rhode Island, to sacrifice Mr. Adams. But the same thing did happen where it was not desired, and where no labor had been spent to bring it about, that is, on the side which supported Mr. Jefferson and Aaron Burr. Each of these gentlemen received seventy-three votes,

---

* Jay's *Life of John Jay*, vol. i. p. 414.

or three votes more than the number necessary for a choice. This did not point out who was to be President; so that the task of choosing between the two devolved upon the House of Representatives, a numerical majority of whom belonged to the federal side, although not a majority, when counted by States, according to the mode prescribed by the constitution for this election. Of course, Mr. Adams was now out of the question. He had nothing more to look forward to than the dreary pageant of three months which the constitution requires every President to enact after substantial power has departed from him.

The first sign of dissolution was the dropping away of the decayed limbs. So soon as General Pinckney was supposed to have failed, the scruples which had haunted the mind of Mr. Wolcott, about holding his office under Mr. Adams, returned with force. On the 8th of November, he addressed to the President a letter of resignation, which was to take effect at the close of the year, that is, about sixty days before the expiration of Mr. Adams's own term. He was not ashamed to add something about affording him suitable time to designate a successor to the official crumbs which he was disposed to leave unconsumed. So adroitly had he conducted himself, that Mr. Adams, though aware of his devotion to the views of Mr. Hamilton, had never ranged him in his mind in the same category with Colonel Pickering or McHenry. To the day of his death he always excepted him from the suspicions of bad faith, which he entertained of the others. Recent disclosures, however, place him in much the most sombre position of the three. From the day of the departure of his comrades, he remained the only person of the cabinet in secret relations with Mr. Hamilton. Not deterred by their dismissal, he seems to have used the warning only to labor the harder to cover the traces of his industrious treachery. His efforts to betray and disgrace his chief, as well by stimulating the disaffection of others wherever he could, as by supplying and revising the materials for the vindictive assault of Mr. Hamilton, are now before the world. It is no part of the present design to dwell upon them further than is necessary to show how deeply Mr. Adams was wronged by this behavior. One of the favorite modes of detraction resorted to by him and his associates was to describe his chief as unreasonably jealous and suspicious. How little he deserved this at the hands of Mr. Wolcott will now appear. Towards the last days of his official term, Mr. Adams, remembering that his old secretary had retired under no favorable pecuniary circumstances, fixed upon him, though long removed from practice in the courts, as a suitable recipient of the lifelong post of judge of the circuit court of the United States, under the law freshly passed for the reorganization of the courts. He did this without prompting or suggestion from any one, out of personal regard, and in the overflowing confidence of his heart in one whom he believed to have been faithful to him, and honorable in all his dealings. Mr. Wolcott betrayed no sensitive delicacy in accepting this most unmerited reward. He did not look back upon the secret letters which might, some day, show him to the world as he really was. He confessed nothing, but cheerfully took the gift from the hand of the man he had so sedulously labored to destroy. In his letter of acknowledgment he promised a change at least for the future. "Believing," said he, "that gratitude to benefactors is among the most amiable, and ought to be among the most indissoluble of social obligations, I shall, without reserve, cherish the emotions which are inspired by a sense of duty and honor on this occasion." There is reason to suppose that from that date to the end of his life, he kept this promise; for letters down to a late period remain among Mr. Adams's papers as evidence to show it. Had it not been for the revival of the memory of these events, in the most painful form of partisan harshness towards Mr. Adams, by the publication of Mr. Wolcott's papers, this exposition, unwillingly made, and based almost exclusively upon the testimony therein furnished, would never have been needed.

The second session of the sixth congress began on the 22d of November, with a speech from the President, destined to be his last. It is remarkable as more exclusively his own work than any of its predecessors. The exordium, which is brief and dignified, alludes in suitable terms to the inauguration of the new seat of government at Washington, where the different departments of government were now for the first time assembled.

"May this territory," he said, "be the residence of virtue and happiness! In this city may that piety and virtue, that wisdom and magnanimity, that constancy and self-government, which adorned the great character whose name it bears, be forever held in veneration! Here, and throughout our country, may simple manners, pure morals, and true religion flourish forever!''

Recommending to the care of congress the territory thus consecrated, he proceeded to give a summary of the relations of the country with foreign nations, and of the state of the negotiations yet pending with Great Britain and France. A treaty of amity and commerce had been concluded with Prussia. Turning from thence to the view of domestic affairs, he touched upon the reduction effected of the military organization, recommended further measures for the establishment of a defensive naval force, and dwelt with some urgency on the necessity of amending the judiciary system. He congratulated the House of Representatives upon the prosperous condition of the revenue during the year, the amount received exceeding that of any former equal period, and concluded with the following somewhat significant exhortation:

"As one of the grand community of nations, our attention is irresistibly drawn to the important scenes which surround us. If they have exhibited an uncommon portion of calamity, it is the province of humanity to deplore, and of wisdom to avoid the causes which may have produced it. If, turning our eyes homeward, we find reason to rejoice at the prospect which presents itself; if we perceive the interior of our country prosperous, free and happy; if all enjoy in safety, under the protection of laws emanating only from the general will, the fruits of their own labor, we ought to fortify and cling to those institutions which

have been the source of much real felicity, and resist
with unabating perseverance the progress of those
dangerous innovations which may diminish their influence.''

This picture of the state of the country was not in
the least exaggerated. The trying crisis caused by the
French revolution was now over, and the people were
just beginning to feel the prosperity, which was about
to come upon them in a flood. All that was needed
was peace, and this was on the point of being secured
to them. The great responsibility which Mr. Adams
had assumed, was completely redeemed by the event.
The neutrality of the country was saved. A few weeks
brought the tidings of the success of the much denounced commission to France, in framing a convention. Straggling murmurs against the insufficiency of
its provisions from some of the malcontents availed
nothing against the general disposition to accept it as
a final settlement of all differences. Only one important objection was raised to it. The second article an-
nulled the old treaties containing the guarantee that
had proved so troublesome, but it left the question of
indemnities on both sides for past grievances, as a
matter to be settled at some more convenient time.
This involved on the one side the question of compensation for surrender of the guarantee, and on the other
the indemnity for injuries done by the spoliations upon
American commerce, during the violence of the revolution. The Senate, not content to leave open a
source of future dissensions, ratified the treaty, with
the exception of this article, which they desired to

have expunged, and of the substitution of a provision that it should be in force for eight years. The President accepted the ratification in this form, but not without leaving on record his own opinion, that the treaty was better as it originally stood. Further negotiations became necessary. Assent to the required modifications was readily obtained from Napoleon, but it was saddled with a little proviso the effect of which went far to prove the correctness of the President's opinion. It was in these words: "Provided that by this retrenchment the two States renounce the respective pretensions, which are the object of the said article." This little condition abandoned the rights of reclamation to the amount perhaps of twenty or thirty millions of dollars, for the most unjustifiable robberies of private property ever committed by a civilized nation. The United States obtained from this surrender of the claims of some of their citizens a great benefit; but to this day those citizens and their descendants have had no reason to draw any favorable distinction between the parties abroad who originally did the wrong, and those at home who profited by sacrificing their rights, and who yet withhold from them even the most trifling compensation. Very fortunately for Mr. Adams, this, the only stain which attaches to that negotiation, does not rest upon his garments.

Two domestic events of note mark this session. The first was the election of a President of the United States for the first time by the House of Representatives. The second was the passage of an act to reorganize the judicial system of the Union.

In the first case it has been already stated, that the

choice was confined between Thomas Jefferson and
Aaron Burr. There was not a doubt in the mind of a
single member, which of the two the popular will intended to make the President. There should not have
been a doubt which should be preferred. Yet such is
the strength of party passions, when once roused, that
no calculation of what will de done can ever be based
upon merely abstract considerations of expediency or
of right. The federalists controlled the voices of six
States, and they neutralized two more. There were
sixteen States, nine of whom were necessary to elect.
But Mr. Jefferson had only eight in his favor. He
therefore could not be chosen without their assent express or implied. It was enough that they had the
power to change the result, for them to be tempted to
use it. The combined fear and hatred of Mr. Jefferson, who seemed to many of them the type of destruction to every thing valuable on earth, perhaps not unmingled with a hope of making terms not absolutely
unfavorable to a revival of their own influence, led
them, as a choice of evils, to give the preference to
Mr. Burr. The violation of the spirit of a popular
election, by a perversion of its forms, had been already
made so familiar to them by the sanction of Mr. Hamilton, that they were little moved by his remonstrances,
now that they were earnestly applied to prevent this to
him very unwelcome result. Such is not infrequently
the consequence of a departure from sound principle
to serve a temporary end.

Mr. Hamilton was not averse to any refinement of
policy short of actually electing Mr. Burr. He wrote
to Mr. Wolcott, that it might "be well enough to

throw out a lure for him, in order to tempt him to start for the plate, and then lay the foundation of dissension between the two chiefs.'' But further than this, he was unwilling to go. There can be no doubt that in this scruple he was right. But he could not fail to foresee that in case of Burr's success he could have no hope of exercising more control over either the chief or those who had elected him than he would have done under Mr. Adams. To him Burr was the most formidable of all opponents, because he lived on his own ground, and baffled him at every turn. But the federalists being mostly from the Northern States, sympathized the more with Burr for that very reason. Parties rarely spend much time in refining. If it was allowable to ''throw out a lure to Mr. Burr,'' the step was easy to giving him a vote. Thus it happened that the federal members took a course, success in which would have proved a misfortune, and wherein failure sunk them forever in the public esteem. Notwithstanding the election of Mr. Jefferson was effected at last by the honest scruples of some, and the timidity of others, who under the guidance of one superior will withdrew their opposition, that triumph gave so great an impulse to the victors, that no credit was ever awarded to those through whom it was attained. In all such political strokes, no medium is to be found between success and utter ruin. The great federal party which had shed so much lustre over the inauguration of the new government, which claimed Washington as its solar orb, and a host of the best and greatest of the revolutionary heroes as its lesser lights, sank in obscurity and disgrace, martyrs to the false and profligate

maxim, that the end will sometimes justify the use of
bad means.

It is one of the inconveniences attending the elective
forms of the federal government, that every fourth year
must be wasted in the process of transition from one
administration to another. Most especially is this
true, when the change becomes at the same time a
change of parties. The acting President is then left
scarcely strong enough to preserve the ordinary course
of business. This inconvenience was most seriously
felt by Mr. Adams. The desertion of Mr. Wolcott
rendered it impossible to find a person, not already in
office, willing to occupy the post of Secretary of the
Treasury for only two months; and what was true in
that case was equally true in every other, the tenure of
which was subject to be terminated by the incoming
President. As a consequence, Mr. Dexter was transferred to the treasury from the war department, whilst
the latter was left temporarily under the same charge.
There was, however, one class of exceptions to this
rule. The federalists, who still held the power in both
Houses, alarmed by the prospect of having Mr. Jefferson at the head of affairs, a man whose opinions
respecting the judiciary were supposed to be radical in
the extreme, determined upon carrying into effect the
other measure of this session, already alluded to, the
reorganization of the federal courts. This had been
often and repeatedly urged by the executive, and was
really called for by the changes that had taken place
in the population and circumstances of the country.
The union of the duties of riding a circuit with those
attached to a seat upon the supreme bench, whilst it

has some advantages, has, in a wide-spread land and under cumulative litigation, objections which become more and more serious with the progress of time. It must sooner or later 'be abandoned. The new act reduced the number of justices of the supreme court in future, and increased the district courts to twenty-three, arranged into six circuits to be travelled by three judges in each. It was not in itself ill devised for the purposes intended, but it happened quite unfortunately that it established a large number of offices with a life-tenure, which were to be filled.

Had the President determined to withhold the appointments, in such a manner as to give the nomination to his successor, a serious difficulty might have been avoided, and the irritation, which ultimately effected the repeal of the act, prevented. Had he been, what the violent federalists not infrequently in their private correspondence say he was, disposed to court his opponents, nothing would have been more easy than to have secured their good-will by a simple omission to act. This course would have been under all circumstances the most advisable. But Mr. Adams, once entertaining the most friendly feelings toward Mr. Jefferson, had had his faith in his principles greatly shaken in the contests of the preceding twelve years, and most especially in regard to his disposition towards the judiciary. He fully believed that the control he might obtain over the courts, by filling them with the extreme men among his followers, would endanger the safety of the government itself. He therefore viewed the power placed in his hands as one which it was a paramount duty to exercise, for the best good of the Union. The last days of the session were therefore spent in a laborious effort to select from the great number of candidates recommended, such as seemed the most capable, honest, and firm to fill these seats.

It naturally followed, that members of the federal party were generally appointed. Mr. Jefferson resented this more than any other act of Mr. Adams's life. But in view of the events which followed his entry into office, the attack made upon the courts, as well as the particular assaults upon several of its officers through he forms of impeachment, it may well be questioned whether the vehement contest on the incidental question of the repeal of this new law, did not prove a shelter to the general system, and ensure it the stability which it has enjoyed ever since. Almost at the same time happened the resignation by Mr. Ellsworth of his high post of Chief Justice of the Supreme Court. Mr. Adams immediately offered the place to John Jay, then Governor of New York; and, upon his declining it on account of his health, he tendered it to John Marshall, his Secretary of State. These appointments excited dissatisfaction on both sides of him. The ultra federalists murmured at the nomination of Jay as useless, and complained that Patterson had been overlooked in order to reward a favorite; the opposition, that the strongest opponent of their chief in Virginia had been set as a check over him. But looking back upon the events of the first half of this century, and upon the combination of qualities, requisite to fill that most responsible and difficult post in such a manner as to consolidate instead of weakening the Union, it is scarcely possible for the most prejudiced man to deny that the selection by John Adams of John Marshall to be Chief Justice of the Supreme Court of the United States was, for its political consequences, second in importance only to that virtually made by the same individual, twenty-five years earlier, of George Washington, as commander-in-chief of their armies.

Thus terminated the official life of Mr. Adams. His Presidency had been one long and severe trial, in the course of which it was his lot to have his firmness and independence of spirit put to the test for the fourth time in his career, under circumstances more appalling than ever before. For the first time his own popularity sank completely under the shock. He retired disgraced in the popular estimation, and his name became a by-word of odium for many years. But he had fully redeemed the pledge into which he entered with himself at the commencement of his career, to "act a fearless, intrepid, undaunted part," though not forgetting "likewise to act a prudent, cautious, and considerate part." And never was a union of these qualities more exemplified than during this administration, in the course of which his inflexible courage had saved the neutral policy, and had removed the obstacles which threatened the prosperity of the nation at the moment that he took the helm.

CHAPTER XI.

ON the 4th of March, 1801, the day upon which
Mr. Jefferson was inaugurated President of the United
States, Mr. Adams retired from public life, after an
uninterrupted course of service of six and twenty years,
in a greater variety of trusts than fell to the share of
any other American of his time. With acknowledged
credit to himself and honor to the country, he had
gone through all of them, excepting the last, and in
that he felt that by a concurrence of adverse circumstances he was visited with censure which neither his
motives nor his acts had merited. Sensitive and ardent
in his temperament, he would not wait to be present at
the installation of his successor, or to exchange the
customary forms of civility in transferring the office.
In this course, as not consistent with true dignity, or
with the highest class of Christian virtue, he was perhaps wrong. It certainly would have been more politic
to have made professions of confidence in Mr. Jefferson. But that was not his way, when he did not entertain them. He shared strongly in the distrust universal
among the federalists, of that gentleman's intentions,
and he believed, not without color of reason, that he
had acted somewhat disingenuously towards himself.

(352)

This was a strong motive for declining to be present at the inauguration, but it was not by any means the only one. Had the party which elected him really made him its head; had it stood unitedly and cordially by him in the policy which he had felt it his duty to prefer, he believed that he should never have been exposed to the necessity of any such trial. But even if, in spite of every exertion, defeat had followed, with a united support, the exultation of the victors might have been easily endured, as an inevitable concomitant of the chances of the popular favor. Such had not been the case. He felt that his most bitter enemies had been of his own household, whom he had offended because he would not submit to be a mere instrument to execute a policy, which he could not approve. Although he did not even then suspect the extent to which he had been circumvented, he knew enough to convince him that he had been a victim of treachery, and that, as such, he must, if he remained, be shown up before both his opponents and his friends. Many of his own side, who had arraigned his policy and attributed to it their overthrow, would draw some consolation to themselves from seeing him pay any penalty, however severe, for having pursued it. Of these a considerable number were in the Senate, friends of the individual who had destroyed him. To them, then, as well as to Mr. Jefferson's followers he was to be made a spectacle, if he should stay to be a part of the pageant. No. His proud spirit would not endure it. He would not consent to enact the captive chief in the triumphant procession of the victor to the capitol.

But in addition to this, there were other and better

reasons for desiring to escape a burdensome ceremonial. The state of his feelings at home was not in harmony with such a scene. He had just passed through the first severe domestic affliction of his life. His second son, Charles, who had grown up to manhood, had been married, and settled in the city of New York with fair prospects of success, had but a few weeks before breathed his last, leaving a wife and two infant children as his only legacy to his father's care. In a note, addressed to Mr. Jefferson, who had opened a letter relating to the matter, which had come by mistake to him after his accession, but which he transmitted unread, Mr. Adams feelingly alludes to this. "Had you read the papers inclosed," he said, "they might have given you a moment of melancholy, or, at least, of sympathy with a mourning father. They related wholly to the funeral of a son, who was once the delight of my eyes, and a darling of my heart, cut off in the flower of his days, amidst very flattering prospects, by causes which have been the greatest grief of my heart, and the deepest affliction of my life." In the state of mind here described, gloomy from the combined pressure of public and private evils, it surely cannot be matter for much wonder that he should resolve to avoid a situation in which his presence would be a severe trial to himself and of no compensating advantage to any one. Yet he was much censured for this act, at the time, by those who knew nothing of the circumstances, and who saw in it only a pettish sally of mortified ambition.

Upon his return to Massachusetts, the legislature, representing a large number of the people of his own

State, who for more than twenty years had not swerved for a moment in their confidence in Mr. Adams, and who saw no reason to withdraw it now, adopted the following address, which was carried out and presented to him at his residence in Quincy by the presiding officers of the two Houses, attended by a numerous escort.

"TO JOHN ADAMS.

"At the moment, Sir, that you are descending from the exalted station of the first magistrate of the American nation, to mingle with the mass of your fellow-citizens, the Senate and House of Representatives of the Commonwealth of Massachusetts, your native State, embrace the occasion to pour forth the free-will offering of their sincere thanks for the many important and arduous services you have rendered your country.

"In the performance of this act, the legislature have but one heart, and that vibrates with affection, respect, and gratitude for your virtues, talents, and patriotism.

"We conceive it unnecessary to detail the character of him, whose life from earliest manhood has been eminently devoted to the public good. This will be the delightful employment of the faithful and able historian.

"Our posterity will critically compare the illustrious characters which have elevated the condition of man, and dignified civil society, through the various ages of the world, and will, with grateful effusions and conscious pride, point to that of their beloved countryman.

"The period of the administration of our general government, under the auspices of Washington and

Adams, will be considered as among the happiest eras of time. The example of their integrity possesses a moral and political value, which no calculation can reach, and will be justly estimated as a standard for future Presidents of the United States.

"We receive you, Sir, with open arms, esteem and veneration; confidently hoping that you will possess undisturbed those blessings of domestic retirement, which great minds always appreciate and enjoy with dignity.

"We devoutly supplicate the Father of the Universe, that you may realize, while you continue on earth, all the happiness of which human nature is susceptible; and when your course shall be finished here, that your spirit may receive the transcendent rewards of the just."

The next year, his fellow-citizens in his own town of Quincy seized the occasion of his birthday to pay their respects to him, and to offer the following affectionate address:

"Sir,—The return of this anniversary cannot fail to awaken in our breasts the warmest sentiments of gratitude and esteem. It recalls to. view the many important events of your public life, events intimately connected with those principles and proceedings which constitute the greatest glory of our country, and which will form some of the most valuable pages in the history of nations.

"We hope the liberty we have taken in personally waiting upon you on this occasion will not be deemed an intrusion. And while we offer you our respectful congratulations, we must beg you to be assured that this visit is the result of feeling and not of ceremony.

"The early and decided part which you took in support of the liberties of America; the series of patriotic and successful exertions, which distinguished you the firm, unwavering, and able friend of these States; the many stations of high responsibility which you filled so much to the advantage of your fellow-citizens throughout our Revolution, gave you an honorable title to their veneration and love.

"But your services to your country did not end with the accomplishment of our Independence. Since that period, it has required, and you have devoted to its cause, the energies of your comprehensive mind. Your civil administration as President of the United States, at a crisis of peculiar difficulty and danger, warded off evils which seemed inevitable, and secured blessings that appeared unattainable. It vindicated the national honor, accommodated serious differences with two of the most powerful nations of Europe, and left the United States, with the means of a speedy extinction of the public debt, a full treasury, and a flourishing commerce, to cultivate the arts of peace.

"May these things be ever held in suitable remembrance. May no untoward circumstances wholly take away the fair prospect we have had of national prosperity and greatness. For you, Sir, we offer our supplications to the Sovereign of the Universe, that your invaluable life may be long preserved. In any critical conjuncture of affairs, may your countrymen yet have the benefit of that foresight, wisdom, and experience

which have so often availed and supported them. And
when you shall finally be called to bid adieu to this
world and its concerns, may the cheering words promised to the good and the faithful, hail you to the man-
sions of blessedness."

October 30, 1802.

But with the exception of a few manifestations of
this kind, the seclusion into which Mr. Adams was at
once plunged, at his farm in Quincy, was profound in
the extreme. No more striking proof of it remains
than his correspondence. The letters addressed to
him in the year prior to the 4th of March, 1801, may
be counted by thousands. Those of the next year
scarcely number a hundred, and he wrote even less than
he received. A few old and tried friends sent kind expressions of their warm regard, which he acknowledged
in the same spirit, but the crowd who had solicited
favors, so long as there were any to grant, moved on
according to immemorial usage, towards the newly-
created fountain of supply. Such are the vicissitudes
of statesmen, as well under the forms of republican
America, as in the courts of kings. To Mr. Adams,
however, this change was most trying as a transition
from a state of the utmost intellectual activity to one
of the most sluggish repose. For years before, he
had looked forward to the event not without some
misgivings as to the possible effect upon his health.
But now that at last it was come, he addressed himself
with such courage as he might to the resumption of the
private occupations within his reach. And, first of all,
he naturally looked back to the early fancy of his life,

from which he had never been weaned by other avocations, abroad or at home, however numerous or important. All the fortune he had inherited or succeeded in acquiring, had been invested in the lands around him. These he set about cultivating and improving; and they furnished his main support for the remainder of his days. At first, under the stimulus of the attack of Mr. Hamilton, he devoted some time to the preparation of a reply; and the next year he entered upon a project of an extended autobiography; but neither of these schemes retained its attraction sufficiently to reach completion. Although invited, in many forms, by the authorities of the State and of the neighboring town of Boston to attend upon public occasions, he accepted them only when it would have been uncivil to do otherwise. His indisposition to take part in new political questions was so decided, that it is scarcely likely it would have been ever overcome, but for one accidental circumstance. He had a son, who had already entered upon a brilliant public career, and whose position was rapidly becoming a prominent one in the contentions of the times.

A detailed examination of the events of this period, as connected with the career of this son, is not within the scope of this work. They will be touched upon, therefore, only so far as may be necessary to explain their effect upon the situation of Mr. Adams during the remainder of his life. From the day of Mr. Jefferson's accession, the federalists, disheartened by the division in their own ranks, and discredited by the failure of the attempt to elect Mr. Burr, gave up united exertion. Mr. Marshall, the representative of one form of opinion, had become chief justice of the supreme court. Mr. Jay, at the close of his term of service as Governor of New York, voluntarily retired into private life. Upon Mr. Adams the whole odium of the party defeat had been concentrated by the victors, with the new President at their head. No prominent man remained, excepting Alexander Hamilton, and he was considered rather as the type of one section than of the whole party. Yet under him rallied the only considerable fragment that kept together after the great defeat. It was composed, in the main, of persons in New England and New York, leaning to extremes in opinion, and with difficulty withheld from violent courses even by the dissuasive counsels of him in whom they placed most confidence. Yet even he appeared to be only counselling delay in order the more completely "to reserve himself for those crises in the public affairs which seemed likely to happen," when the vindictive spirit of Aaron Burr, irritated by his haughty yet officious enmity, took advantage of an indiscreet remark made by him at a public meeting, to force him into the field of combat in which he fell. Thus it happened that in 1804 all those persons who could be regarded in any general sense as heads of opposition to the new administration were removed from the scene, at the same time that a treaty with France was negotiated, by which the splendid acquisition of Louisiana was secured to the Union. Neither did the attempt to stir up strife within the ranks of the victorious party avail to impair the authority of the new President. It fared no better in the hands of the disaffected Burr, meditating mysterious projects of a new empire in the west, than in those of John Randolph, discontented by the want of deference to his unreasonable demands. The consequence was a perfect consolidation of the power of the new government, the re-election of Mr. Jefferson by the votes of all the electors excepting fourteen, and the ability to entail the succession to the Presidency at the end of his second term, upon the person of James Madison, his confidential friend and long-tried coadjutor.

Under this process the federalists crumbled away until few traces remained of the once powerful association, south or west of the Hudson. The moderate men, despairing of its revival, either withdrew from public action altogether or permitted themselves to sink into the ranks of the majority. Neither was this tendency altogether imperceptible in New England, where the federal ascendency had been the most marked, and where it yet maintained itself. But the withdrawal of Mr. Adams, which had thrown the direction of the party into the hands of that portion of it known to be particularly associated with Mr. Hamilton, threatened to deprive it of a considerable share of strength, obtained from the popular confidence reposed in his character and services. Mr. Hamilton, in his exploring journey before the election, had come to the conclusion that although the "strong-minded men" were generally in sympathy with himself, those of the second class and the body of the people were too much disposed to follow Mr. Adams. The consciousness of this had been the cause of the great reluctance manifested by Hamilton's friends to the open hostility which he had thought it proper to declare. And after the election was decided, it still prompted an avoidance of any enlargement of the breach then made. The friends of the new government were too numerous to render it advisable to hazàrd the alienation of a single person who could be in any way induced to continue in opposition. Enmity to Mr. Jefferson was a common bond still to be relied on to keep together those who might entertain few other sentiments in unison. Hence, bitterly as they continued to feel towards the person who had rejected their advice, and whom, for that reason, they had sought in secret to destroy, the "strong-minded men" deemed it expedient to avoid every occasion for pushing further the differences that had already taken place.

So far as John Adams was concerned, no motive remained to do so. He had determined upon absolute retirement from public life and all its concerns, and had declared this intention in his reply to the address of the Massachusetts legislature. But there yet remained a representative of him in the field whose position and influence it was not easy to disregard, or prudent to overlook. Mr. Adams's eldest son, John Quincy Adams, the companion of his voyages, and of his European life, after eight years of creditable service in diplomatic stations abroad, which had removed him from all the scenes of contentious politics at home, had returned to Massachusetts, with a reputation for abilities, character, and learning exceeded by that of no one of his generation in the commonwealth. The claims of such a man upon the popular confidence, it was dangerous to neglect. Yet it is not possible to imagine that those persons who had been engaged in the clandestine movements to betray the father, even to the limited extent as yet laid open to the public eye, could be likely to entertain much cordiality in advancing the son. For they could scarcely fail to impute to him some share of filial indignation for the manner in which he knew that his father had been treated. Yet in the ardor of their hostility to Mr. Jefferson, they were ready to overlook a great deal. Besides, the alienation of Mr. Adams might be more dangerous to their ascendency than an attempt to conciliate him by a show of confidence. So they acquiesced in a policy of union, which, whilst it conceded a certain share of support to him, might secure in return a union of the more moderate men upon persons holding opinions like their own. It was in this spirit that Mr. Adams was brought forward in the autumn of 1802 as a candidate for a seat in the House of Representatives, in the Boston District, whilst Colonel Pickering, the most vehement of his father's enemies, was presented in the same way to the county of Essex. Such coalitions are seldom hearty, especially at first. This one did not prove so. The people appeared indifferent, and neither candidate was chosen. Mr. Adams failed by less than sixty, Colonel Pickering by about a hundred votes.

But though defeated here, an opportunity very soon occurred when the same policy of equivalents could be carried out more successfully in another form. Two vacancies occurred at once in the Senate of the United States. The two branches of the legislature which were to fill them contained a great number of intermediate men. An attempt to push Colonel Pickering through proved unsuccessful, and a perseverance in

it threatened to be followed by the election of an opponent.   Under these circumstances recourse was had to
Mr. Adams, then himself a member of the State Senate,
and understood not to be manageable, as a party man.
By assenting to his election to one of the places, a way
was made for the attainment of the other by Colonel
Pickering.   The consequence was the election of the
two to sit as colleagues representing Massachusetts in
the federal Senate.   A more incongruous mixture could
scarcely be conceived.   It was plain that the smoulder-
ing fires had been covered for the moment, only to
kindle into a fiercer conflagration upon occasion of the
first conflict of opinion which might spring out of the
disturbed condition of public affairs.

Neither was that occasion long wanting.   So long
as Mr. Jefferson's domestic policy was in question,
and the effort to break down the judiciary, first, by
the repeal of the organic law of 1801, and afterwards
by the successive impeachments of judges, was continued, there was no risk of a division.   But when the
country became involved in new difficulties from the
warfare waged among the European powers, the course
to be pursued was not so clear.   The place in which the
injury was most felt was upon the high seas, and those
who suffered were the eastern commercial States carrying on a profitable neutral trade.   The temper of the
belligerents had not been softened by the peace of
Amiens, and the resumption of arms became the signal
for a course of retaliatory warfare unexampled in any
former contest.   To America this was hurtful, as a
neutral power having rights of trade with each side
which were too often disregarded by the other.   But

of the two the action of Great Britain was by far the
most irritating, because her maritime supremacy came
the most directly into collision with American commerce.   Her revival of the rule of '56, for the express
object of cutting off a profitable neutral trade with the
colonies of her enemy, occasioned the capture and
condemnation of many vessels.

Yet unpleasant as were the relations made by these
events they would scarcely have caused a breach, had
they not been followed up by the claim of a right to
search American national ships for deserters, and to
seize any persons who might be designated as British-
born subjects.   It was the case of the frigate Chesapeake boarded by the officers of The Leopard, who
took out of her, in a most arrogant and insulting manner, four of her men, which justly roused the indignation of the people of the United States.   At this day,
it is difficult to understand how there could have been
a moment's difference of opinion on the necessity of
resenting so insolent an assumption.   Yet the fact cannot be controverted that the disposition to do it was
much less strong in the commercial region, the citizens
of which were immediately liable to suffer from it, than
in the purely agricultural sections of the interior.
There were even found leading men disposed to excuse,
if not to defend, the pretensions of Great Britain.
The times were not favorable to the decision of any
point of public policy solely upon its merits.   The
violent opponents of Mr. Jefferson were disposed to
see in every act of his towards England a disposition
to play into the hands of Napoleon, then believed by
them to be meditating the subjection of the world;

whilst on the other hand, these suspicions were met with a counter belief that those who were willing to overlook such aggressions secretly meditated a betrayal of their country to the dominion of their ancient step-mother. In times of alarm, party passions thrive on extremes of opinion. The hatred thus engendered is never satisfied with less than the reciprocal imputation of crime. If Mr. Jefferson and his counsellors were on the one side said to be sold to France, on the other, Colonel Pickering and his coadjutors of the Essex junto, were set down as in secret conspiracy with the British ministry.

In the midst of the turmoil John Adams and his son occupied a difficult position. Although by no means satisfied with the general coldness of Mr. Jefferson towards the commercial States, they were not so far carried away by their feelings as to overlook the superciliousness of Great Britain. They had known it by personal experience in its most offensive shapes, and they felt that submission to it in any form was not the most likely way to put an end to it for the future. Hence it happened that upon the occurrence of the outrage on The Chesapeake both of them hesitated not a moment in expressing their indignation, and their earnest wishes for measures of redress. Finding the federalists with whom he was connected unprepared to listen to his suggestions of immediate action, John Quincy Adams determined to signify his own opinion at all events. He therefore attended the public meeting called in Boston to that end. It was not called as a party meeting; but his presence among those generally ranked as opponents who naturally constituted the greater part, was no sooner perceived, than by general acclamation he was summoned to take part in the deliberations. The resolutions were confined to the objects for which the meeting was called; yet the act of Mr. Adams was construed among the federalists as ominous of the division which soon afterwards fell out.

It is not necessary to go into this history further than it may show the influence which it had over the action of the subject of this narrative. It is sufficient to this purpose to say that among other measures occasioned by the attack on The Chesapeake, was a proclamation issued by Mr. Jefferson, interdicting British armed vessels from entering the harbors of the United States. The British ministry on their part, conscious of the indignity which had been committed by the rashness of their officer, betrayed anxiety to atone for it rather as an exceptional act of incivility, than by disclaiming the right of search itself. In this spirit, whilst they determined upon sending a special minister to make negotiations and explanations confined to that single outrage, they accompanied the act by issuing the king's proclamation recalling all British seamen from service under the flags of foreign nations, which was followed by other measures of hostility to the neutral trade of America by no means calculated to promote reconciliation. Colonel Pickering, however, viewing the policy of the administration as one designed to precipitate a war with Great Britain, drew up a paper expressive of his views upon the questions in dispute between the two governments, in the course of which he was carried so far as to palliate, if not directly to defend, the claim made in the king's proclamation. This paper roused the indignation of John Adams, and for the first time since his retirement, he broke silence by publishing an examination of the grounds of the pretension. This paper is included in the general collection of his works. Thus, in conjunction with a more general reply to Pickering drawn up at the same time by his son, a new issue between the parties was formed, an issue which subsequent events widened into a perfect breach, presenting on the one side all of the federalists who had been dissatisfied with his administration driven to extremes in opposition, and on the other the whole weight of Mr. Adams's authority thrown on the side of Mr. Jefferson and the most vehement of his ancient enemies.

Had Great Britain been actuated during this period by a tithe of the conciliatory temper which has been manifested in her relations with the United States of late years, it cannot admit of a doubt that the difficulties which led to the war of 1812 might have been removed; but her ministers and people yet smarting under the recollection of the failure to uphold her sovereignty in America, instinctively shrank from every concession to men whom they still regarded too much in the light of successful rebels. Still impressed with the exclusive commercial notions of the preceding century, they saw with a jealousy little disguised, the plenteous returns flowing into the coffers of their old subjects from a fortunate neutrality in the wars which were bearing them down; and they lost no opportunity so to apply the harshest principles of international law as to seize as much as they could of this abundance for their own benefit. Negotiations carried on whilst such a spirit prevailed, could end in nothing valuable. Napoleon had, early in his career, learned the lesson how uncertain a science is that diplomacy which rests its expectations only upon the supposed interests of peoples or governments. The passions form the great elements of calculation, at the same time that they defy all human sagacity.* This remark was never more true than during the long series of events, dating from the French Revolution, in which he himself played the chief part. The evidences of it are thickly strewed along the course of these times, in the shape either of orders in council, paper blockades, and imperial decrees, or in the more bloody yet quite as profitless butcheries of the Nile, Trafalgar, and Copenhagen, of Austerlitz, Jena, Borodino, Leipsic, and Waterloo. A conciliatory spirit, guided by a benevolent regard for the welfare of millions of the race, would have saved all these horrors in a day; but the delirium of the sovereigns of these times proved the truth of the poet's verses on a scale in comparison with which the sufferings of the Greeks which he lamented were but as solitary accidents.

And in this wanton strife Great Britain was not slow to take her part. Instead of forbearance and moderation, her tone was domineering and her temper savage; and nowhere was this more sensibly felt than in the bearing of her naval officers on the high seas, from the admiral of the red down to the cabin-boy. Furthermore, among all the foreign nations with which they had to deal, none were so much exposed to this harsh treatment as Americans. The temper of the old king had engrafted itself upon the feelings of the aristocracy,

---

* *Mémoires du Roi Joseph*, tome i. p. 68.

and what is their temper will be sure to crop out in the
official tone of the army and the navy. Under this
trial the administration of Mr. Jefferson was doomed
the more severely to suffer from the fact that the impression as to his leanings to France had become
general in England. To reproach him at this day for
resenting these manifestations of ill-will with too much
violence, would be wide of the truth. The error, if
any was committed, was of an opposite kind, in carrying forbearance to the point of timidity. If fault there
was, it was in half-way contrivances which proved weak
and inefficacious at a moment when helplessness injured
Americans more than the power did which insulted
them; but embargo and non-intercourse were, under
the circumstances in which the people had chosen to put
themselves, the only alternative. Mr. Adams, as well
in his earliest labors in the revolutionary struggle, as in
his later appeals to the pride of his countrymen during
the difficulties with France, had ever urged the establishment of a naval force at least adequate to defend
the seaboard and to protect the national commerce on
the ocean; and, during his administration, the foundation of such a power had been so well laid, that, with
a moderate and gradual development, it would by this
time have been strong enough to do essential service.
But this was one portion of his policy which had been
the most severely denounced by his opponents. So that
when Mr. Jefferson was elevated in his place it was laid
aside as having caused a wasteful expenditure of the
public money. The statesmanship of self-protection
was dwarfed into an economical array of Liliputian
gun-boats, and the commercial marine was left to shift

for itself if pushed out to sea, or to rot at the wharves if kept at home. Confined to this alternative, it was certainly less mortifying to preserve the character of the country by a voluntary secession from the Ocean, than passively to suffer every thing calling itself American to become a prey to the raging passions of the European belligerents; and either was better than the suggestion, which was whispered in some quarters, if not openly favored, of submission to the British pretensions.

To the possibility of such a step as this last, J. Q. Adams, not less than his father, was most resolutely opposed. Their joint experience had produced no clearer lesson than this, that Great Britain seldom respected the rights of any nation on the sea, whose power did not make itself feared. The tone of George Canning had not been such as to inspire much confidence in any immediate change of her old habits. So they declared themselves on the side of the government in maintaining, at all events, the rights of America. From this moment they were no longer ranked among the remnants of the federal party. The consequences were soon important to them. The opposition to the federal government in Massachusetts, greatly fortified by the severe pressure upon the community of its anti-commercial measures, determined to anticipate the customary period of election of a new senator, in order the more significantly to mark the withdrawal of their confidence from the incumbent.

These particulars, which will find space for fuller development in the biography of the son, are here alluded to for the purpose only of tracing the progress of the irritations which ended in reviving the controversies of an earlier time. Some of the more violent federalists, not confining themselves to the topics before them, and provoked by the interposition of Mr. Adams in support of an administration which they abhorred, strove to impair whatever influence might remain to him, by a recurrence to the charges contained in Mr. Hamilton's pamphlet. Such is party warfare, from the ferocity of which no man who seeks strongly to affect public opinion, in times of agitation in a free country, can ever hope to be exempt. In the day of it, Mr. Adams had collected the materials for a replication to that attack, but partly from his own indifference to perfecting any literary labor, partly in consequence of the fate of his assailant, and perhaps from the fruitless nature of the contest, he suffered them to lie unused, until they had ceased to attract his attention. The stimulus of this assault now roused him to look them up. It so happened that the columns of a newspaper in Boston, then seeking to extend its circulation, were freely offered to him by the proprietors. This informal mode of publication was peculiarly tempting to him, as it released him from the necessity, always burdensome, of methodizing and polishing his composition. At first he proposed to confine himself simply to a defence of the mission to France, which constituted the *gravamen* of Mr. Hamilton's attack; but once engaged in the review of his past life, he enlarged his plan, until it extended itself to the publication of a large part of his most valuable papers. These labors were continued from time to time for the space of three years. A portion, embracing perhaps two-thirds of the communications, was collected, and published in numbers, which make together an octavo volume, entitled, "Correspondence of the late President Adams, originally published in the *Boston Patriot*, in a series of Letters." This book is now very rarely to be met with.

No more unfortunate time for the attainment of the object which the writer had in view could have been selected. He had borne with injustice and misrepresentation so long, without defending himself, that it would have been wise to let them take their course, at least for the remainder of his life, and to reserve himself, by a calm and careful preparation of his papers for a more impartial age, to establish the truth. There can be no question that the most unfavorable moment to gain proselytes, even to the most convincing arguments, is when the person attempting it, himself under great momentary irritation, is addressing persons who are listening under still more. Especially is this the case when the subject discussed has any bearing whatever upon immediate interests, on which the whole community has divided into parties. But Mr. Adams suffered himself to be so much censured, without reply, as to make him begin to doubt of any future reversal of the verdict, unless he should interfere at once and plead his own cause. To this opinion he was the more impelled by a fear that if he should prepare his papers for posthumous publication, some unlooked-for accident or domestic vicissitude might, after all, intervene to disperse or to destroy them before they could ever reach the public. A singular mishap of this sort had occurred, under his immediate observation, in the case of Samuel Adams, and still another, of a different kind. in that of Dr. Franklin. He therefore determined, at all hazards, to proceed. The consequence was a perpetuation of his most important documents, it is true, but under circumstances most adverse to any beneficial effect, either to history or to his own reputation. Scattered through the pages of a newspaper of very limited circulation, during three years, without order in the arrangement, and with most unfortunate typography, the papers might, indeed, be described as safe, but it was the safety of a treasure which an individual buries in the ground in his lifetime, and leaves to some straggler of a distant age, perchance to hit the spot where it may with labor be brought to light.

It is owing to the defects enumerated that no attempt has been made to reproduce this publication in its original form in the collection of his works. That part of it which relates to the nomination of Mr. Murray, although marked by too much asperity towards Mr. Hamilton and his other opponents, is yet in itself so complete an exposition of his own view of that measure, that it has been transferred entire. From the remainder, such extracts have been taken as help in any way to elucidate the documents to which they refer, whilst those documents themselves have been arranged on a more methodical and comprehensive plan. In this way it is believed that nearly, if not quite all of material importance in that publication has been preserved. The form itself is of little value. The task of authorship was always irksome to Mr. Adams. He seldom assumed it excepting upon the spur of some immediate impulse, and he never carried his labors further than the preparation of the manuscript. The consequence is that he suffered even more than writers commonly do from the careless typography of the newspapers in that day.

The accession of Mr. Madison to the Presidency, a result which Mr. Jefferson much favored, was the signal of a division among the friends of government, and of a more conciliatory policy towards the moderate federalists. The latter had been already manifested in the appointment of William Pinkney, of Maryland, to a special duty, and afterwards to the permanent mission in Great Britain. The policy might have been carried even to the restoration of good feelings at home and of more friendly relations with England, but for the interference of a portion of the Senate in dictating to the new President the person he should make Secretary of State. It did, however, extend to the appointment of John Quincy Adams to be the first accredited minister of the country at the court of St. Petersburg. His father naturally viewed this act as a relaxation, the first he had experienced since the accession of Mr. Jefferson, of the harshness manifested towards himself by the party in power. The same event embittered the hostility of his federal opponents, who had now, for the first time, gained an exclusive ascendency in Massachusetts. This state of things opened the way to a restoration of friendly feelings with Mr. Jefferson, who was now out of power, like himself, with nothing left to overcome the natural dictates of his heart. The interposition through which it was reached, was that of a common friend, Dr. Benjamin Rush, of Philadelphia, whose voluntary services smoothed away all the obstacles formed by the long estrangement. Some explanation of their nature will not be out of place.

The character of Thomas Jefferson presents one of the most difficult studies to be met with by the historian of these times. At once an object of the most exalted eulogy among those who made him their political chief, and of the bitterest execrations of his opponents, it is not very easy, between the two, to trace the lines which truth and justice alike demand. As an original thinker, there can be little doubt of his claim to stand in the first rank among American statesmen. His, too, was the faculty, given to few, of leading the many, by impressing their minds with happily concentrated propositions. More ardent in his imagination than his affections, he did not always speak exactly as he felt towards either friends or enemies. As a consequence, he has left hanging over a part of his public life a vapor of duplicity, or, to say the least, of indirection, the presence of which is generally felt more than it is seen. Sometimes, indeed, when his passions become roused by personal rivalry, it shows itself darkly enough. Cautious, but not discreet, sagacious, though not always wise, impulsive, but not open, his letters, as printed since his death, have scarcely maintained for him the character he enjoyed among his followers whilst living. The most obvious deficiency is the absence of repose of mind, and of consistency in heart. The great lead he early took in the Revolution naturally brought him in frequent relations with Mr. Adams, generally friendly, though, considering the striking discordance of their characteristic traits, they could never have been intimate, but sometimes hostile.

The first instance took place during the perilous days of 1775, when both were enlisted with ardor in the work of pushing the country forward to independence. Here was a common opponent and a common interest. The fields of labor only were diverse. Mr. Adams, the eldest in public life as well as in years, careless of external fame as a writer, preferred the natural channel to his impetuosity supplied by the unrestrained freedom of debate within the walls of congress, whilst Mr. Jefferson, avoiding that arena of conflicting opinions, chose rather the course which gave full play to the happy facility of his written word. Never was there a more fortunate combination to advance a great object. Mr. Adams hewed out the road, vigorously but roughly, may be, for the pioneers, whilst Mr. Jefferson smoothed and widened it for the nation to follow; and each felt the value of the other in the common task. Here they separated, Mr. Jefferson to do other duty in his native State, Mr. Adams presently to cross the water. The next time they met was many years later, in Europe, when Mr. Adams had become the representative of his disenthralled countrymen at the court of their former sovereign, and Mr. Jefferson filled the same position in the presence of the monarch of France. The duty imposed upon the two by congress to open negotiations of commercial treaties with all the powers of Europe once more entailed an intimacy and frequent correspondence, which there was nothing to prevent from growing into friendship. Mr. Jefferson, in a letter to Mr. Madison, recorded the impression he had of Mr. Adams at this time, which gives him much less credit for penetration than he deserved, whilst it does full justice to his nobler qualities. Mr. Adams, on his side, measured Mr. Jefferson with even more friendly eyes, and, if he was aware of any qualifications, gave no utterance to them. An interchange of visits and frequent civilities, so long as they remained in Europe, continued to preserve their social relations upon the kindest footing.

During this period no incidents occurred to draw out the lurking contrasts of their characters. But scarcely was the constitution adopted, and the two were called to fill stations only one grade beneath the first, when events took place which had the effect of setting them in opposition to each other. They not only clashed in opinions, but became the types of opposing ones before the world. The great cause of this change was the breaking out of the French Revolution. Mr. Jefferson hailed it as the harbinger of a new era on earth, whilst Mr. Adams saw in it only the image of a ship in a tempest without helm or anchor. But this difference of sentiment would not of itself have sufficed to disturb the private feelings of the parties, had it not been for an instance of the duplicity already referred to, which gave a shock to Mr. Adams's confidence such as he did not for a long time get over. The facts were these. During the spring of the year 1791, the United States Gazette of Philadelphia had been publishing, in numbers, a summary of Davila's work on the Civil Wars of France, with commentaries, which were well understood, though not expressly acknowledged, to be from the pen of Mr. Adams. Not unaware of their imputed origin, and much disturbed at what he thought their pernicious tendency, Mr.

Jefferson welcomed, with great satisfaction, the arrival, from the other side of the Atlantic, of Thomas Paine's pamphlet on the Rights of Man, and approved the project of republishing it in America as an antidote to their poison. Wishing to express his thanks for the use of an English copy, which had been lent to him to read, he was impelled to add, in his note, the reasons why he rejoiced that the work was about to be reprinted. Prominent among these was an allusion to the heresies upon Davila. That Mr. Jefferson had not the remotest idea his note would ever be seen by the public, cannot admit of a doubt. Great, then, was his consternation, when he found it paraded at large, with his name attached, as a prefix to recommend the pamphlet publication.

This incident attracted much attention in Philadelphia, where it was regarded as an indecorous attack intentionally made by one high officer of the government against another. Pressed by this exposure, which imputed to him far more than he probably meant, he endeavored to escape from it by volunteering an explanation directly to Mr. Adams. This brought from the latter, then at home in Quincy, a frank reply, which, in its turn, elicited a rejoinder, explicitly disavowing any intention, by the terms of the unlucky note, to allude to Mr. Adams or any of his writings. With this explanation, Mr. Adams professed himself satisfied. Unfortunately, however, for Mr. Jefferson, a private letter of his, addressed to General Washington at the very time, has since been published, in which he expressly says that he *did* mean, in his note, to allude to the Discourses on Davila. From this contradiction there seems no outlet of escape. It is not a pleasant task to allude to it, neither would it be necessary, were it not essential to show that if Mr. Adams did not easily relinquish the suspicions, which Mr. Jefferson describes him as too liable at all times to entertain, the facts prove that he was not without abundant justification.

Indeed, it can scarcely be denied that the publication of Mr. Jefferson's letters since his death, has fixed rather than relieved this shade upon his character. It is, however, much confined within the period between 1790 and 1801. Whilst on the one side, he is professing a profound respect and attachment to General Washington, on the other, he is communicating privately to Philip Mazzei in Europe the most significant insinuations of the political apostasy of that chief. So his broader private charges made against Mr. Adams, implying danger to the republican institutions of the country from his devotion to the British theory of government, are not easily reconciled with the spirit of the letter he addressed to him on the 28th of December, 1796, upon his election to the Presidency, which was committed to the discretion of Mr. Madison to deliver. That gentleman wisely decided to suppress it chiefly for two reasons. The first, because of the false attitude in which the act would place the writer towards his own political friends. The second, because of the danger of putting such admissions in the hands of an opponent whom it might ultimately be necessary to try to break down. It would seem to be plain that either there had or there had not been solid reasons for opposition to the elevation of Mr. Adams. If there were such, how could

they have been made less so by the fact of his triumph?
Yet Mr. Jefferson's letter gave no hint of serious obstacles to congratulation on his success.   If, on the other
hand, there were no grave reasons, what were his friends
to think of all the argument, the remonstrances and
the denunciations of monarchical tendencies, that had
formed the base of the opposition of which he had been
hailed as the chief?   The only escape from this dilemma
is in the supposition that Mr. Jefferson, by his letter,
hoped and intended to scatter seeds of division between
Mr. Adams and his friends to such a degree as to para-
lyze the influence of those deemed the most dangerous
section of the federalists.   But this would be to attribute
to him an Italian refinement of policy far beyond the
simple notions of the country and of that time, or the
general character of the writer.   The idea is not, therefore, to be entertained for a moment.   What the judgment of Mr. Adams would have been had this remarkable
letter ever reached him it is not easy to pronounce. But
it is certain that he never at any time knew of its having
been written.   The only demonstration which did come
to his knowledge was that made two months later when
Mr. J. assumed the Vice-President's chair.   His tone
had then been tuned simply to self-gratulation that the
reins of government had not fallen into his hands, but
rested rather with Mr. Adams.   Even this declaration was going rather too far for a perfectly straight-
forward man.   For if he conscientiously believed one
half of what he has left on record, then he should have
regarded his own failure of an election and Mr. Adams's
success as serious public calamities.   Neither was the
earnest anxiety shown to suppress all publication of his

private correspondence, much relieved by the accidental exposure, from time to time, of the pecuniary
assistance he had rendered to the most profligate and
unworthy calumniators of his opponents. It is no part
of the design of this work unnecessarily to dwell on
these unpleasant topics. But they are material to explain the motives of Mr. Adams's course, and the causes
of his withdrawal of confidence from Mr. Jefferson at
the close of his administration. He then fully believed
him to be a false and dangerous man ; and, so believing,
he acted up to his conviction. The refusal to give any
assurances as to his future course, was what determined
Mr. Adams to take the extraordinary step of filling all
the vacant places under the revised judicial system before his accession. On the other hand, this proceeding
very naturally offended Mr. Jefferson. Indeed, it was
a stretch of authority of that sort which can be too
easily twisted to the justification of the very abuses it
is designed to prevent, ever to be a safe measure in
popular governments. And the result of this example
is not without use as an illustration.

But no sooner is the conflict over, and Mr. Jefferson
fully established in power, without risk of further rivalry
with his opponent, than the shades of his character
begin to disappear, and his better nature again struggles for the mastery. He has left on record the fact
that he desired to confer on Mr. Adams the most lucra-
tive post in New England, a step the inconsistency of
which with the professions on which they came into
power, his friends in that quarter seem to have felt
much more keenly than he. He further states that he
was deterred from prosecuting his wish by the sugges-

tion that the advance would not be well received. Perhaps in this he was right; but the public manifestation of any such confidence would have done no disservice to his own character for magnanimity, however coldly it might have been met, whilst it would have greatly served to shield Mr. Adams from the ferocious and unsparing denunciations which his partisans, during his administration, were in the habit of pouring out upon him. And all of them were carried on, so far as the public could see, without the smallest effort on his part at counteraction. So little was Mr. Adams in the way of suspecting the existence of any good-will, that a trifling incident which occurred in Massachusetts was well calculated to impress him with a notion of the prevalence of quite an opposite spirit. The number of commissioners of bankruptcy was diminished by the repeal of the judiciary law in such a manner as to render it necessary to deprive some of the incumbents of their places. John Quincy Adams had received his appointment from the district judge under the law. He was now selected for removal under the authority vested in the President, although others, not a whit more in political sympathy, were retained. In the absence of all explanations, and none were offered, but one construction could be put upon such a proceeding. Yet Mr. Jefferson was not probably intending any such petty hostility as this implied. The prejudices which he had succeeded in rousing among his followers, especially in New England, probably exceeded his power to control. But the act had its natural effect on Mr. Adams. Hence, when Mr. Jefferson endeavored to revive his ancient relations with him through an open-

ing casually furnished by Mrs. Adams, his effort met
with a colder reception than it deserved. The estrangement continued complete until after Mr. Jefferson's retirement had released him from his obligations to his
partisans. On the other hand, the same event rescued
the motives of Mr. Adams from all liability of misap-
prehension. It then needed only the intervention of
some common friend like Dr. Rush, to bring the two
once more into kindly relations. The bitterness of
party warfare, which had prompted them to be mutually
unjust, gradually softened away, and during the remainder of their lives, though they never again met face
to face, they kept up a correspondence by letters upon
indifferent topics of literature, theology, and general
politics, which will probably retain a permanent interest with posterity.

Thus passed the life of Mr. Adams in peaceful retirement, for many years. His correspondence began to
grow upon him, and he divided his time between
reading on a more extensive scale than ever, and writing to his numerous friends. He devoted himself to a
very elaborate examination of the religion of all ages
and nations, the results of which he committed to paper
in a desultory manner. The issue of it was the formation of his theological opinions very much in the mould
adopted by the Unitarians of New England. Rejecting
with the independent spirit which in early life had driven
him from the ministry, the prominent doctrines of Cal-
vinism, the trinity, the atonement, and election, he was
content to settle down upon the Sermon on the Mount
as a perfect code presented to man by a more than
mortal teacher. Further he declined to analyze the

mysterious nature of his mission. In this faith he lived with uninterrupted serenity, and in it he died with perfect resignation.

The termination of the war with Great Britain by the signature of the treaty of Ghent, closed the disputes connected with European politics, which had raged with greater or less fury for nearly a quarter of a century. Mr. Adams, as a leading actor, had shared largely in the bitterness of the strife. He had been made the object of the most fierce and unrelenting attacks from opposite quarters, and had in his turn been impelled to say and to write much of his opponents which a calm review would scarcely venture to defend. All this contention ceased with the return of peace. The fragment of the ultra-federal party, which had been revived into importance in New England and New York by the unpopularity of the war, and which with singular rashness had staked every thing upon the most intemperate opposition to the course of Mr. Madison, perished under the reaction that followed. Mr. Monroe was elevated to the Presidency without a struggle; and he immediately organized an administration which went into office upheld by the full confidence of the country. Of this administration, John Quincy Adams was the member to whom the department of foreign affairs was assigned; and the selection was ratified by a general expression of good-will in New England. This revolution was felt by his father in a greatly increased manifestation of the popular regard towards himself. From this time to the end of his life the traces of an ever-growing reaction are visible in the extension of his correspondence, which, in spite of his seclusion from public affairs, became almost as large as it had been when he had numerous offices to bestow. Not a shadow now remained on this score to disturb the natural serenity of his mind. It is highly honorable to Mr. Jefferson, that his active and unsolicited testimony, generously given to the value of the public services of his ancient opponent, and extensively spread among the large class over whose minds his authority was yet unbounded, had a great effect in accelerating this change. It was a cheering consolation to the declining days of the old statesman, whose integrity not even his most bitter enemies had ever really disputed, the prospect of losing which had at an earlier moment filled his mind with anxiety and gloom.

So entirely had party strife disappeared upon the second election of Mr. Monroe, that no division took place in the popular votes in the several States. In Massachusetts, Mr. Adams was placed on the list of electors and was chosen without opposition. He was made President of the College, and gave his vote for James Monroe as President and Daniel D. Tompkins, as Vice-President. With a single exception in New Hampshire, prompted by personal regard for John Quincy Adams, the electors were unanimous; the first instance since Washington went out of office, and not improbably the last that may occur in the American annals.

Shortly after the joyful event of the return of his son from his eight years' absence in the diplomatic service of the country, Mr. Adams was destined to meet with the severest affliction that had ever yet befallen him. His wife, who had gone through the vicissitudes of more than half a century in his company; who had sympathized with him in all his highest aspirations, and had cheered him in his greatest trials; who had faithfully preserved his worldly interests, when he was unable to be present to guard them himself; who had enlivened his home and had shared his joys and his pains alike, was taken ill with a typhus fever, in the autumn of 1818, and died on the 28th of October. He was at this time eighty-three years of age, and of course had little reason to expect long to survive her; but to him her loss was a perpetually recurring evil; for she had been the stay of his household. Her character had adapted itself to his in such a manner as to improve the good qualities of both, so that her loss threw over his manner ever afterwards, a tinge of sadness not natural to him; and the sprightly humor, which made so agreeable a part of the letters addressed to her in her lifetime, as it did of his daily conversation, ceased in a degree to appear.

He now began to indulge in the latest privilege of old age. He recurred to the various events of his life, and sought to compare his remembrance of them with that of the few contemporaries who yet survived. Many facts of importance seemed to him in danger of being forgotten, and the services of some individuals entirely overlooked. What especially stirred him was the publication of Mr. Wirt's Life of Patrick Henry, because it seemed to claim the merit of originating resistance to the pretensions of Great Britain too exclusively for the State of Virginia. This brought him forward in explanation of the action of James Otis, concerning whom he supplied a great part of all the

information that has been preserved. The series of
letters, relating to this subject, written at a very advanced age to Judge Tudor, abound in details and
anecdotes which would not otherwise have come down
to us. Many of the facts have been substantially confirmed by the testimony of Governor Hutchinson, the
last volume of whose history was not brought to light
until after Mr. Adams's death. The most remarkable
feature of these late letters is the vigor of imagination
and freshness of feeling with which they are written;
they overflow with the desire to do honor to those over
whose memory time was rapidly closing, and yet whose
services had not been without their claim upon the
public gratitude. In this way he did much to perpetuate the recollections of honorable events in the
career of Otis, of Hawley, and of Samuel Adams, and
the labor was to him a most grateful tribute to their
worth.

He was now eighty-five years old, and his physical
frame, strong as it had been, was slowly but surely
giving way under the sap of the destroyer. But his
mind still worked with vigor, when an occasion happened which fully developed the regard in which he
was held by the people of his native State. The time
had come when the District of Maine, which had been
long attached to Massachusetts, though not an integral
part of her territory, demanded an independent government, and an admission into the Union on an equal
footing with the parent State. Massachusetts assented,
and a separation was effected; but this event carried
with it a necessity of adapting the forms of the constitution of the State to the circumstances of her greatly

abridged limits. This could be done only by calling a convention to amend it. Arrangements were made accordingly. Mr. Adams was unanimously elected a delegate by the people of his native town, just as he had been forty years before, when the instrument now to be amended had been originally framed. Great pains were everywhere taken to select for this body such citizens as had become most distinguished for abilities, learning, or weight of character. The absence of party divisions just then favored such an object remarkably. The result was, the convocation of a popular assembly such as was never gathered from so limited a territory before, and such as may not soon be seen again. The three learned professions, the commercial, the agricultural, and the mechanic interests, all were represented by an amount of intelligence, of culture, of social and of moral worth, such as any Commonwealth of far greater dimensions might well be proud to show.

The sessions of this convention were opened on the 15th of November, 1820, and were continued until the 9th of January, 1821. When Mr. Adams, in his eighty-sixth year, with a form yet erect, though tremulous with age, made his appearance on the second day, he was received by the members of this brilliant assembly, all standing, with demonstrations of the utmost respect and regard. The dignified office of presiding over its deliberations had been unanimously tendered to him through a committee, instructed to present to him the following resolutions adopted on the motion of Isaac Parker, then the respected Chief Justice of the Supreme Court of the Commonwealth:

"Whereas, the Honorable John Adams, a member of this Convention, and elected the President thereof, has for more than half a century devoted the great powers of his mind, and his profound wisdom and learning, to the service of his country and mankind:

"In fearlessly vindicating the rights of the North American provinces against the usurpation and encroachments of the superintendent government:

"In diffusing a knowledge of the principles of civil liberty among his fellow-subjects, and exciting them to a firm and resolute defence of the privileges of freemen:

"In early conceiving, asserting, and maintaining the justice and practicability of establishing the independence of the United States of America:

"In giving the powerful aid of his political knowledge in the formation of the constitution of his native State, which constitution became in a great measure the model of those which were subsequently formed:

"In conciliating the favor of foreign powers, and obtaining their countenance and support in the arduous struggle for independence:

"In negotiating the treaty of peace, which secured forever the sovereignty of the United States, and in defeating all attempts to prevent it; and especially in preserving in that treaty the vital interests of the New England States:

"In demonstrating to the world, in his defence of the constitutions of the several United States, the contested principle, since admitted as an axiom, that checks and balances in legislative power are essential to true liberty:

"In devoting his time and talents to the service of the nation, in the high and important trusts of Vice-President and President of the United States:

"And lastly, in passing an honorable old age in dignified retirement, in the practice of all the domestic virtues, thus exhibiting to his countrymen and to posterity an example of true greatness of mind and of genuine patriotism:—

"Therefore, Resolved, That the members of this Convention, representing the people of the Commonwealth of Massachusetts, do joyfully avail themselves of this opportunity to testify their respect and gratitude to this eminent patriot and statesman, for the great services rendered by him to his country, and their high gratification that, at this late period of life, he is permitted by Divine Providence to assist them with his counsel in revising the constitution which, forty years ago, his wisdom and prudence assisted to form.

"Resolved, That a committee of twelve be appointed by the chair, to communicate this proceeding to the Honorable John Adams, to inform him of his election to preside in this body, and to introduce him to the chair of this Convention."

Grateful for this honorable testimonial to the value of his past services, Mr. Adams was sufficiently sensible of his failing strength to reject all idea of assuming the arduous labors of the post thus offered. He therefore returned to the committee the following answer:

"FELLOW-CITIZENS,—An election at my age and in my circumstances by the free suffrages of so ample a representation of the fortunes and talents, the experience and wisdom, the authority, the virtues, and the piety of the ancient and renowned State of Massachusetts, I esteem the purest and fairest honor of my life; and my gratitude is proportionally ardent and sincere. I pray you, gentlemen, to present to the Convention my most cordial thanks.

"Your enumeration of services performed for this country recalls to my recollection the long services and succession of great and excellent characters with whom I have had the honor to act in the former part of my life, and to whose exertions I have endeavored to add my feeble aid; characters, who have been employed by Divine Providence as instruments in preserving and securing that unexampled liberty which this nation now possesses; that liberty, which is the source of all our happiness and prosperity; a prosperity which cannot be contemplated by any virtuous mind without gratitude, consolation, and delight.   May it be perpetual!

"Gentlemen,—As my age is generally known, it will readily be believed that my forces are too far exhausted to perform the arduous duties of the high office which the benevolence of the Convention has assigned to me.   I am, therefore, under the necessity to request permission of the Convention to decline the appointment, and to pray that some other gentleman may be elected, whose vigorous age and superior talents may conduct their deliberations with more convenience to themselves, and with greater satisfaction to the people of the Commonwealth at large."

In the proceedings Mr. Adams took great interest, but his bodily frame, now easily susceptible of derangement from any change of the long-settled habits of a uniform life at home, refused the test of daily attendance during the severity of the winter season. Only once or twice did he venture upon any remarks. A report of what he said is given in the published volume of the debates. It is characteristic, and in perfect consistency with the views which he had steadily held through life. These views were singularly misrepresented so long as temporary objects were to be served by weakening his influence over the popular mind, but there is now no motive left to consider them as other than they are. They may be in brief described as the system of a Whig of the Revolution, born of purely English stock, but transplanted to America; republican in its character, and popular, without being democratic, in its tendencies; conservative in its forms, with but a slight leaning to aristocracy. On this last point, nothing is more remarkable than the extent to which his character was misconceived. In the simplicity of his daily habits he would have stood the test of comparison even with Mr. Jefferson, whom the great body of the people had learned to regard as the embodiment of all republican ideas.

There was one change in the old constitution which Mr. Adams labored, though ineffectually, to procure. It was a modification of the third article of the Bill of Rights, an article which he did not himself draw when he furnished the rest, in such form as would do away with the recognition of distinct modes of religious faith by the State. This amendment had been sug-

gested by Dr. Price in his comments upon the constitution, published soon after it was made, though it is
not likely that Mr. Adams remembered it. Not able to
make his voice clearly heard by the members, he had
recourse to the agency of others to effect his object;
but it was in vain. The old Puritan feeling which began with laboring to establish a Christian Commonwealth, was yet alive, and refused to recognize Jews
or heathens as perfect equals with Christians before
the law. The proposition was gently put aside; the
spirit of it has, however, since found its way, by the
operation of an amendment, into the system of government.

This appearance in the convention made a fitting
close to the public career of Mr. Adams. His few remaining years were passed serenely at his residence in
Quincy, where he kept up the habit of receiving strangers, who came from abroad, or visitors from other
States, attracted by curiosity to see him. Once a year,
his time was enlivened by the presence of his son, John
Quincy Adams, now Secretary of State, and himself
arrived at a position in the popular estimation, which
seemed to open a prospect of his elevation to the
Presidency, as the successor of Mr. Monroe. It was
this circumstance which gave rise to the last attempt
to disturb the peace of Mr. Adams's declining years.
Not long after his retirement in 1801, and whilst smarting under the irritation, caused by the sense of injustice
done to him by members of both contending parties, the
same which produced the papers in the *Boston Patriot*,
a maternal relative of his, then bordering upon in-
sanity, which at last ended in suicide, drew from him,

by force of earnest expressions of sympathy, and under
the seal of the strictest confidence, the most unreserved
expression of his sentiments respecting the chief actors
and events in the later portion of his public life. Not
until long after the catastrophe that befell the recipient
of these letters, and the rise of John Quincy Adams to
be a prominent candidate for the Presidency, did an
inducement occur to betray confidence by bringing
them to light. The heir of the deceased person then
earned by the transfer of them to the political opponents of the son, a claim upon their gratitude in case
of their attaining power, which was ultimately recognized by the gift of a subordinate place in the Boston
custom-house. By such means the letters were published
to the world. It may fairly be doubted whether the
injury done by them to the prospects of John Quincy
Adams was ever an equivalent even for the pitiful
reward paid for the breach of trust.

At any rate, they appeared too late to disturb the
equanimity of the father. Mr. Jefferson and Colonel
Pickering, the two surviving individuals most harshly
reflected upon in them, appear to have perused the
papers with very opposite emotions. The former justly
considered them as the relics of a conflict in which he
had already given as well as taken blows enough not to
seek to renew it in his last days. The latter felt it his
duty to leave behind him a general replication to all
the charges ever made against him, which might defend
his memory from the revival of them after his death.
At this day it would seem as if a less virulent production would have better answered to protect his fame.
Bitter as it was, the perusal of it excited in Mr. Adams

no disposition to protract the controversy. The day for such passions had gone by with him. The returning good-will of his countrymen was healing all his wounds. He regretted the publication of his own letters, not from any anxiety for himself, for his career was run, and by the substance of the opinions, already expressed in other forms, on public affairs he was ready to abide, but on account of the spirit which the betrayal of his most private feelings in a season of irritation might renew in others, after his own had subsided into peace. Even with Colonel Pickering, the last as he ever had been the most vindictive of his enemies, he had no further hostility to wage.

With the public these pamphlets made little impression. The original motive for printing seemed so unworthy, that they excited little response and obtained but a limited currency. They have been rather more referred to in later times as authority for facts on one side or the other of public questions; but for obvious reasons they are entitled to but a moderate share of weight; and for the reason that they never were intended by the writer for the public eye, no part of the letters thus betrayed has been admitted to a place in the present work. Neither have they been relied upon to sustain the narrative in this biography.

Tranquil as Mr. Adams had become in his last days, and happy in his correspondence with the remnant of his old compeers, he was not indifferent to the struggle which was going on for the office of President of the United States. His son was now a mark for the same shafts which had been aimed at him thirty years before, and it was not unnatural that he should await with emotion the favorable or adverse issue that might attend it. From youth to age his son had been a faithful one to him, never varying in his efforts to promote his comfort and his happiness, always supplying abundance of material to gratify his highest pride. To have such a son rewarded by the people of the United States by an elevation to the highest station in their gift, was an aspiration which he could hardly be sanguine enough to indulge, though the conviction that he was fully worthy of it had been long cherished in his mind. It was reserved to him to live to see the fulfilment of his hopes.

By reason of the multiplication of candidates consequent upon the disintegration of parties, no election of President was made at the usual period for the popular choice. As a consequence, the decision fell, for the second time since the formation of the government, upon the House of Representatives. The only formidable competitor of Mr. Adams was General Jackson; and between them the friends of the minor candidates were compelled to choose. The choice of Mr. Adams was effected by the adherents of Mr. Clay, who controlled the votes of four States. But, at that moment, the supporters of the fourth candidate, Mr. Crawford, were understood to be likewise disposed to prefer him, had circumstances made a decision on their part necessary. As a consequence, John Quincy Adams was declared to be elected. The event brought to his father numbers of congratulatory letters, some specimens of which merit insertion here :

     " WASHINGTON, 12 February, 1825.

"Receive the most cordial congratulations from an old friend of the father and the son, who on this occasion feels much for you, and for him ; and who will be happy on the Bunker Hill anniversary to express in person the patriotic and individual sentiments which have been known to you for near half a century.

    " Most truly and affectionately,

       "Your old friend,

          " LAFAYETTE."

The next is from an individual who had been active and efficient in his opposition to the father in former days, and who, as a member of the House of Representatives from Louisiana, had not contributed to this election ; but his feeling at the time may be understood from the terms of his congratulation :

"I cannot avoid seizing this occasion of congratulating you on an event which gives you the rare felicity of seeing your son succeed to that high station in which you yourself were once placed by the suffrage of the nation. Although circumstances did not permit me to contribute to this event, I am not the less convinced that his administration will prove honorable to himself and advantageous to his country.

    " I have the honor, etc.,

       " EDWARD LIVINGSTON."

The next is from one of the sufferers under the old Sedition Law, who as editor of the *Bee*, a newspaper in Connecticut, had been subjected to prosecution for his attacks on Mr. Adams's administration :

"NEW YORK, 4 March, 1825.

"VENERABLE SIR,—As you may now have some respite from the respectful attentions of your immediate friends on the auspicious result of the recent Presidential election, I take the liberty of asking permission, also, to congratulate you upon an event so honorable to yourself, so creditable and beneficial to our country, and so fortunate for the distinguished subject of the popular choice.

"We perceive, Sir, in the election of your son, a signal proof that republics are not forever insensible to personal merits, nor always ungrateful to faithful servants; and that the long-wished time has at length arrived, when good sense has triumphed over party spirit, and patriotism prevailed over political hostility.

"It is to your glory, Sir, that your son has proved himself worthy of your instructions, your wisdom, and your experience, and become confessedly the fittest and most deserving object to succeed, after time has restored the empire of reason, his father in the highest confidence and trust of a great and free people.

"I remain, Sir (changed with the times, *tempora mutantur*, since 1798, and notwithstanding my trial of the Sedition Law), with the most sincere deference, esteem, and veneration, and desirous of contributing my mite to the consolations of a political Simeon,

"Your very obed't humble servant,

"CHARLES HOLT."

But the question will naturally arise, how did the individual most deeply interested in this result announce it to his father? The answer may be briefly given.

Immediately after the decision in the House of Representatives, Rufus King, then one of the senators of the State of New York, dispatched from the capitol the following note to the son, apprising him of what had taken place:

"SENATE CHAMBER, 9 February, 1825.

"MY DEAR SIR,—We have this moment heard the issue of the election, and I send you and your venerable father my affectionate congratulations upon your choice as President of the United States on the first ballot of the House of Representatives. I include your father, as I consider your election as the best amends for the injustice of which he was made the victim.

"To me and mine, the choice has been such as we have cordially hoped for and expected.

"RUFUS KING."

This interesting note from one who had been himself a prominent actor in the times to which he alludes, the recipient immediately inclosed in another of his own, which he sent to his father. It ran thus:

"WASHINGTON, 9 February, 1825.

"MY DEAR AND HONORED FATHER,—The inclosed note from Mr. King will inform you of the event of this day, upon which I can only offer *you* my congratulations, and ask your blessings and prayers.

"Your affectionate and dutiful son,"

"JOHN QUINCY ADAMS."

Mr. Adams survived this event little more than a year. He was now at the age of ninety, infirm in body, but yet preserving a remarkable activity of mind. Unable to see clearly enough to read, or to guide a pen to write, he still retained so much interest in present objects as fully to employ the services of members of his immediate family, both in reading to him and in writing after his dictation. What he most disliked was the mere vegetation of extreme age; rather than to fall into which he would cheerfully listen to any book, however trifling, which might at the moment be attracting the fancy of younger generations. The brilliant fictions of Walter Scott, then in the height of their popularity, the sea stories of Cooper, and even the exaggerated, but nervous verse of Byron, were all welcome, in the intervals when he could not obtain what he better relished, the reminiscences of contemporaries, or the psychological speculations of more profound writers in England and France. His avidity for new literature was so well understood that he seldom failed of a supply from the good-will of kind friends in the neighboring city. This condition was varied by a single ride daily taken in fine weather, around the vicinity, in the scenery of which he ever delighted, and by conversation with friends and visitors who chanced to call and see him. Such was his habit after exercise in walking had become too fatiguing to his yet heavy frame. Thus ebbed away the remnant of his being, gently and insensibly, as Cicero so happily describes: "Semper enim in his studiis laboribusque viventi non intelligitur quando obrepat senectus. Ita sensim sine sensu ætas senescit. Nec subito frangitur, sed diuturnitate extinguitur."

The relatives of Mr. Adams were not, however, unaware that the spring of 1826 opened upon him with enfeebled powers. This became so observable in the month of April as to warn them of what would ere long take place. He was stretching over his ninety-first year. That year was generally viewed with uncommon interest as marking the lapse of the first half century of the national history. The Fourth of July approached, and on every side sprang up a demand for a more than common celebration of that anniversary. The eyes of all involuntarily turned towards the few who yet lingered of the survivors of 1776, and especially to the two individuals most identified with the action which had made the day forever famous. John Adams and Thomas Jefferson yet lived. They were thought to be still able to come forward and crown with their presence the joyous festivities of the jubilee. With what interest would the younger generations view these time-honored servants of freedom, once more brought together in presence of the nation, after twenty-five years of separation, to shake hands for the last time with each other, to take note of the happiness and prosperity they had done so much to promote, and to receive the warmest expressions of gratitude from millions of grateful hearts. Stimulated by these ideas, invitations poured in from all quarters, to secure the desired meeting at some favorite and convenient place. Even the neighbors of Mr. Adams, though they well understood his strength to be unequal to a distant excursion, yet flattered themselves that he would be able at least to honor their comparatively small gathering with his presence. The sanguine hopes thus excited were all destined to be equally disappointed; for the objects of them were even then not wholly insensible to the nature of the far more imperative summons that was awaiting them. As the time drew nearer, the townsmen of Mr. Adams became more and more aware of the progress of his decline. But if they could not have him in person, they still desired to obtain from him some last word or sign of cheer to his friends and neighbors upon the interesting occasion. To this end the individual who had been selected to make the oration, was deputed to pay him a visit, and communicate their wishes. He did so; and he has briefly recorded the result in a diary, which he left behind him. It was on Friday, the 30th of June, at nine o'clock in the morning, that, according to his account, he walked down to see Mr. Adams. His record is as follows: "Spent a few minutes with him in conversation, and took from him a toast, to be presented on the Fourth of July as coming from him. I should have liked a longer one; but as it is, this will be acceptable. 'I will give you,' said he,

'INDEPENDENCE FOREVER!'"

He was asked if he would not add any thing to it, and he replied, "Not a word."

The visitor, evidently not one of the laconic school, in objecting to this toast as not long enough, may raise a smile in the present day. Looking back from this distance of time, it would seem as if the addition of another word must have spoiled it. In that brief sentiment Mr. Adams infused the essence of his whole character, and of his life-long labors for his country.

The visitor had not come too early, for the symptoms

of debility became more and more alarming every
moment. There was no suffering, except from the labor
of respiration, but this increased so steadily, that early
on the morning of the 4th Mr. Adams's medical adviser,
Dr. Holbrook, predicted his patient would not last
beyond sunset. In the mean time the celebrations went
on in Quincy, as everywhere else. No more interesting
festival has ever occurred. From one end of the
country to the other, the names of Adams and Jefferson
were coupled, wherever Americans were gathered together, in accents of gratitude and praise. All remnants of party passions were completely drowned in the
strong flood of national feeling which overspread the
land. At Quincy, the exercises passed and the banquet
began. The orator of the day here again records the
following: "I presented the toast I obtained from the
President, and it was received with unceasing shouts."

As these shouts were rising to the skies, shouts which
might have been caught by his ears, had they been
longer sensitive to receive them, the spirit of Mr. Adams
was passing away. The sands of a long, a varied, and
a memorable life were run out. A noble and a pure
heart, the aspirations of which had ever been for the
advancement of his country and the welfare of his race,
had ceased to beat. The record already quoted adds
that "the intelligence of the President's death was received as the company were beginning to leave the
hall." It was not a moment auspicious to further manifestations of noisy joy, although such a death could not
convey with it any of the common feelings of sadness.
It was a fitting close of a brilliant day. The setting
sun spread its rays over even the dispersing vapors only

to give a more serene majesty to the golden splendors of the sky. Could it be given to a man to choose the hour and moment of his exit most glorious to his name and most in harmony with his life, none within the wide range of mortal experience can be imagined more to be desired than this.

Yet, strange as it may seem, another incident was coming in to give a second and still more remarkable association with the occasion. It is stated of Mr. Adams that the last words he ever uttered, so far as they could be gathered from his failing articulation, were these: "Thomas Jefferson still survives." Long as the two had been travelling in parallel lines to the common goal, ever observant of their relative position, such an idea might naturally occur to Mr. Adams, especially at a moment which brought them so freshly together in the minds of all other men. But he was mistaken. The fact was not as he supposed. Thomas Jefferson did not survive. He, too, had reached this anniversary, and he, too, had been summoned, but at an earlier hour, to immortality. Marvellous as it might seem, perhaps exceeding, in respect of its strange parallels, many a wonder transmitted from a mythological age, yet the event was to be indelibly stamped on the memory of America, that John Adams and Thomas Jefferson, who had inaugurated the independence of the nation on the 4th of July, 1776, exactly fifty years afterwards, years not unmarked with other coincidences quite extraordinary, if this closing one had not thrown them all into the shade, were almost simultaneously translated, in the midst of the acclamations of millions of their race, to the judgment of their God.

No greater sublunary blessing could have remained in store for them.   For if the opinion ascribed to Solon be just, when asked by Crœsus, the rich Lydian monarch, whether he had ever seen a man more blessed than he, that he named two brothers, Cleobis and Bion, who once put themselves to the wagon and drew their mother to Juno's temple ; and then, after sacrificing and feasting, went to rest and died together in the height of their reputation of filial piety; how much more deserving to be called blessed is the life of these two, who drew their nursing-mother, against strong resistance, to the temple of liberty, and who, after a long period of services and labors devoted to her welfare, went to the same rest under auspices a thousand-fold more sublime !   The moral of the story of Cleobis and Bion has, in the incidents which attended both the lives and the deaths of the two great men of America, an application by so much the wider as it expands the beautiful idea of completed duty from the narrow circle of a single household to the ever-unfolding area of a nation's home.

As the news of this singular coincidence spread over the land, it raised everywhere a thrill of emotion such as has never been caused by any other public event. It was not the wail of grief, such as is drawn forth by the sense of privation by the loss of valuable lives. The advanced age of these persons, if nothing else, neutralized that.   It was the offspring of a mixture of feelings, the chief of which were surprise at the strangeness of the occurrence, veneration for the men themselves, and delight in the splendor which it would forever reflect upon a page of the national annals.

Certainly, the fabulous passing away of the first Roman king, nearly on the same anniversary, in the midst of elementary chaos, does not compare with it in grandeur. Men loved to meet each other and to dwell on the most minute particulars, as they were sedulously laid before the public by the newspapers, and to read the comments raised to unusual eloquence by the tone of the general mind. The first feelings were followed by enthusiastic demonstrations of respect to the memory of the dead. The most distinguished orators and statesmen were summoned to prepare eulogies or memoirs, which were delivered at times set aside for the performance of appropriate services. In this way a large number of orations and addresses were produced, which are not without their value as a permanent contribution to the literature and history of the United States. Among them it is not inappropriate to make particular mention of that delivered by Daniel Webster, on account of the felicity with which he succeeded in weaving into the form of a speech in favor of independence energetic passages scattered in Mr. Adams's writings, and in animating the whole with somewhat of the ardor of the individual he sought to personate. So successful has this attempt been regarded by some, that to this day the belief is entertained that the speech is indeed that which Mr. Adams actually made. Other addresses are valuable for authentic particulars and curious anecdotes carefully collected at the time, which have thus been rescued from the oblivion which commonly overwhelms the personal reminiscences of contemporaries. As time goes on, it is by no means unlikely that these various productions will be regarded with ever-growing interest, not simply for the facts, more or less correctly given, in which they abound, but also as marking an epoch in American history—the close of its heroic age.

Mr. Adams died, leaving many descendants, some of the fourth generation, among whom he distributed, by his will, the limited estate which he had inherited or acquired. The bulk of this consisted in farming lands round about him, the income of which barely sufficed to maintain him in his later days, even in the simple and frugal manner in which he lived. Indeed, so rapid was the decline in the returns of this sort of property, after the peace of 1814, that he was induced to propose a transfer of his largest and most burdensome estate of Mount Wollaston to his eldest son, in exchange for a fixed annuity for the rest of his life, a proposal which was at once acceded to, and faithfully executed. A portion of his lands, together with his library, he decided, in 1822, to convey to the inhabitants of Quincy, as a token of his good-will towards them. His main object in giving, among other things, the very spot memorable as the birthplace of John Hancock, and the residence, at one time, of Josiah Quincy, Jr., was to make upon it a foundation for a school of the highest class, and a library, forever to remain open for the encouragement of the highest and best aspirations of future generations of the youth in his native place.

In Mr. Adams's vocabulary, the word *property* meant land. He had no confidence in the permanence of any thing else, hence he left little else behind him. The opinion was inherited by his son, John Quincy

Adams, who, in consequence, purchased, at the settlement of the estate agreeably to the will, the lands his father left. Fortunately for both, their simple habits created no need of straining the sources of an annual income to minister to the demands of luxury or to the vanities of an extraordinary state. They lived free from pecuniary obligations of every kind to others, a fate which has not always attached to the incumbents of the highest executive posts in America; and they died leaving the same estate greatly increased in nominal value, but little more productive than when they acquired it.

In figure John Adams was not tall, scarcely exceeding middle height, but of a stout, well-knit frame, denoting vigor and long life, yet as he grew old, inclining more and more to corpulence. His head was large and round, with a wide forehead and expanded brows. His eye was mild and benignant, perhaps even humorous, when he was free from emotion, but when excited, it fully expressed the vehemence of the spirit that stirred within. His presence was grave and imposing, on serious occasions, but not unbending. He delighted in social conversation, in which he was sometimes tempted to what he called rodomontade. But he seldom fatigued those who heard him; for he mixed so much of natural vigor, of fancy, and of illustration with the stores of his acquired knowledge, as to keep alive their interest for a long time. His affections were warm, though not habitually demonstrated, towards his relatives. His anger, when thoroughly roused, was, for a time, extremely violent, but when it subsided, it left no trace of malevolence behind. Nobody could see

him intimately without admiring the simplicity and
truth which shone in his action, and standing in some
awe at the reserved power of his will.   It was in these
moments that he impressed those around him with a
sense of his greatness.   Even the men employed on his
farm were in the habit of citing instances, some of which
have been remembered down to the present day.   At
times his vehemence would become so great as to make
him overbearing and unjust.   This was most apt to happen in cases of pretension or any kind of wrong-doing.
Mr. Adams was very impatient of cant, of sciolism, or of
opposition to any of his deeply-established convictions.
Neither was his indignation at all graduated to the
character of the individuals who might happen to excite it.   It had little respect of persons, and would
hold an illiterate man, or a raw boy, to as heavy a responsibility for uttering a crude heresy as the strongest
thinker or the most profound scholar.   His nature was
too susceptible to overtures of sympathy and kindness,
for it tempted him to trust more than was prudent in
the professions of some who proved unworthy of his
confidence.   Ambitious in one sense he certainly was ;
but it was not the mere aspiration for place or power.
It was the desire to excel in the minds of men, by the
development of high qualities, the love, in short, of an
honorable fame, that stirred him to exult in the rewards
of popular favor.   Yet this passion never tempted him
to change a course of action or to suppress a serious
conviction ; to bend to a prevailing error or to disavow an odious truth.

In two things he was favored above most men.   He
was happily married to a woman whose character was

singularly fitted to develop every good point of his; a
person with a mind capable of comprehending his, with
affections strong enough to respond to his sensibility,
with a sympathy equal to his highest aspirations, and
yet with flexibility sufficient to yield to his stronger
will without impairing her own dignity. In this blessed
relation he was permitted to continue for fifty-four
years, embracing far more than the whole period of his
active life; and it is not too much to say that to it he
was indebted not merely for the domestic happiness
which ran so like a thread of silver through the most
troubled currents of his days, but for the steady and
unwavering support of all the highest purposes of his
career. Upon the several occasions when his action
placed him in the most critical and difficult positions,
when the popular voice seemed loud in condemning
the wisdom or the patriotism of his course, her confidence in his correctness seems never to have wavered
for a moment. Not a trace of hesitation or doubt is
to be seen in her most confidential communications;
on the contrary, her voice in those cases came in to
reinforce his determination, and to urge him to persevere. Often she is found to have drawn her conclusions in advance, for several of her letters bear on the
outside the testimony of her husband's admiration of
her sagacity. The soothing effect this must have had
upon him, when chafed, as his temper not unfrequently
was, by the severe friction to which it was exposed in
the great struggles of his life, may easily be conceived.
An ignoble spirit would have thrown him into depres-
sion; a repining and dissatisfied one would have driven
him frantic. Hers was lofty and yet cheerful, decided

and yet gentle. Whilst she understood the foibles of his character and yielded to them enough to maintain her proper authority, she never swerved from her admiration of his abilities, her reliance upon the profoundness of his judgment, and her pride in the integrity of his life. And if this was her state of feeling, it was met on his part by a devotion which never wavered, and a confidence scarcely limited by a doubt of the possibility of error. A domestic relation like this compensated for all that was painful and afflictive in the vicissitudes of their career ; and its continuance to so late a stage in their joint lives left to the survivor little further to wish for in this world beyond the hope of a reunion in the next.

The other extraordinary blessing was the possession of a son who fulfilled in his career all the most sanguine expectations of a father. From his earliest youth John Quincy Adams had given symptoms of uncommon promise, and contrary to what so frequently happens in such cases, every year as it passed over his head only tended the more to confirm the hopes that had been raised at the beginning. A kindly nature received from early opportunities of travel and instruction in foreign lands, not the noxious seeds which so often germinate only to spread corruption, but a generous and noble development as well of the intellect as of the affections. At twenty years of age his father saw in him the outline of a full-grown statesman, a judgment which time served only the more unequivocally to confirm. But it was not merely in the circumstances of his brilliant progress as a public man that his parent had reason to delight. As a son, affectionate, devoted, and pure, his parents never failed to find in him sources of the most unmingled satisfaction. In whatever situation he was placed, and however far removed from them in the performance of his duties, he never forgot the obligations which he owed, to soothe by every effort in his power the hours of their declining years. The voluminous correspondence that was the offspring of this relation, furnishes an affecting proof of the tenderness and the devotion of the son to his parents, and of their implicit trust and grateful pride in their child. And the pleasure was reserved to the father rarely enjoyed since time began, of seeing his son gradually forcing his way by his unaided abilities up the steps of the same ascent which he had trod before him, until he reached the last and highest which his country could supply. The case is unexampled in the history of popular governments. And when this event was fully accomplished, whilst the son was yet in the full enjoyment of his great dignity so honorably acquired, it was accorded to the old patriarch to go to his rest on the day above all other days in the year which was the most imperishably associated with his fame. Such things are not often read of even in the most gorgeous pictures of mortal felicity painted in Eastern story. They go far to relieve the darker shadows which fly over the ordinary paths of life, and to hold out the hope that, even under the present imperfect dispensation, it is not unreasonable to trust that virtue may sometimes meet with its just reward.

The mortal remains of John Adams and of his wife repose side by side in sarcophagi of stone, under a temple, in the town in which they resided in life, constructed since his decease, and consecrated to the worship of God. And a modest marble tablet, affixed to one of its walls within, surmounted by a bust of him from the chisel of Horatio Greenough, bears the following inscription prepared for the benefit of later generations, by his eldest son:

LIBERTATEM, AMICITIAM, FIDEM RETINEBIS

D. O. M.

Beneath these walls

Are deposited the mortal remains of

JOHN ADAMS.

Son of John and Susanna (Boylston) Adams,

Second President of the United States;

Born $\frac{19}{30}$ October, 1735.

On the Fourth of July, 1776,

He pledged his Life, Fortune, and sacred Honor

To the INDEPENDENCE OF HIS COUNTRY.

On the third of September, 1783,

He affixed his seal to the definitive treaty with Great Britain,

Which acknowledged that independence,

And consummated the redemption of his pledge.

On the Fourth of July, 1826,

He was summoned

To the Independence of Immortality,

And to the JUDGMENT OF HIS GOD.

This House will bear witness to his piety;

This Town, his birthplace, to his munificence;

History to his patriotism;

Posterity to the depth and compass of his mind.

At his side
Sleeps, till the trump shall sound,

ABIGAIL,

His beloved and only wife,
Daughter of William and Elizabeth (Quincy) Smith;
In every relation of life a pattern
Of filial, conjugal, maternal, and social virtue.
Born November $\frac{11}{22}$, 1744,
Deceased 28 October, 1818,
Aged 74.

Married 25 October, 1764.
During an union of more than half a century
They survived, in harmony of sentiment, principle, and affection,
The tempests of civil commotion;
Meeting undaunted and surmounting
The terrors and trials of that Revolution,
Which secured the Freedom of their Country;
Improved the condition of their times;
And brightened the prospects of Futurity
To the race of man upon Earth.

PILGRIM.

From lives thus spent thy earthly duties learn;
From fancy's dreams to active virtue turn;
Let Freedom, Friendship, Faith, thy soul engage,
And serve, like them, thy country and thy age.

www.ingramcontent.com/pod-product-compliance
Lightning Source LLC
Chambersburg PA
CBHW032037050726
47590CB00001B/36